D0213182

Understanding Parkinson's Disease

A Personal and Professional View

Richard B. Rosenbaum, M.D.

Westport, Connecticut
London

Library of Congress Cataloging-in-Publication Data

Rosenbaum, Richard B., 1946–

  Understanding Parkinson's disease : a personal and professional view / Richard B.
Rosenbaum.

    p. cm.

  Includes bibliographical references and index.

  ISBN 0–275–99166–0 (alk. paper)

  1. Parkinson's disease. I. Title.

  RC382.R67 2006

  616.8'33—dc22   2006026802

British Library Cataloguing in Publication Data is available.

Library of Congress Catalog Card Number: 2006026802
ISBN: 0–275–99166–0

First published in 2006

Praeger Publishers, 88 Post Road West, Westport, CT 06881
An imprint of Greenwood Publishing Group, Inc.
www.praeger.com

Printed in the United States of America

The paper used in this book complies with the
Permanent Paper Standard issued by the National
Information Standards Organization (Z39.48–1984).

10 9 8 7 6 5 4 3 2 1

For my wife, Lois Rosenbaum; without her, nothing.

Contents

Acknowledgments   xi

Introduction   xiii

1. THE DIAGNOSTIC CONVERSATION—DIAGNOSIS
    AND PROGNOSIS OF PARKINSON'S DISEASE   1
    Making the Diagnosis   1
    James Parkinson and the Shaking Palsy   3
    Jean Charcot and Better Examinations   6
    Checking Diagnostic Accuracy   7
    Specificity and Sensitivity   9
    Prognosis   13
    The Hoehn and Yahr Scale   15
    The Unified Parkinson's Disease Rating Scale   17

2. PATHOLOGY OF PARKINSON'S DISEASE   21
    What Part of the Brain Fails in Parkinson's Disease?   21
    Nerve Cell Connections   27
    Chemical Pathology of Parkinson's Disease   31

3. IS THERE AN EPIDEMIC OF PARKINSON'S DISEASE?   39

    Epidemiology of Parkinson's Disease   39

    John Snow—The Father of Epidemiology   40

    Koch's Postulates   42

    Investigating Clusters of Parkinson's Disease   43

    Kuru and Creutzfeldt-Jakob Disease   44

    Does Smoking Cause Parkinson's Disease?   46

    Causation versus Association—The Hill Criteria   47

    Epidemiology of Smoking and Parkinson's Disease   48

    Pesticides, Head Trauma, and Parkinson's Disease   51

    Parkinson's at the Manor   52

4. CAUSES OF PARKINSON'S DISEASE   55

    Does an Infection Cause Parkinson's Disease?   55

    When Prophecy Fails   58

    Do Toxins Cause Parkinson's Disease? An Answer
    from the Frozen Addicts   60

    Do Genes Cause Parkinson's Disease?   67

    All Disease Is Genetic Disease   77

5. MEDICATIONS FOR PARKINSON'S DISEASE   83

    The Herbal Tradition   84

    Herbal Treatment of Parkinson's Disease   86

    Awakenings—L-Dopa Therapy   94

    Dopamine and Schizophrenia—The Dopamine
    Receptor   102

    Rational Drug Therapy—Trying to Prevent Progression of
    Parkinson's Disease   109

    Coenzyme Q_{10}—Another Quest for Neuroprotection   117

    The Challenges of Taking L-Dopa   122

6. IMAGES OF THE BRAIN—A PICTURE OF THE
    BRAIN IS WORTH A THOUSAND WORDS   135

    Imaging and Diagnosis   136

    Imaging and Presymptomatic Diagnosis   141

    Imaging and Disease Progression   143

7. A BETTER MODEL OF PARKINSON'S DISEASE   145

    Dopamine Nerve Cells Connect to Many Parts
    of the Brain   146

    Dopamine is One of Many Neurotransmitters
    That Are Important in Parkinson's Disease   150

    Patients with Parkinson's Disease Lose Cells from
    Many Areas of the Brain   151

8. BRAIN SURGERY FOR PARKINSON'S DISEASE   155

    Can Destroying Part of the Brain Be Good?   155

    "Brain Transplantation"—Implanting New Brain Cells   162

    Gene Therapy   168

9. LIVING WITH PARKINSON'S DISEASE   175

    Mood, Behavior, and Parkinson's Disease   175

    Can L-Dopa Make People Gamble?   177

    Are Parkinson's Disease and Alzheimer's Disease Related? 184

    Sleep and Parkinson's Disease   187

    Fall and Injury Prevention   196

10. CONCLUSIONS   203

    What Happens to Brain Cells to Cause Parkinson's Disease? 203

    Living Better with Parkinson's Disease   209

    The Story of Parkinson's Disease Is Not Finished   214

Appendix: Reading about Parkinson's Disease   215

Glossary   219

Notes   229

Index   239

Acknowledgments

This book began as a series of talks on how to do research that I presented to a class of high school students who were learning about medical research at Oregon Health and Science University (OHSU). Dr. James Rosenbaum, Dr. Edward Neuwelt, and I began the class in the late 1990s. Each year since then, questions from many students have refined the lecture material. Drs Tammy Martin and Kendra Farris have joined us in teaching the class and many other scientists from OHSU have mentored the students. In 2002, I began writing this book while a guest at the Rockefeller Foundation Villa Serbelloni in Bellagio, Italy. My wife, Lois Rosenbaum, has steadily provided advice, encouragement, and insightful critiques. My daughter, Laura Rosenbaum, and my niece Dr. Lisa Rosenbaum gave me valuable suggestions. A number of other friends and family have read the manuscript and provided welcome advice: Debbie Pollack, Barry Pelzner, Dr. Howard Rosenbaum, Dr. Marcia Kahn, Ken Rosenbaum, Sue and Dennis West, Kendra Farris, and Jennifer Jasaitis.

Dr. John Nutt and his colleagues in the Movement Disorders Clinic at OHSU have given my father the best possible neurological care.

Douglas Katagiri drew all the illustrations.

Amy Roth and Peggy Baldwin at the Providence Portland Medical Center library have given me invaluable bibliographic assistance. Stan Wakefield arranged my contact with Praeger-Greenwood where Debbie Carvalko has been my helpful editor.

My debt to my parents and to my patients with neurologic disease is apparent throughout the book.

Introduction

On a rainy afternoon, I sat with my parents in their assisted-living apartment, reading aloud from this manuscript. In it I tell many of their stories, and I wanted to be sure that they were comfortable with these shared intimacies. My father, 90, was slumped in his armchair. I thought he was asleep until he suddenly suggested, "Be sure to include in the book how disturbing drooling can be when you have Parkinson's disease."

At 87, my mother's memory and attention span can be as brief as a blink; she took advantage of the break in the reading to make a phone call to her mother. Sadly, my grandmother died 15 years previously, and my mother started to get upset when the operator told her that the phone had been disconnected. I calmed my mother by simply saying that I would take care of things. She sat down and listened again but interrupted after a couple of paragraphs, "Don't you think this book is much too complex for most people?"

"Mother," I replied defensively, "with your intelligence, if you had Parkinson's disease, you would want to understand it in all its complexities, and you could always skip any passages that were too scientific."

Many people want to understand Parkinson's disease, which slowly damages the brain, impairing not only muscular abilities but also many other bodily functions. It affects nearly one million Americans, so most people have a friend or relative with it. The late Pope John Paul II had Parkinson's disease, and throughout the years we sadly watched him moving more and more slowly during his public appearances. The disease develops gradually, usually late in adult life. About one percent of those over the age of 60 have Parkinson's disease, and by age 80 perhaps one person in five has at least some minor motor slowing or stiffness such as that caused by the disease. Former U.S. Attorney General Janet Reno has Parkinson's disease. Her hand tremor and stiffened facial expression are sometimes evident when she is on television. She has graciously and elegantly shown that many people with this disease can remain active for years in intellectually and physically demanding jobs. The actor Michael J. Fox has Parkinson's disease. His illness began at an unusually young age, and he has become a vigorous and effective spokesperson for medical research. The boxer Muhammad Ali has Parkinson's disease. We do not know the cause of most cases of Parkinson's disease, but Ali's illness may have been caused by the repeated brain bruising he sustained during his career as a boxer.

Living with Parkinson's disease challenges patients, family members, and caregivers. Those with Parkinson's disease must live with the illness for the rest of their lives. We are just beginning to find ways that their action and decisions might slow its progress. However, people can choose *how* they will live with Parkinson's disease and can actively participate in planning their treatment They have autonomy; they have choices to make. Those who understand their illness are most likely to benefit from and be happy with their own decisions.

Because I am a neurologist, I spend much of my professional life talking with people with serious illnesses of the nervous system. When I meet a patient for the first time, we usually spend about an hour together. During much of that time I am listening to the patient's story and then doing a neurologic examination so we have only the last fraction of the hour to discuss the key issues of diagnosis, prognosis, and treatment. Most patients want and need much more information about their illnesses than they currently have. I try to recommend books and Web sites to them. They speak with friends and do Internet searches. I wish that I had an entire day or more to educate my patients. Usually they return to my office regularly for many years, and we gradually teach each other.

Someone with Parkinson's disease or other serious illness faces many decisions. Should I believe the diagnosis that I have heard from my physician? What is my prognosis? Should I change my life plans? Should I take the medications that the physician has prescribed? Do I need to take them just as instructed? Should I look for nontraditional and alternative therapies? Should I think about brain surgery? The list of questions is infinite.

In *Understanding Parkinson's Disease,* I try to help readers make these decisions by teaching about the disease, its course, causes, and treatments. I want to show how I think about the advice that I give. Most of us

cannot go to medical school, but if patients can understand how physicians analyze the disease, patients and physicians will communicate and
collaborate better.

Ideally, I should tell my patients the facts, answering their questions
clearly and truthfully in simple language uncluttered with medical lingo.
The truth is that the facts can be fuzzy or inexact. Everyone's illness has
a distinct course and many idiosyncrasies, and each treatment must be
individualized. Even more difficult, the best therapy when I write this
book may not be the best therapy by the time it is read because new
experiments and discoveries are constantly redefining *Understanding
Parkinson's Disease.*

In this book I have written about Parkinson's disease as if I were
teaching students when we have a semester to study together. I have
reviewed some of the history of how scientists have learned about it
and explained some of the experiments that have been particularly
important in this understanding. I have tried to minimize long words
and complex details, yet some readers will find sections of the book
too scientific. Each chapter starts simply and becomes more complex;
the key points are outlined early in the chapter. The reader should feel
free to skip to the start of the next chapter if the reading slows like
parkinsonian footsteps.

My goal is for *Understanding Parkinson's Disease* to make living with
Parkinson's disease easier, not only in practical matters such as taking
the best medication, preventing falls, or avoiding depression, but also,
equally important, by offering hope and autonomy to patients and those
close to them.

CHAPTER ONE

The Diagnostic Conversation—Diagnosis and Prognosis of Parkinson's Disease

Making the Diagnosis

"Dad, how long have you had Parkinson's disease?" I asked my father while we relaxed in my living room after dinner one evening in 1994. As he had walked from the dinner table, bald and a bit portly, he looked his 79 years, but I noticed no slowing or hesitation in his movement. To a son's eye, his gaze was energetic, optimistic, and ageless. Then, for the first time, I saw his right hand shaking in his lap and with little forethought blurted out the question. He replied calmly, "Do you think I have Parkinson's?" I was surprised, not by his equanimity, but because he had missed his own diagnosis.

I asked the question very casually. In some ways, recognizing that a family member has Parkinson's is not so unusual. Most people know someone or have watched people with the disease. It does not take a neurologist to diagnose Parkinson's disease. The characteristic tremor, inexpressive face, slow movement, and stooped posture of those with Parkinson's have become so familiar that many without medical training can tell if someone has it as easily as we all can recognize a cold or the flu.

For anyone, discovering a progressively debilitating illness is life changing. For Dad and me our laconic interchange reverberates particularly because we are both physicians. When I told him that he had Parkinson's disease, we knew that I was offering a very well-educated, professional opinion.

"I am a neurologist," I reply to a cocktail party question about my job. I know from experience that this can stop the conversation dead, or sometimes it elicits a monologue about a friend or family member who has Alzheimer's disease, stroke, multiple sclerosis, or another devastating illness. Even worse, in the noise of competing conversations, "urologist" is heard, and I am told stories of incontinence and impotence.

Few neurologists are noted casual conversationalists. They are cerebral, at times precise, rarely loquacious. I love the story about the two balloonists who got lost in the clouds and landed in a field to get their bearings. They hailed a man standing nearby and asked where they were. The man replied, "You're in my field." One balloonist said to the other, "Isn't it just our luck to run into a neurologist at a time like this?" His companion asked, "How do you know he's a neurologist?" "Because what he said is precisely true and totally useless."

Sometimes the humor lands close to the mark. Neurologists do take pride in how we can help our patients by careful examination and diagnosis. A woman came to my office because she was afraid that her facial nerve was deteriorating. A year before, she had had Bell's palsy, paralysis of one side of her face. The facial weakness is usually caused by a herpes virus, worsens over a few days, and then recovers in six months or less. My patient was concerned because a year after the first attack of palsy, the affected side of her face seemed stiffer and more swollen. I watched her face closely while she told me her story. I asked her to raise her eyebrows, blink, keep her eyes closed, smile, and whistle. I took time to hear her detailed medical history and checked her thoroughly to confirm that with the exception of her face, her nervous system responded normally. After the examination, I was able to tell her that her abnormal facial movement was a sign of nerve healing rather than of a new or progressive nerve disease. My treatment for her was education and reassurance. I disagree with the balloonist; for many patients, simply understanding what is happening to their bodies is therapeutic.

It is true that until recently, we rarely had worthwhile drugs for neurological diseases. Fortunately, the current generation of neurologists is hardly useless. We have powerful new treatments for Parkinson's disease, Alzheimer's disease, stroke, multiple sclerosis, epilepsy, migraine, and many other illnesses. This therapeutic explosion comes from basic science and clinical research in genetics, pharmacology, cell biology, toxicology, epidemiology, and many other disciplines. Both neurologists and patients depend on research scientists, often collaborating from many fields, to develop and test therapeutic advances.

Neurologists never learn to operate on the brain the way neurosurgeons do. While the surgeons are learning to cut, we devote our training to diagnosis and treatment. We are the experts on identifying

Parkinson's disease and many other diseases of the brain or nerves. My own training was at some of the finest neurological centers in the world—Harvard, Stanford, the National Institutes of Health, and the University of California at San Francisco. When I finished formal training in 1977, I moved back to Portland, Oregon, where I had grown up. Many of my classmates went into research, but I returned to practice neurology in the same clinic where Dad had worked for years as an internist. My partner as a neurologist is my cousin, Robert. He trained at two other famous neurological programs, Johns Hopkins and the Mayo Clinic, but institutional rivalry does not intrude on our long friendship. My father and Robert's father, a general surgeon, were our mentors. We continued to teach each other and to learn from our patients. In 1994 I knew a lot about Parkinson's disease. I had cared for hundreds of patients. In 1994 I did not think deeply about how much more I would be learning about Parkinson's disease, new ways of treatment, exciting new research about its cause, a more intimate understanding of its toll, and ultimately, I hope, a better ability to be a physician for those with it and other neurological diseases.

When I asked my father how long he had had Parkinson's disease, I assumed that he had already made a simple self-diagnosis. He had graduated from medical school in 1938, served in the U.S. Army in one of the first MASH units in World War II, and finished postgraduate training at the Mayo Clinic in rheumatology, the specialty that cares for arthritis. When he moved to Portland and opened his clinic in 1948, there was one neurologist in the city. Most patients with Parkinson's disease saw internists or family physicians. The neurologist consulted only on atypical or unusual cases. There was really no need for specialists' opinions because there was essentially no effective treatment. Any internist should be able to tell if someone has Parkinson's disease. During his career Dad certainly had cared for many parkinsonian patients. He was an accomplished, even brilliant, diagnostician. Why had he been surprised when I offered the diagnosis? Had his clinical acumen waned so quickly after retirement? Did he use psychological denial of illness so that he knew the diagnosis in some part of his brain but would not admit it to himself? Had the illness crept up on him so slowly that he hardly noticed the changes? He and I have talked about this, and neither of us knows the answer.

James Parkinson and the Shaking Palsy

The tradition that you do not have to be a neurologist to diagnose Parkinson's disease goes back to James Parkinson himself. Born in 1755, he lived in an age of change, the time of the American and French revolutions. England's own revolution was industrial. He was fully engaged in the political and intellectual activity of the day, not only as a general physician and surgeon, but also as a prolific pamphleteer, whose subjects were as diverse as radical politics, gout, geology, and appendicitis.

There were no neurologists in 1817 when Parkinson wrote his pamphlet *An Essay on the Shaking Palsy,* in which he described six men who had tremor and impaired movement. For centuries, physicians had known that tremors could occur in a wide variety of illnesses. Parkinson reported on six people whose tremors were accompanied by other findings that he described as "involuntary tremulous motion, with lessened muscular power, in parts not in action and even when supported; with a propensity to bend the trunk forwards, and to pass from a walking to a running pace: the senses and intellects being uninjured." Parkinson noted that the tremor usually first appeared in a hand, arm, or foot, and then gradually spread, often within a year, to other areas. Eventually, the sufferer began to bend forward, especially while walking. The initial tremor might be little more than an annoyance, but Parkinson observed that eventually, "the submission of the limbs to the directions of the will can hardly ever be obtained in the performance of the most ordinary offices of life."[1]

Parkinson brought this disease to the attention of English and European physicians, but the disease was not new. It had been described by Indian physicians millennia before 1817. In the second century the great Greek physician Galen mentioned patients with resting tremors. Some medical historians suggest that Parkinson observed so much because of changing epidemiology. Cities were growing. People were leaving the farms. Perhaps toxic pollution from the industrial revolution increased the incidence of the disease, or the growth of cities brought enough people together that clusters of illness were evident. Others point to the many diseases that were first named in the nineteenth century because of intellectual changes in how physicians studied illness.

We do not know how thoroughly Parkinson examined these six patients. He described them in a few paragraphs. He reported that he saw one of the patients only from a distance and made the diagnoses of two others after meeting them in the streets. He named the condition *paralysis agitans,* combining the Latin words for "weakness" and "shaking."

As a clinical neurologist, I always schedule an hour for my first meeting with a patient. I listen to his or her complaints, take a complete medical history, and do a physical examination before offering my initial opinion of diagnosis, the need for tests, and possibilities of treatment. For patients with Parkinson's disease, this ritual is usually an afterthought to making the diagnosis, which is often apparent when I first see the patient walk from the waiting room.

A medical history is a very stylized conversation. I start by asking the patient to tell me about the problem that brings him or her to my office. I listen carefully, take notes, and avoid interrupting. I encourage a friend or family member to accompany the patient and offer details. I want the patient to provide the narrative of the illness because particulars like timing of symptoms, modifying factors, and effects on daily activities can tell the tale of the diagnosis. Of course, once the patient has finished, I usually need to fill in gaps with more directed questions.

The medical history of Dad's illness has been strikingly similar to the illnesses of Parkinson's patients. Parkinson wrote that symptoms began very gradually: "So slight and nearly imperceptible are the first inroads of this malady, and so extremely slow is its progress, that it rarely happens, that the patient can form any recollection of the precise period of its commencement."[2] Looking back for the first harbingers of incoordination, Dad, who always welcomes the chance to tell a story, recalls that when he was 65 years old, in 1980, his handwriting seemed clumsier when he signed prescriptions. He remembers his extravagant purchase of a thick-barreled Mont Blanc pen in hopes that he would write more easily, but his writing did not improve when he tried the new pen.

In 1985 my father and I were examining a patient together and trying to decide whether the patient had Parkinson's disease. I checked the tone in the patient's arm. To check arm tone, I put one of my hands on the patient's elbow and used my other hand to grasp the patient's hand as if we were shaking hands. I asked the patient to relax while I gently flexed and extended the elbow. A person with increased tone will have muscle resistance to this movement, even when completely relaxed. The neurological term for this muscular resistance is rigidity. The patient had a very slight increase in tone; for comparison I checked Dad's tone because he was about the same age as the patient. In clinical scientific studies, patients are often compared to well individuals of the same age, so-called age-matched controls.

My comparison of this one patient with a single age-matched control was too haphazard to qualify as a scientific study. The patient and my father both had the same mild increase in tone. At that time Dad had no other hints of Parkinson's disease, and I dismissed his increased arm tone as a sign of his age.

Dad's right hand began to shake in the mid-1990s. At first the tremor was limited to this hand. This type of asymmetry is very common early in Parkinson's disease. Eventually, both hands were clumsy, and my mother had to button his shirts for him. For many years he remained agile on his feet. About 1999, he had trouble getting up from a chair. This was his first evidence of another parkinsonian feature called bradykinesia, which means slow movement. In the last few years he has been increasingly unsteady on his feet, which is most apparent when he tries to turn quickly. More and more, he has tripped and sustained minor injuries. This difficulty relying on his footing is called postural instability.

Jean Charcot and Better Examinations

When a twenty-first-century neurologist does a history and physical examination, the techniques derive from neurologists of the later nineteenth century. Scientific advances are often propelled by the development of new methods and techniques. During the first part of the nineteenth century, little was added to Parkinson's description of paralysis agitans. However, beginning in the 1860s, Jean Charcot, in Paris, was leading a new era in neurology by a new technique: very careful physical examination. Working at the Salpêtrière, a large Parisian hospital for the chronically ill, he examined many of the residents in detail, followed their illnesses over time, and often was able to study the pathology in their brains by doing autopsies when they died.

In the vibrant Paris of the later nineteenth century, Charcot was for neurology what the impressionists were for art. He taught a new way of seeing. Charcot aspired to be an artist before he chose medicine as a career. He emphasized careful visual inspection of the patient and skill-fully sketched his observations. His lectures became famous in Paris. On Fridays he gave formal presentations; on Tuesdays his lectures were more informal. One Tuesday, he began,

> Gentlemen: Those among you, who, this morning passed through our wards, were probably surprised to find collected there so great a number of female patients, in whom tremor seems to constitute the paramount or at least the most striking symptom of the disease which they labor under. This gathering of patients forming a genus apart, I purposely contrived. In that way, I desired to enable you to recognize, by means of a comparative study, certain shades of distinction and even marked differences which the examination of isolated cases does not allow you so readily to discern.[3]

Charcot showed his students that the tremor of patients with paralysis agitans was a repetitive rhythmic shaking, occurring four to six times each second while the patient was relaxed. The tremor is often visible in the hands resting in the patient's lap and decreases or disappears when the hands are moved or used. The repetitive tremulous motion of the tip of thumb against the side of index finger is classically called pill rolling, emphasizing the appearance that the patient is rolling a small object between the first two digits. Charcot looked carefully at patients' handwriting and saw that the tremor affected the writing more on the upstroke than on the downstroke. Charcot also described limb rigidity, discovered when the examiner tries to move the limb of a patient who is attempting to relax. He noted that careful examination of muscle strength somewhat surprisingly showed that most patients with this condition had no weakness of individual muscles. Paralysis means weakness, so Charcot disagreed with Parkinson's choice of the name "paralysis agitans." Charcot renamed the shaking palsy "Parkinson's disease."

By the end of the nineteenth century, the principal or cardinal features of Parkinson's disease were well known: tremor, rigidity, brady-kinesia, and postural instability. Physicians knew the progressive nature of the disease, which usually begins asymmetrically in one limb, worsens gradually over years, and eventually leads to severe immobility. The anatomy, physiology, cause, and treatment remained mysterious, but my father's diagnosis of Parkinson's disease would have been as clear to Charcot in 1880 as it is to me now.

Many neurologists, myself included, are attracted to neurology because it is one of a few medical specialties in which diagnosis and treatment still rely heavily on the physician's observations made during history taking and physical examination. Clinicians diagnose Parkinson's disease solely by these techniques; there is no accurate blood test, electrical test, or X ray that is diagnostic of Parkinson's disease. During the patient's life the opinion of an experienced clinician determines the diagnosis.

When I teach beginning students about Parkinson's disease, Dad often volunteers to join me as an exemplary patient. As a physician, he is very comfortable making this traditional contribution to medical education. The students listen to his history and watch me examine him, and we discuss how clinicians make diagnoses. We debate whether diagnosis is a scientific process or an art of pattern recognition.

The answer, as with so much of medicine, is that diagnosis is both science and art. One aspect that is clearly scientific is the clinicians' willingness to test and retest their ideas. We use experiments to quantify the accuracy of our diagnostic skills.

Checking Diagnostic Accuracy

Some patients listen to their doctors' diagnostic pronouncements as if they were hearing the truth from an oracle. In contrast, physicians are constantly aware of how difficult it is to be certain that they have made a correct diagnosis. To understand this, let's analyze the complexities of diagnostic imperfection. If a clinician were a perfectly accurate diagnos-tician for Parkinson's disease, a patient would always have Parkinson's disease when the clinician made the diagnosis and never have Parkinson's disease when the clinician said the disease was absent. We can envision this in a two-by-two table comparing the clinician's proposed diagnosis to the proven diagnosis (Table 1.1). When the clinician correctly says the disease is present, the diagnosis is called a true positive; when the clinician correctly says the disease is absent, the diagnosis is called a true negative. As shown in the table, incorrect diagnoses can be false positives or false negatives.

Investigators checked neurologists' diagnostic accuracy by performing brain autopsies on 100 consecutive people whom British neurologists had diagnosed as having Parkinson's disease.[4,5] The British have been famous in the medical community for the training and skill of their neurologists.

The autopsied brains were viewed by neuropathologists, specialists in studying brain, spinal cord, or nerve tissue to understand disease of the nervous system. Later, I shall describe the well-defined pathological characteristics of Parkinson's disease. Some are visible to the unaided eye; others are seen only under the microscope. Surprisingly, the neuropathologists confirmed the diagnosis of Parkinson's disease in only about three-quarters of the cases!

The reports from the neuropathologists of diagnostic errors by clinicians are very important to neurologists, who can respond in various ways. First, the neurologists look carefully at the skills, methods, and diagnostic criteria used by the neuropathologists. Who has the diagnosis wrong—the clinician or the pathologist? Perhaps the pathologists' diagnosis should not be the gold standard for the correct diagnosis. Errors in pathological diagnosis might arise from erroneous pathological diagnostic criteria; methodological errors, such as not examining the brain carefully or using incorrect stains and techniques; or from unreliable observations or interpretations by the pathologist. In this study, there were no obvious errors by the neuropathologists.

Second, neurologists need to reevaluate the clinical diagnostic criteria for Parkinson's disease. The initial diagnostic criteria emphasized the cardinal features of Parkinson's disease (tremor, rigidity, bradykinesia, postural instability), with added weight given to response to treatment

TABLE 1.1: Comparison of Clinicians' Diagnoses of Parkinson's Disease to the Proven Diagnosis

	Clinician's diagnosis—Parkinson's disease	Clinician's Diagnosis—Not Parkinson's disease
Proven diagnosis—Parkinson's disease	True positive	False negative
Proven diagnosis—Not Parkinson's disease	False positive	True negative

with a drug called L-dopa, or levodopa. In these diagnostic criteria the investigators make a distinction between parkinsonism and idiopathic Parkinson's disease.

Parkinsonism means having signs like tremor, rigidity, bradykinesia, and postural instability. Some people have parkinsonism without truly having Parkinson's disease. For example, certain medications, like the strong tranquilizer drugs haloperidol (Haldol) or chlorpromazine (Thorazine), cause some people to develop the characteristic movement difficulties of a person with Parkinson's disease, but fortunately, these characteristics disappear after the medication is stopped, and the drugs do not cause the pathological changes of Parkinson's disease in the brain.

In other words, parkinsonism has a differential diagnosis. Parkinson's disease is the best-known cause of parkinsonism, but reversible drug tox-icity is another common cause of parkinsonism. There are rarer causes of parkinsonism, often irreversible, that the neuropathologists can sepa-rate from Parkinson's disease (Table 1.2).

One of my students said that when we call a disease idiopathic, we are admitting that we are idiots about its pathology. His etymology is a little imaginative, but it is a way to remember that *idiopathic* is a medical term that means "of unknown cause." We know the causes of few cases of Parkinson's disease; therefore most cases are idiopathic. Someday our understanding of Parkinson's disease will be so clear that few or no cases will remain idiopathic. When that happens, the term *Parkinson's disease* may fall into disuse and be replaced by a term or terms that emphasize the causes or pathologies of the disease.

Specificity and Sensitivity

The British investigators reexamined the diagnostic criteria and found that neurologists could have modified the diagnostic criteria for idiopathic Parkinson's disease to improve diagnostic specificity. Diagnostic specificity is one important measure of any diagnostic test or set of diagnostic criteria. Diagnostic criteria are more specific if

TABLE 1.2: Differential Diagnosis of Parkinsonism

Parkinson's disease

Reversible drug-induced parkinsonism

Parkinsonism due to brain damage from encephalitis

Parkinsonism due to brain trauma

Parkinsonism due to multiple strokes

Normal pressure hydrocephalus

Other neurodegenerative diseases (multiple systems atrophy, progressive su-pranuclear palsy, etc.)

they lead to fewer false positive diagnoses. If you have a mammogram, screening for breast cancer, or a PSA blood test, screening for prostate cancer, and the test has low specificity, a positive result on the test might lead to extensive additional testing and much anxiety before the positive result is shown to be a false positive.

If the British clinicians had reserved the diagnosis of Parkinson's disease for those people in whom tremor was the predominant symptom, they would have improved specificity to 96 percent. Unfortunately, only 11 of the 76 patients with pathologically confirmed Parkinson's disease had the tremor-predominant form of the illness, so clinicians who used this very specific diagnostic criterion would have overlooked many people who actually had the disease. These instances when the clinician misses the presence of disease are called false negatives. A test or diagnostic criteria has less diagnostic sensitivity if it is associated with more false negative results. When the diagnostic criterion was tremor-predominant disease, the diagnostic sensitivity was only 14 percent.

In every diagnostic setting, there is a balance between specificity and sensitivity. More specific diagnostic criteria are almost always less sensitive. A screening test for cancer that is insensitive may minimize anxiety-provoking false positive results at the cost of deceptively reassuring false negative results that miss the opportunity for early cancer detection. Every woman who has a mammogram should be concerned about false negative or false positive reports from the radiologist who interprets her films. A normal report might be a false negative, so it is vital that she continues regular breast self-examination and has follow-up examinations by her physicians and mammographers. Conversely, an abnormal report is frequently a false positive, so many women have costly, uncomfortable, nerve-wracking breast biopsies that ultimately show no cancer.

The balance between false positives and false negatives, between improving diagnostic sensitivity and improving diagnostic specificity, is a problem that affects every medical test or set of diagnostic criteria. Beyond science, this problem extends to all other settings where we try to detect or identify something. Imagine designing a burglar alarm system for your home. Should you put detectors only on the front door, on all the doors, on the windows? If you choose only the front door, you will not have a very sensitive alarm system because someone could enter another door undetected. The lack of alarm when someone entered the back door would be a false negative for the alarm system. One alternative choice is to put detectors on all the doors to decrease the chance of false negatives and thus increase the sensitivity of the system. The system might still have some false negatives; for example, someone might enter through a window or have a clever trick to turn the system off. Every time we try to improve the burglar alarm, by testing more doors, by testing windows, or by adding other refinements, we increase the risk of false positives and therefore decrease the specificity of the alarm; a door left ajar or a bird hitting a window might set off a false alarm if we increased the sensitivity of the alarm system.

Airport security detectors are another everyday example of diagnostic accuracy, sensitivity, and specificity. Security screening is designed for high sensitivity. The result is that travelers are hassled by frequent false positives. The specificity is low, so that to detect a few very dangerous terrorists, the screeners confiscate scads of nail files from the harmless but absent minded.

In contrast, in the American criminal justice system, we believe that everyone is innocent until proven guilty. We insist on high specificity because we never want to punish the innocent, so inevitably, we lose some sensitivity and allow some false negatives, some criminals to escape conviction. Of course, no matter how much the courts strive for high specificity, avoiding the false positive of an unjust conviction, the specificity is still less than 100 percent. Inevitably, we read a few stories of those incorrectly convicted of a crime, only to be exonerated years later. Technological improvements, like identification using DNA, can decrease both false positives and false negatives, but even a theoretically perfect identification test must have an occasional error because of measurement errors, machine failures, or human imperfection.

Many nonphysicians accept medical diagnoses as proven facts. They do not realize that the delicate balance between sensitivity and specificity means that no diagnostician is always right. In contrast, physicians recognize that each diagnosis that they make has a chance of being incorrect. The scientific physician must respond to this constant chance of diagnostic error. One response of clinicians to learning of their inaccuracy is to check the consequences of their mistakes. When I diagnose Parkinson's disease, which is worse: to miss the diagnosis and delay treatment, or to make a false positive diagnosis, which can lead to unnecessary treatment and worries?

Physicians are taught early in their training *primum non nocere* (first do no harm). When neurologists learn that they are imperfect at diagnosing Parkinson's disease, they can concentrate on improving their diagnostic skills for diagnoses that are most amenable to treatment or are most dangerous if overlooked. Clinicians are often uncertain about a diagnosis because clinical tests always have false positives and false negatives. Therefore clinical care often proceeds with a trial dose of medication or reexamination over time, while the diagnosis remains unproved.

The way an illness changes over time gives the clinician clues to its diagnosis. An old saw is true: the last neurologist to examine a patient usually looks like the smartest neurologist. Michael J. Fox has written about his Parkinson's disease, illustrating this point. He tells of first noting his symptoms in November 1990:

> I woke up to find the message in my left hand. It had me trembling. It wasn't a fax, telegram, memo, or the usual sort of missal bringing disturbing news. In fact, my hand held nothing at all. The trembling was the message.[6]

He quickly consulted a neurologist, who, despite carefully examining the actor, was unable to make a correct diagnosis. By missing the diagnosis of Parkinson's disease, the neurologist made a false negative diagnosis. When he saw the first neurologist, Fox had tremor but neither slow movement, nor rigidity, nor postural instability. False negative diagnoses are common in patients early in the course of Parkinson's disease before all the cardinal features have developed.

Fox's tremor persisted, and he became slow and clumsy. By the summer of 1991, his left side moved more stiffly than his right. The difference was particularly noticeable when he was jogging. At summer's end he consulted another physician, who correctly diagnosed Parkinson's disease.

Medicine remains both an art and a science; it is as much about caring for people as it is about scientific facts. That is why I am still embarrassed about how artlessly I announced my father's diagnosis. I had learned many clinical skills from him and certainly knew better. Early in my career, a patient with Parkinson's disease came to me for a second opinion. The diagnosis was evident from the first minute, but I did not pronounce it until I had heard his story and examined him. "Thank you for being so thorough in your examination and explanations," he said. He had been dissatisfied with one of my skilled colleagues, who had prematurely offered the diagnosis of Parkinson's disease on first sight, without taking time to convince the patient that he had investigated his complaints. They say, "The patient needs to know how much you care before he cares how much you know." My only excuse for not offering my father the same clinical compassion is that the family is far different from the clinic.

Every year, Dad tells the students the story of how he learned his diagnosis. He has never seemed perturbed by my sudden revelation. Because his son is a neurologist, he probably learned his diagnosis a bit earlier in the course of his illness than most patients do. He responded with equanimity, which was always his style for facing challenges. Physicians cannot care for their family members, and I quickly directed my father to another neurologist for care. Making the diagnosis is only the first chapter in the long story of this illness.

Making a diagnosis should be a conversation between neurologist and patient. The conversation starts with the formalized process of going over the medical history and proceeds with the physician offering his opinion about the diagnosis, at times explaining why the diagnosis is tentative or uncertain; educating the patient about the illness; answering questions; and arranging to continue the discussion at future follow-up visits.

Prognosis

I speak with my father a few times each week. We talk about my practice, my wife, and his grandchildren. I ask what he and Mom have done that day. He usually has a humorous anecdote about one of his old friends, a bittersweet story of failing memory, injury from falls, or other challenges of aging. He occasionally asks me questions about his illness, checking my opinion of the medications that his physician prescribes or inquiring about an experimental treatment that he has read about in the newspaper. He has had Parkinson's disease for more than a decade, yet he has never asked me about his prognosis. His reticence comes from his own experiences with prognosticating for his patients and with his own previous illness.

Dad had a very busy practice. Even at age 70, he was seeing 30 patients a day. By this age, he would come home, after 10 hours in the office, exhausted and hoarse. His hoarseness led him to a throat specialist, who did a biopsy. The specialist reassured Dad that he had a benign polyp on his vocal cords. Unfortunately, the hoarseness persisted for many months, and Dad consulted a second specialist, who discovered throat cancer. The initial reassuring diagnosis had been a false negative.

My mother called my office and told me about the cancer. I felt a surge of hormones and neurotransmitters. My heart was pounding, and my hand was trembling. I am sure that my mother was even more upset than I was, but we spoke quietly on the phone, each pretending to be calm.

I rushed to the medical library to read about the prognosis, about his chances for survival, for regaining his voice, for a cure. I learned that his future was very uncertain and that his physicians would need more information, like X rays showing how far the tumor had spread, before offering any predictions. I drove to my parents' house and walked into their den with trepidation. I can still visualize Dad, sitting in his armchair, looking healthy and croaking with John Wayne–like bravado, "We're going to beat this." The drama was heightened by his uncharacteristic theatricality.

I was shocked that he was so certain about the prognosis. One of his favorite stories dated to his internship, when he was assigned to talk to a patient about a biopsy result. As instructed by his teachers, Dad told the man that he had a cancer that would kill him within six months.

When the patient was alive a year later and the diagnosis of cancer was disproved, Dad vowed never again to make predictions of life and death. Of course, now predicting his own survival, he was responding as patient, not as physician, and whether he was speaking from denial or hope or intuition, everyone in the family gained strength from his attitude.

Diagnosis and prognosis are closely linked. Both words are built on the Greek root for "knowledge." To diagnose is to know distinctions. Dad's stories of cancer misdiagnosis, of false positives and of false negatives, further illustrate the fallibility of medical diagnosis and the importance of reassessing diagnoses over time.

To prognose is to know the future. One of the great insights of Hippocrates, the Greek forbearer of all modern physicians, was that once he made a diagnosis, he could study the natural evolution of a disease and then offer a prognosis, a prediction of the future, when he later saw others afflicted with the same condition. Hippocrates advised his students to use knowledge of prognosis to impress patients. He thought patients were likely to trust a physician who made correct predictions. Unfortunately, if diagnosis is uncertain, prognosis is even more so, and I have learned from Dad to be very wary of offering prognoses.

Dad's shoot-from-the-hip self-prognosis was miraculously correct. Radiation therapy cured his cancer, and his voice gradually recovered. Stories of cancer are often dramatic, ending in death or in recovery, and Dad's cancer story literally had a Hollywood ending. He wrote a book about his illness, initially published as *A Taste of His Own Medicine*. In 1991 the book was reissued as *The Doctor* and made into the movie *The Doctor*, with William Hurt playing the role of my father.

If you closely watch the DVD of the movie, you can catch a glimpse of my parents in cameo roles. Dad had no visible hints of parkinsonism during his brief film career. In the movie William Hurt walks down the hall of the hospital with a train of junior physicians. My father is sitting in a chair, playing the role of senior physician, talking to my mother, who is playing a patient's wife. When Hurt walks by, my father speaks a single line to his colleague: "Hi." After 12 takes the scene was still wrong. Hurt realized that on the stage, Dad was out of his element. He gave Dad a quick acting lesson, and take 13 was in the can.

A story of Parkinson's disease from beginning to end does not have the same drama. The insidious course of the disease has been known at least since 1817, when Parkinson emphasized eventual deterioration in his description of the shaking palsy. Over the years my father's Parkinson's disease has certainly shown very slow but relentless decline. After the success of *The Doctor*, Dad began a second career, traveling the country and speaking about the experiences of doctor-turned-patient. He loved going first class, receiving honorary degrees, and telling his stories to large audiences. Finally, embarrassment about his tremor took away his joy in public speaking. He never was willing to talk to audiences about Parkinson's disease the way he loved to tell about beating cancer.

Physicians call the untreated course of an illness its "natural history." Hippocrates and his successors studied the natural history of diseases long before we could treat them successfully. However, despite powerful modern therapies, physicians still study the natural history of diseases, charting how they change over time, not only to teach patients about their illnesses, but also to make diagnoses.

Each illness has a distinct pattern of development. A neurologist would not confuse a stroke, which starts very suddenly, quickly reaches its maximum severity, and then improves, with Parkinson's disease, even if both cause tremor and slow movement on one side of the body. Even though I am cautious about prognosticating, I do not hesitate to tell a stroke patient to expect improvement. For some strokes I can offer more information, like "your leg strength will return faster than your arm strength." I have to add that I cannot predict the speed or final extent of the recovery.

Rarely, when a stroke patient comes to my office for a follow-up appointment, I am told that my promise of recovery was wrong. When this happens, I must recheck the diagnosis. Has the patient had another stroke? Has some other illness interfered with the natural history of recovery? Diagnosis and prognosis are closely linked, and when I observe the patient over time, I learn more about both.

For patients with progressive illnesses like Parkinson's disease, the diagnosis is often obscure early in the illness. Remember the initial misdiagnosis of Michael J. Fox when his only early abnormality was tremor, before he had the other characteristics of Parkinson's disease, like rigidity, slow movement, and instability on his feet.

The Hoehn and Yahr Scale

Like all physicians, I first learned the natural history of illnesses from my teachers and enforced my knowledge by observing my patients, but a more accurate sense of prognosis comes from compilations of many patients. In 1967, neurologists Margaret Hoehn and Melvin Yahr reported on this aspect of Parkinson's disease based on observations of hundreds of patients seen at the College of Physicians and Surgeons in New York between 1949 and 1964.[7] They proposed a scale of disability caused by the disease (Table 1.3), which is now a standard, relatively simple way to classify the disease severity.

TABLE 1.3: Hoehn and Yahr Stages of Parkinson's Disease

Hoehn and Yahr stage	Clinical findings
Stage I	Symptoms mostly on one side of the body with little loss of function.
Stage II	Symptoms on both sides of the body, but balance is normal.
Stage III	Symptoms on both sides of the body, and balance is imperfect.
Stage IV	Severe impairment of movement and balance but still able to walk without help.
Stage V	Severe impairment of movement; unable to walk without help or even confined to bed and chair.

Adapted from Hoehn MM, Yahr MD. Parkinsonism: Onset, progression, and mortality. *Neurology.* 1967;17:427–442.

Clinical scales, like Hoehn and Yahr's, let us sort patients in order of severity, but they do not have the precision of a scale that weighs objects. Two pounds is always twice as heavy as one pound. A patient with stage II Parkinson's disease is more impaired than a patient with stage I disease but is not exactly twice as sick.

Hoehn and Yahr successfully used their scale to document the variation in disease progression. For example, nearly three-eighths of their patients had deteriorated to stage III or worse within five years of the onset of symptoms; on the other hand, one-third of patients who had been ill for over a decade were still in stage I or II. They were able to correlate the duration of the illness with the risk of reaching stage IV or dying.

As a physician, I may be tempted to take disease stagings like this, which exist for hundreds of diseases, and apply them to my own patients, thinking that I have become an adroit prognostician. However, if I want to extrapolate these observations to my own patients, I need to consider whether the patterns of referral that lead patients to a famous hospital like Physicians and Surgeons are similar to those that lead patients to my office. For example, the patients might be referred to a specialty clinic because they have more severe disease. Furthermore, Hoehn and Yahr's observations offer only a little help to me and to my patients as we think about the future because they give few clues about what determines the rate of worsening. We still know very little about why one patient worsens quickly, whereas another has a very slow, relatively benign illness. The prognosis of Parkinson's disease is so variable that I cannot offer patients the same details that I offer stroke patients.

By 2003, my father was clearly in stage III. He was living independently but moving slowly and walking unsteadily. He occasionally fell.

He sustained cuts and bruises but fortunately, no broken bones. How long did it take him to reach stage III? Reflecting on the beginning of his illness, we see one problem with the Hoehn and Yahr prognostication. Do we date the onset of his problems to the mid-1990s, when his tremor first appeared, or to the early 1980s, which he currently recollects as the time of the first appearance of his handwriting difficulty? Any prognosticating scheme that relies on patients' memories of early symptoms will suffer from large variations in human skills for self-observation and recollection.

The year 1967 was seminal in the history of Parkinson's disease. Prior to 1967, there was little effective treatment for the disease. Technically speaking, Hoehn and Yahr did not observe the natural history of the disease because they prescribed for their patients the paltry drugs then available, but these treatments probably did not have major effects on the risks of disability or death. In 1967 George Cotzias and his colleagues published their first paper on the use of L-dopa in the treatment of Parkinson's disease.[8] Most current studies of Parkinson's disease treatment show the prognosis of treated Parkinson's disease, a prognosis improved by modern therapies.

The development of more powerful therapies sparked the development of better ways to assess disease severity. To test new treatments, investigators need ways to measure disease before and after treatment. The measure needs to be objective, which means both that it provides a quantifiable rating of the disease and that it is reliable and reproducible. A bathroom scale is useless if every time you step on it, it reports a widely different weight; an unreliable clinical scale is equally useless.

A measure of Parkinson's disease needs to provide clinically meaningful divisions of disease severity, just as the Hoehn and Yahr scale clearly divides the disease into varying stages of interference with body function. However, because the Hoehn and Yahr scale has only five divisions, it can overlook treatment effects that might be very beneficial to a patient but insufficient to reclassify the patient to a lower stage.

The Unified Parkinson's Disease Rating Scale

Researchers devised the Unified Parkinson's Disease Rating Scale (UPDRS) to measure the disease better.[9] It is now widely used to assess treatment of Parkinson's disease, and a new version is in preparation. I will describe the UPDRS in detail now because we will return to it frequently when reviewing results of different treatments.

The UPDRS rates a patient on 31 different items, each with a score of 0 to 4 (Table 1.4). The rating scale covers three areas: mentation, behavior, and mood (4 items); activities of daily living (13 items); and motor examination (14 items). The full UPDRS also includes items for

TABLE 1.4: The 31 Items on the UPDRS Divided into Three Major Categories; Each Item Is Scored from 0 to 4

Mentation, mood, and behavior	Activities of daily living	Motor examination
Intellectual impairment	Speech	Speech
Thought disorder	Salivation Swallowing	Facial expression
Depression Motivation/	Handwriting	Tremor at rest
initiative	Use of eating utensils	Action or postural
	Dressing	tremor
	Hygiene Turning in bed	Rigidity Finger taps
	Falling	Hand movements
	Freezing while walking	Rapid alternating
	Walking	movements
	Tremor	Foot agility
	Sensory complaints	Arising from chair
		Posture
		Gait
		Postural stability
		Body bradykinesia

Adapted from Gancher S. Scales for the assessment of movement disorders. In: Herndon R, ed. *Handbook of Neurologic Rating Scales.* 1st ed. New York: Demos Vermande; 1997:81–106. Original published by S. Fahn and R. L. Elton, members of the UPDRS Development Committee, in Fahn S, Marsden CD, Calne DB, Goldstein M, eds. *Recent Developments in Parkinson's Disease.* Vol. 2. Florham Park, NJ: Macmillan Health Care Information; 1987:153–164.

complications of therapy. A healthy person has a UPDRS of 0; a patient with the most severe Parkinson's disease could have a UPDRS of 146. Table 1.5 shows examples of how individual items are scored.

TABLE 1.5: Examples of Scoring of UPDRS Items

Score	Tremor (effect on daily activities)	Arising from chair (findings on examination)
0	Absent	Normal
1	Slight, infrequent	Slow
2	Moderate, bothersome	Pushes self up
3	Severe, interferes with many activities	Tends to fall back or retry
4	Marked, interferes with most activities	Needs help

Adapted from Gancher S. Scales for the assessment of movement disorders. In: Herndon R, ed. Handbook of Neurologic Rating Scales. 1st ed. New York: Demos Vermande; 1997:81–106. Original published by S. Fahn and R. L. Elton, members of the UPDRS Development Committee, in Fahn S, Marsden CD, Calne DB, Goldstein M, eds. Recent Developments in Parkinson's Disease. Vol. 2. Florham Park, NJ: Macmillan Health Care Information; 1987:153–164.

Changes in a UPDRS score during a patient's life provide further insight on the natural history of the disease. Typically, motor scores are the first to increase. Tremor is the earliest symptom of Parkinson's disease for about three-quarters of patients, so when Michael J. Fox first noted his tremor, he had a UPDRS of less than 10, with all the points derived from measures of tremor or finger and hand movements. Gradually, other measures of motor abnormality increase. Only later do the functional items measuring impairment in activities of daily living become more abnormal. For most patients the scores for abnormalities of mentation, behavior, and mood are the last to increase, but there are wide variations: Depression is an early symptom for a minority of patients, whereas many others are fortunate enough to never develop mental abnormalities.

The UPDRS provides a single number describing the status of a patient with Parkinson's disease at any given moment. However, this number should not be mistaken for a perfect measure of the disease. The scoring of each item requires subjective judgments by the patient or the examiner. Furthermore, the relative scores must be interpreted with caution. No one should assume that a person with a tremor score of 4 (interferes with most activities) is exactly twice as ill or twice as disabled as one with a tremor score of 2 (bothersome). There is no way to know which is worse: a tremor score of 2 plus an arising from chair score of 4 (needs help) or a tremor score of 4 plus an arising score of 2 (pushes self up), even though either combination gives a UPDRS score of 6.

The UPDRS provides some twenty-first-century data on the prognosis of Parkinson's disease. Despite its imprecision, we can use the UPDRS to trace the early disease course. For example, a group of 16 patients with Parkinson's disease so mild that they needed no specific antiparkinsonian medication had average UPDRS scores of 24. As expected, most of the score (18 points) came from motor abnormalities, some (5 points) came from impaired daily activities, and very little (1 point) was from mental impairment.[10] Most of the patients were in Hoehn and Yahr stage II. These patients were rechecked about 16 months later. Most had not changed their Hoehn and Yahr stage, but their average UPDRS had worsened by 12 points, gaining approximately 1 mental point, 6 motor points, and 5 daily activities points. The UPDRS here is clearly much better than the Hoehn and Yahr scale in documenting changes in the disease over months, but it does not completely solve the prognosis problem. First, even in this small group of patients, there was much variation so that some gained many more UPDRS points than others. More important, while this scale quantifies the disease, it offers only a peek at how the disease affects the patient's life. The patient who inquires about prognosis may wish for a fuller portrait of the future, but modern physicians, despite our attempts at quantification and evidence-based medicine, can still seem like ancient soothsayers who foretell the future with riddles.

Why has my father never asked me his prognosis? Of course, there are many reasons for not asking a question, including not wanting to know the answer. I believe that as a physician, he is all too aware not only of the progressive nature of his illness, but also of how fallible physicians are as prognosticators. For prognosis, just as for diagnosis, some patients seem to expect exact facts from their physicians, while physicians are continually aware of scientific imprecision and strive to improve scientific evidence and to understand just how inexact that evidence is.

Of course, everyone knows that the future is not predictable. Patients who ask about prognoses must know that their physicians' answers will be inexact. Asking for prognosis, however, is about much more than asking for facts. All of us, ill or well, have hopes for the future and want some control over our fate. When I speak with neurological patients about their future, I emphasize how they can modify and improve their symptoms. I encourage them to exercise, learn about their illnesses, and join me in planning their treatments. I stress that scientific investigations are likely to offer them new treatments and to eventually cure or prevent Parkinson's disease.

In this era of scientific medicine we know amazingly little about whether the patient-physician conversation changes prognosis. Did Dad's optimistic outlook improve his chance of surviving throat cancer? If he asked more about the prognosis of his Parkinson's disease, would the knowledge hurt or help? What therapeutic words and actions should I use with my patients when we talk about their illnesses? For now these questions belong to the art of medicine.

CHAPTER TWO

Pathology of Parkinson's Disease

What Part of the Brain Fails in Parkinson's Disease?

To prevent or cure Parkinson's disease, we need to know how the brain is causing the disease; we must understand the basic science of the disease. By tradition, the first two years of medical school are devoted to learning the disciplines that underpin scientific medicine. My father in the late 1930s, myself in the late 1960s, and my niece and nephew in the first years of the new millennium all struggled with subjects like anatomy, biochemistry, or cell biology, impatiently awaiting the days when we knew enough to begin treating patients. The neurosciences are some of the most complex of these so-called basic sciences. A family joke is that we need a video called *Baby Charcot* to show to the next generation in their cribs so that neuroscience will be easier for them in medical school. To introduce causes and treatment of Parkinson's disease in the video, we would start with some anatomy and pathology: In Parkinson's the main site of brain cell failure is called the substantia nigra. When viewed under the microscope, the diseased cells in this part of the brain have characteristic abnormal inclusions that are called Lewy bodies.

When Parkinson described the shaking palsy in 1817, he suggested that the disease was caused by an abnormality in the upper part of the spinal cord in the neck and that as the disease progressed, the abnormality extended into the very back end of the brain, the medulla, where it connects to the spinal cord. Parkinson was wrong. He was off by only a couple of inches, but in the dense connections of the brain, a fraction of an inch makes the difference between health, paralysis, or death.

In his own defense Parkinson apologized that he was unable to study the brains of his patients after they died. He was well aware that his observation of living patients was just the start of the scientific investigation of an illness. He apologized in his essay that "mere conjecture takes the place of experiment; and, that analogy is the substitute for anatomical examination, the only sure foundation for pathological knowledge."[1]

During Parkinson's lifetime the very concept that diseases are localized to parts of the brain as opposed to being caused by diffuse brain dysfunction was debated. Many of his contemporaries believed that the brain was a single, uniform organ without specific areas to control individual muscles, perceive specific sensations, or perform complex activities like language, memory, and emotion. They thought of the brain as if it were a bowl of jelly rather than a network of nerve cells. At least Parkinson was on the right side of this debate; the shaking palsy is due to failure of a localized, relatively small group of brain cells.

One of his six patients had an experience that bears directly on the question of localized functions in the brain. More than a decade after this man's shaking palsy began, he awoke one night with nearly complete paralysis of his right face, arm, and leg. The tremor, which had been on both sides, had suddenly ceased on the paralyzed right side but continued on the left side of his body. This new right-side paralysis was characteristic of a stroke, a sudden partial interruption of brain function.

Strokes cause abrupt loss of brainpower. One stroke might take away strength on one side of the body or in one limb; another might cause loss of vision; a third might distort speech. A severe stroke might destroy multiple abilities such as strength, feeling, speech, and vision. A stroke is caused by a local block of blood flow to or bleeding into part of the brain. The timing of strokes is quite distinct from the timing of Parkinson's disease. The sudden onset of the stroke contrasts to the gradual appearance of parkinsonian tremor and slowed movement. A stroke reaches its worst state shortly after onset, then neurological function can recover over days, weeks, or months, contrasting with the relentless deterioration of Parkinson's disease. Parkinson's patient had a relatively mild stroke and largely recovered his strength in about two weeks; when he recovered from the stroke, his right-sided tremor reappeared.

The tremor disappeared until the patient recovered from the stroke because the part of the brain that controls tremors is separate from the part that controls strength, and tremor can only occur if strength exists. The arm weakened by a stroke became too weak to tremble.

Examination of peoples' brains after they die with neurological disease is one way to answer the question of whether the brain has localized or uniform functions. This method played a major role in the nineteenth-century study of the brain and remains important today. At the time of autopsy, shortly after death, the brain is as flimsy as soft gelatin, too fragile to cut and study accurately. However, if the brain is removed from the skull and preserved in formalin, it becomes firm and can easily be sliced. For many years, brain cutting has been a tradition of neurological training and research. Neurologists gather in the conference room of the neuropathology department. After the case history is read, each physician offers an opinion on what the brain will look like. The neuropathologist then takes a broad, long knife and slices the brain like a loaf of bread.

When a person dies after a stroke, the brain slices usually show a scar in the particular area of the brain that had been injured by the stroke. By comparing the sites of scars with the abilities lost by stroke victims, neurologists have learned much about which portions of the brain influence which bodily functions. Parkinson's patient who had had a stroke that paralyzed his right face, arm, and leg must have temporarily damaged nerve cells in the area that connects the brain to the spinal cord and controls strength in the arms and legs.

In the United States, perhaps three-quarters of a million people have a stroke each year, so as a neurologist, I see many more patients with strokes than with Parkinson's disease. I have benefited from this long tradition of matching stroke symptoms to brain pathology. After I examine a patient who has had a stroke, I usually have a very good idea of what part of the brain has been injured.

About one-fifth of patients who have a stroke die from it. Most stroke victims, like Parkinson's patients who had the temporary arm weakness, recover, and we do not look directly at the brain to confirm the pathology. However, modern MRI and CT brain scans are excellent at showing stroke pathology. I regularly look at the scans to confirm my clinical deductions, getting feedback to improve my skills at localization and to help future patients.

Those nineteenth-century scientists who thought that the brain was a uniform mass of jelly were wrong. Many other experiments over the last 200 years have firmly established that many abilities are localized to specific areas of the brain. Experiments have included injuring small areas of the brains of experimental animals, watching the results of electrically stimulating brain tissue, and, more recently, taking images of the brain during different activities. Now, we know a great deal about the parts of the brain that control our abilities like strength, touch, vision, hearing, or speech, but neuroscientists are still debating the exact mechanism of parkinsonian tremor.

My father is color-blind. This has nothing to do with his Parkinson's disease but does explain one blind spot in his medical practice. When he was an intern, he was expected to do the laboratory work on his patients.

If a patient needed a blood count or urinalysis or sputum examination checking the cause of a fever, the intern collected the specimen, walked down the hall to a small laboratory on the ward, stained the slides, and looked through the microscope. Unfortunately, many medical stains use red dyes, the bane of someone with red-green color blindness. I do not know how he got through his internship, but as soon as Dad started his own practice, he hired a laboratory technician. As a child, I loved to hang around his office. I would sit in the laboratory, watching the technician work, but I never saw Dad use the microscope.

Color blindness is inherited on the X chromosome. Men get the gene from their mothers, not from their fathers, so it is not surprising that I have normal color vision. When I started medical school, I brought the family microscope with me. I could easily see the colored stains, but when I went to classes to study pathology or other disciplines where I needed my microscope, I used it unenthusiastically, sneaking out early whenever possible. Having watched Dad practice medicine, I mistakenly believed that anything that required the microscope was not really relevant to becoming a good physician.

Fortunately, medical science is a collaboration of many tastes and talents. I might have avoided pathology class, but I understand now that modern neurology grew from the work of nineteenth-century pathologists, who examined brains from patients who had died with various neurological diseases and learned the sites of many brain functions. For example, Charcot carefully compared clinical findings of neurological disease and postmortem brain pathology using brain-cutting techniques similar to those still in use. He contributed new information on the pathology of diseases like multiple sclerosis and amyotrophic lateral sclerosis, but Charcot and his contemporaries never discovered the brain pathology underlying Parkinson's disease, despite studying the brains of many patients who had died with the disease.

Then, in 1905, Tretiakoff established that patients who died with Parkinson's disease lacked normal color in a part of the brain called the substantia nigra. This structure is in the upper back part of the brain called the midbrain. Substantia nigra, meaning "black substance," is named for the black pigment in its cells, blackness that is present in all normal adults (Figure 2.1A). The color difference between normal brain and parkinsonian brain is so evident to an untrained eye that it is hard to believe that 88 years passed between the time Parkinson wrote *On the Shaking Palsy* and the time someone noted the absence of black in the substantia nigra in those with the disease.

Parkinson's disease can destroy about one-half million brain cells in the human substantia nigra. Each of us normally has trillions of brain cells, so for every brain cell lost in a patient with Parkinson's disease, millions of other healthy cells remain in the brain. Trying to find which cells are missing in Parkinson's disease is like trying to tell if a handful of stars have disappeared from the sky. If it were not for the loss of black pigment, the absence of cells in Parkinson's disease would have taken even longer to discover.

In the late nineteenth century, new stains for brain tissue were major technological advances. You might say that in those days, neuropathologists vied to stain their reputations. Alzheimer, in 1897, immortalized his name when he showed that a woman with dementia had unusual microscopic plaques and tangles in her brain; he relied on a new stain introduced by his friend Nissl. Golgi won a portion of the 1906 Nobel Prize for Physiology or Medicine based largely on his work developing a new stain for nerve cells. Modern neuropathologists still use Nissl stain, Golgi stain, and many others.

On microscopic examination and using appropriate stains, the brains of patients who die with Parkinson's disease have distinctive abnormal material in some nerve cells. The masses of abnormal material form round or oval structures, called inclusions, inside cells (Figure 2.1C). About 1912, Freiderich Lewy saw these inclusions in patients with Parkinson's disease. A few years later, Tretiakoff named them "Lewy bodies." The substantia nigra is the main site where Lewy bodies are found in patients with Parkinson's disease.

Lewy bodies are now recognized as a pathologic hallmark of idiopathic Parkinson's disease. The British study of diagnostic accuracy for Parkinson's disease that I mentioned in chapter 1 relied on Lewy bodies and other changes in the substantia nigra as the pathological proof of the diagnosis. In the last few years, genetic research has greatly enhanced understanding of these inclusions, and I will often refer to Lewy bodies in future chapters.

Lewy, like many of his contemporaries, learned from careful observations rather than from controlled experiments. Looking back years later, he recalled his excitement when he had first found the bodies and thought that he knew the pathological basis of parkinsonism. However, after examining dozens of brains, he became confused because the presence or absence of the bodies did not perfectly predict whether a brain came from someone with Parkinson's disease.

One source of confusion was that Lewy bodies are also found in other conditions and in other areas of the brain. In particular, the inclusions are common in another neurodegenerative disease called Lewy body dementia, which shares some overlap with clinical features of Parkinson's and Alzheimer's diseases.

Recently, improved stains for Lewy bodies have given a new view of evolving pathology of Parkinson's disease. The abnormalities appear first low in the brain stem, affecting nerve cells that control the heart and the gut, and also near the front of the brain, affecting nerve cells important to the sense of smell. Both these areas are far from the substantia nigra. These newly discovered pathological findings might

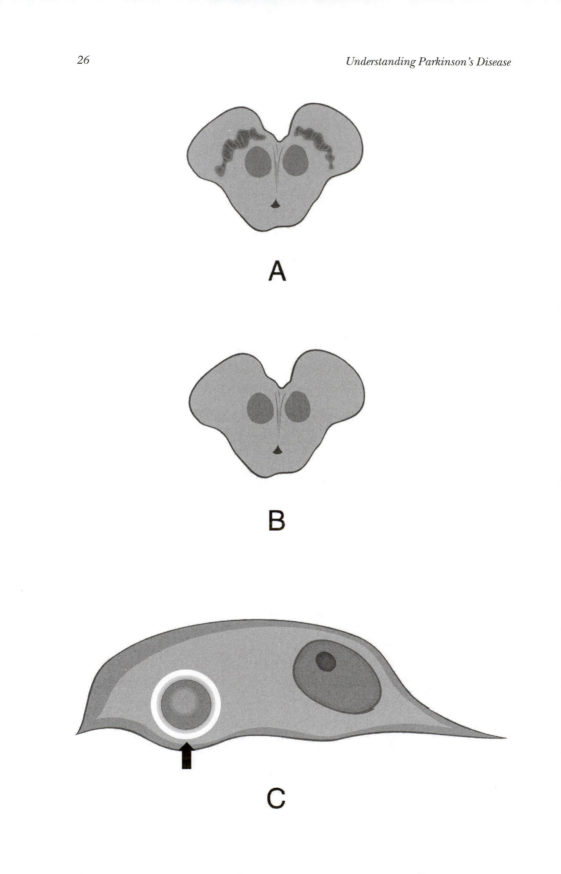

A

B

C

explain old clinical observations that patients with Parkinson's disease can recall losing their senses of smell and developing constipation years before their tremor and other motor problems appeared. Lewy did not live to see this extension of our knowledge of Lewy bodies, so we do not know if he would be more or less confused today.

Dad was a very good medical student. When he graduated from medical school, he knew what Parkinson and Charcot had never learned. When tested, he could recite that patients with Parkinson's disease lose cells and pigmentation in the substantia nigra and have Lewy bodies in their brain cells. I suspect that he would have forgotten this bit of trivia within a few years. Most physicians forget basic science details outside their own specialties once they master the underlying principles needed for clinical medicine.

Sadly, even if he recalled the story of Lewy bodies in the substantia nigra, this knowledge would not have helped him fight his Parkinson's disease. However, modern investigators are vigorously improving our knowledge of what part of the brain fails in Parkinson's disease. We have to extend our knowledge beyond which cells fail and learn how and why the cells fail. We have to improve our localization of brain function to specific molecules like proteins and genes. We will soon cure and prevent Parkinson's disease based on the continued research of neuroscientists, and then I will be delighted when I can struggle to understand more of the basic science of Parkinson's disease.

Nerve Cell Connections

Brain cell communication is key to normal brain function. In Parkinson's disease, part of the communication fails. In 1906 Camillo Golgi and Santiago Ramón y Cajal won the Nobel Prize for Physiology or Medicine for their pioneering brain research. Each championed a model of how nerve cells connect. Golgi was born in northern Italy in 1843, trained as a physician, and began research at the University of Pavia. However, in 1872, feeling financial pressure, he left the university to care for

---

FIGURE 2.1: The pathological characteristics of Parkinson's disease are the loss of black pigment from the substantia nigra of the midbrain and inclusions, called Lewy bodies, within nerve cells. (*A*) Slice of a normal human midbrain. The substantia nigra is the shaded area toward the top. (This is near the actual size of the human midbrain, which is about four centimeters wide.) (*B*) Slice of a midbrain from a patient who died with Parkinson's disease. Note the absence of pigment from the substantia nigra. (*C*) Microscopic view (enlarged more than 1000 times) of a nerve cell from the substantia nigra of a patient who died with Parkinson's disease. In this view the dendrites and axon are not visible. The arrow points to a Lewy body, the round structure with a light halo within the cell. (Drawn by Douglas Katagiri.)

patients at a hospital for the chronically ill. He continued his research activities in a small kitchen. In this humble laboratory he developed a new stain for brain tissue. The Golgi stain used silver to specifically highlight individual nerve cells. Among hundreds of cells, only a few might pick up the silver stain, but the stained cells could be traced in better detail than ever before.

Using his stain to study brain cells, Golgi proposed a model of brain cell connections. Golgi's model, called the network theory, depicted the nervous system as a network of continuously connected cells, with information flowing through nerve cells just as water flows through the interconnected pipes of a city's water system. In his 1906 Nobel Lecture Golgi acknowledged that the majority of those studying the subject rejected his theory, and then he proceeded to argue its merits.[2]

In contrast, Ramón y Cajal's theory, called the neuron theory, was that each nerve cell was a separate entity, nearly touching other nerve cells but not actually sharing cellular contents with its neighbors: "The nerve elements possess reciprocal relationships *in contiguity* but not *in continuity.*"[3] Cajal (he preferred to use his mother's last name) had been given a superb microscope by the Spanish government in appreciation for research he did during a cholera epidemic. Working in Madrid, he had improved Golgi's stain and made intricate drawings from his microscopic study of brain tissue, showing the complex interweaving of nerve cell branches. In Ramón y Cajal's model the axon of one nerve cell came very close to other nerve cells, but a gap separated the cells.

Sherrington, an English brain researcher, popularized the term *synapse* for this discontinuous connection between nerve cells. The gap between the cells is called the synaptic cleft. When Sherrington wrote of synapses in the late nineteenth century, he referred to a purely hypothetical structure; no microscope then available was powerful enough to see a synapse in enough detail to prove its existence (Figure 2.2A).

Ramón y Cajal often used embryonic or developing brain tissue to study how nerve cells came together. To explain this strategy, he compared the intertwining cells to trees in a forest: "The roots and branches of these trees in the gray matter terminate in that forest so dense that ... there are no spaces in it, so that the trunks, branches, and leave touch everywhere.... Since the full grown forest turns out to be impenetrable

---

FIGURE 2.2: Models of the synapse evolved during the twentieth century. (*A*) Ramón y Cajal envisioned the synapse as a point of contact between two nerves. (*B*) Loewi and Dale showed that chemical neurotransmitters carried messages across the synapse. (*C*) The neurotransmitters are stored in small packets in the nerve terminals. (*D*) Neurotransmitters act by attaching to receptors (white arrow) on the postsynaptic nerve cell. Neurotransmitters are inactivated by enzymes (MAO and COMT) and by being absorbed back into the presynaptic cell via the dopamine transporter protein (gray arrow). The packets of neurotransmitter in the presynaptic cell are medicated by the black arrow. (Drawn by Douglas Katagiri.)

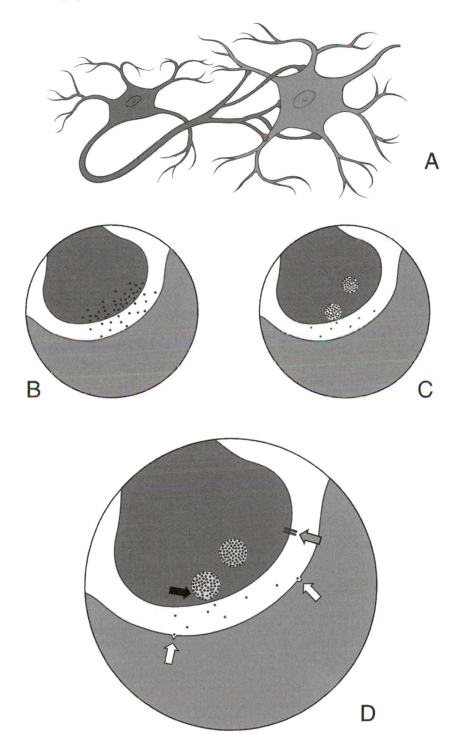

and indefinable, why not revert to the study of the young wood, the nursery stage, as we might say?"[4]

Over the last three centuries, advances in understanding Parkinson's disease have sprung new techniques and technologies. For Ramón y Cajal, one new technique was attention to nerve cell development, and the new technologies were improved stains, particularly the Golgi stain. Ramón y Cajal often praised Golgi for this pioneering contribution, despite Golgi's refusal to recognize the superiority of Ramón y Cajal's nerve cell connection theory. However, in his autobiography, Ramón y Cajal wrote of his frustration with Golgi's failure to concede the intellectual debate or acknowledge the scientific contributions of others, calling Golgi "one of the vainest and most self-worshipful men of talent that I have ever known."[5]

Ramón y Cajal had a more realistic model of nerve connections than Golgi, yet Ramón y Cajal's model did not explain how one cell sent messages to the next across the synapse. Understanding how cells communicate has been a major theme of neuroscience in the twentieth and twenty-first centuries. Coming chapters show increasingly sophisticated models of synapses. Improvements in the model suggest new experiments to improve it further, and improvements in the model can have very useful implications, suggesting better treatments for disease.

Ramón y Cajal has much to teach scientists, particularly about dedication to and enjoyment of their work. He was a meticulous observer. His precise drawings of his microscopic views are peerless; he saw the nervous system as an aesthetic wonder:

> Really, the garden of neurology offers the researcher captivating spectacles and incomparable artistic emotions. My aesthetic instincts find their full satisfaction. Like the entomologist catching colorful butterflies, my attention pursued, the garden of the gray matter, the delicately and gracefully shaped cells, the mysterious butterflies whose wing beats might some day reveal the secret of mental life.[6]

Ramón y Cajal's hard work schedule was legendary. Once, on a trip to England, he stayed at Sherrington's home. The Sherringtons were puzzled because Ramón y Cajal always carefully locked his bedroom door. Later, they learned that after a busy day of meetings, Ramón y Cajal would stay up late, alone in the bedroom, peering through the microscope that he had brought from Spain, never pausing in his research.[7]

Ramón y Cajal learned from and worked in concert with a host of microscopists, pathologists, and neuroanatomists. These scientists' chief research method was careful observation. Often, the controls for their observations were informal comparisons to their own experiences, what today would derisively be called historical controls. Scientific methodology is now much more sophisticated, but Ramón y Cajal remains the father of neuroscience because of many contributions, especially his perfection of the neuron theory in preference to the network theory.

Chemical Pathology of Parkinson's Disease

In 1967, when physicians like Dad could treat Parkinson's disease only with drugs derived from traditional herbal medicines, I started medical school. I cannot recall when I first heard of Parkinson's disease, but at that time I knew nothing of its treatment. By coincidence, 1967 was the year that George Cotzias revolutionized the treatment of Parkinson's disease. He showed that swallowing large doses of the amino acid L-dopa could greatly diminish the symptoms of the disease. Prior to 1967, the few drugs available to treat Parkinson's disease had had mild benefits at best. After 1967, patients took L-dopa and had marked improvement in mobility. Cotzias's innovative use of L-dopa evolved from decades of experiments by many investigators.

In this chapter I will go into a fair amount of technical detail about synapses, neurotransmitters, and L-dopa. If you want to skim the basic science and move ahead to more clinical chapters, the key points in this chapter are summarized in Table 2.1.

The progressive understanding of Parkinson's disease from Ramón y Cajal to Cotzias came from a growing knowledge of how nerve cells send or transmit messages across synapses. Ramón y Cajal showed that there was a gap between cells, but he could not see the gap with his microscope, and his careful studies did not explain how messages crossed the gap. Looking at Ramón y Cajal's model of the synapse, scientists did not see solutions to the problems of Parkinson's disease. However, as investigators learned more, they improved models of the synapse.

TABLE 2.1: Key Points about Dopamine in the Brain

1. Dopamine is a brain neurotransmitter.

2. Most of the dopamine nerve cells in the brain carry messages from the substantia nigra to brain areas called the putamen and caudate.

3. The dopamine is stored in the caudate and putamen in small packets within nerve cells.

4. When dopamine nerve cells fire, the dopamine is released from the packets into the synaptic cleft to carry messages to the nerve cells on the other side of the synapse.

5. The dopamine effect in the synaptic cleft is turned off when the dopamine is taken back into cells or broken down by enzymes called COMT and MAO.

It was nearly 60 years after Ramón y Cajal won the Nobel Prize that a model of the synapse became sophisticated enough to inspire treatment of Parkinson's disease with L-dopa.

Synapses connect not only nerves to nerves, but also nerves to muscles, including the heart muscle. In 1921 Otto Loewi found that a chemical called acetylcholine is a messenger between a nerve and the heart. This was the first proof that chemicals can transmit information across synapses; chemicals that do this are now called neurotransmitters. Loewi's discovery began a gradual increase in our knowledge of synapses. In 1902, Loewi, who began his research in Germany, was working in London when he met a Cambridge-trained scientist named Henry Dale. They became lifelong friends. Dale complemented Loewi's research by showing that neurotransmitters carried messages between nerve cells and ordinary muscle cells and between two abutting nerve cells. In 1936 they shared the Nobel Prize for Physiology or Medicine (Figure 2.2B).

In 1970 the Nobel Prize in Physiology or Medicine was given to Sir Bernard Katz, Ulf von Euler, and Julius Axelrod. Katz studied the release of acetylcholine from the nerve at the nerve-to-muscle synapse. He did many of his experiments using very small wires, called microelectrodes, inserted into muscle cells to measure the electrical changes in cells caused when acetylcholine was released from the nerve. He deduced from electrical experiments that the acetylcholine must be stored in the nerve terminal in small packets. Electron microscopic pictures show these packets as bubble-like structures located at the tip of the axon where it forms the membrane on one side of the synapse. This membrane is called the presynaptic membrane.

In his 1970 Nobel Lecture Katz noted that his observations applied only to the peripheral nervous system, the nerves beyond the brain and spinal cord. Loewi and Dale had already shown that in the peripheral nervous system, acetylcholine was the neurotransmitter for some nerves and norepinephrine or epinephrine were the neurotransmitters for others.

Ulf von Euler, the second recipient of the 1970 Nobel Prize, showed that norepinephrine, rather than epinephrine, was the predominant neurotransmitter in sympathetic nerve cells in the peripheral nervous system. He and his colleagues ground up sympathetic nerves and isolated small nerve particles that were rich in norepinephrine. Electron microscopic pictures showed that these particles rich in norepinephrine were the presynaptic packets of the sympathetic cells. These experiments by Katz and von Euler added another dimension to the model of the synapse: The neurotransmitter is stored in the tiny packets at the tip of the axon. When an electrical impulse, traveling down the axon, reaches this tip, the neurotransmitter is released from the axon.

These experiments, studying peripheral nerves with microelectrodes or grinding up nerves and then looking at particles under an electron microscope, seem unrelated to the brain. Even by 1970, little was known about neurotransmitters in the central nervous system. It is unlikely that Loewi, Dale, Katz, or von Euler thought of Parkinson's disease while they designed and interpreted their experiments. However, subsequent experiments have shown that the brain cells that degenerate in Parkinson's disease store the neurotransmitter dopamine in their presynaptic packets.

We now know that neurotransmitters are found in nerve cells throughout the central nervous system and are the principal way that nerve cells communicate with each other. There are many different neurotransmitters, but each nerve cell has a single chief neurotransmitter. In the substantia nigra, the site of the greatest nerve cell loss in patients with Parkinson's disease, dopamine is the neurotransmitter, so I will frequently refer to these as dopamine nerve cells. (A more technical name is dopaminergic neurons.)

Electrical impulses reach the tip of an axon and start sending information across the synapse by releasing small packets of neurotransmitter. An information system needs a way to turn off as well as to turn on. Julius Axelrod shared the Nobel Prize in 1970 for his contribution to understanding how the neurotransmitter messages were turned off. He found that two enzymes were important for inactivating epinephrine and norepinephrine after they were released from the nerve terminal. Enzymes are proteins that facilitate chemical reactions in the body. The names of all enzymes end with the suffix *-ase*. The enzymes that Axelrod studied are MAO (monoamine oxidase) and COMT (catechol O-methyltransferase). Epinephrine, norepinephrine, and dopamine are all in a class of chemicals known as catechols. COMT breaks down catechols when they are in the synapse, after they have been released from the nerve axon. MAO breaks down catechols when they are in the nerve axon, except that once the catechols are inside a synaptic packet, they are protected from breakdown by MAO. Together, these enzymes, MAO and COMT, help control the amount of dopamine in a synapse. Today, physicians can prescribe drugs that manipulate these enzymes to treat Parkinson's.

Axelrod worked his way up from the bottom of the laboratory ladder to the Nobel Prize. When he graduated from college in 1933, he began working as a laboratory assistant, first in bacteriology and later in chemistry. He did not received his Ph.D. until 1955, by which time he was already working at the U.S. National Institutes of Health (NIH) on the experiments that were so important to understanding neurotransmission. At the risk of seeming to be the Forrest Gump of Parkinson's disease, I will admit that when I was working at the NIH in the mid-1970s, I rode the bus to work every morning with a quiet older man. We both read silently in our seats. At the end of the two years I learned that I had been sitting near Axelrod but had never spoken to him.

Axelrod and others injected radioactively labeled norepinephrine into veins of animals. They found that the radioactivity became concentrated at the sympathetic nerve synapses. Using electron microscopy, they saw the radioactive norepinephrine in the presynaptic packets. If a sympathetic nerve was stimulated after it had taken up radioactive norepinephrine, some radioactivity appeared in the blood, but the nerve quickly reabsorbed most of the radioactivity. If Axelrod cut a sympathetic nerve, gave it time to degenerate, and then injected the radioactive norepinephrine, he did not find the radioactivity at the synapse for that nerve. Figure 2.2C shows a model of the synapse based on work like that of von Euler, Katz, and Axelrod.

Neurotransmitter action in the synaptic gap between the nerve cells, the synaptic cleft, can be turned off not only when enzymes destroy the neurotransmitter, but also when nerve cells reabsorb the neurotransmitter from the synapse. This reuptake into the cell of the neurotransmitter stops the chemical from working in the synapse and also replenishes the nerve cell supply of neurotransmitter for refilling packets and later release.

Arvid Carlsson was among three neuroscientists who won the Nobel Prize in 2000. In the 1950s he began research on the catechols. He used a new fluorescent staining technique to see and measure catechols in tissues. This technique helped show that after norepinephrine is released from the presynaptic packets of an axon, the same axon can reabsorb the norepinephrine from the synaptic cleft. This reuptake of the norepinephrine is important because it stops the neurotransmission at the postsynaptic nerve cell and replenishes the norepinephrine in the presynaptic nerve cell.

All the experiments that I have described so far in this chapter studied the peripheral nervous system. In the 1950s, very little was known of the synapses of the central nervous system. Scientists were uncertain whether the central nervous system cells worked like the peripheral nervous system cells.

The anatomy of the nervous system can be viewed in many ways: appearance to the naked eye (e.g., white matter versus gray matter); microscopic appearance of different cell types; and specific functional areas, such as those that control strength or those that control vision. In the late 1950s and early 1960s, investigators studied a new kind of anatomy, a chemical anatomy of the brain. If small pieces of the brain are removed, ground up, and then analyzed for chemical content, each area of the brain has a distinctive composition. Some call this "grind and find" neuroscience. It requires strict attention to detail because the chemical composition of the brain tissue can change rapidly after death.

Investigators did not realize at first that a clue about Parkinson's disease would be the brain distribution of dopamine, which was already known to be a neurotransmitter in the peripheral nervous system.

Four-fifths of the dopamine in the brain is in two deep gray matter areas called the caudate and putamen (Figure 2.3). The rich supply of dopamine in the putamen and caudate can be seen using the fluorescent catechol stains.

A drug called reserpine provided a hint to the relation between Parkinson's disease and dopamine. Reserpine is another herbal derivative, extracted from a plant called rauwolfia. For years, rauwolfia, and more recently, reserpine, have been used as mild sedatives and for treatment of high blood pressure. Unfortunately, some people who are treated with reserpine or rauwolfia develop signs of parkinsonism! Fortunately, the parkinsonism disappears after the reserpine is stopped. Research into how reserpine causes parkinsonism led to a major advance in the treatment of Parkinson's disease.

Axelrod, Carlsson, and others had already found in the peripheral nervous system that certain drugs could block the reuptake of norepinephrine into the presynaptic packets. Some of these drugs simply block reuptake; others, such as reserpine, not only block reuptake, but also release norepinephrine that is stored in the presynaptic packets. The reserpine releases the norepinephrine inside the cell, where MAO inactivates it.

Arvid Carlsson studied the effect of reserpine on the chemical composition of rat brains. Carlsson showed that animals treated with reserpine developed motor slowing, that these reserpine-treated animals were missing dopamine in their brains, and that treatment with L-dopa restored the dopamine and improved the animals' ability to move. Reserpine not only depletes norepinephrine from peripheral nerves, but also depletes dopamine from the putamen and caudate.

I recently heard Carlsson speak when he visited the Oregon Health and Sciences University. He recalled that as early as 1959, he had proposed at research meetings that brain dopamine deficiency might cause parkinsonism, but his ideas were met with skepticism.[8] One of those who strongly doubted his hypothesis was the Nobelist Sir Henry Dale.[9] As shown by Golgi and Ramón y Cajal, or Carlsson and Dale, personal disagreements between passionate, brilliant investigators often fuel scientific debate and lead to new discoveries.

Fortunately, researchers pursued Carlsson's findings. Once again, research progressed using fluorescent staining that further revealed the chemical anatomy of dopamine. The stain made dopamine-containing cells appear green when viewed using a microscope equipped with fluorescent light. Other catechols appear yellow or green with the same stain.

The brains of patients with Parkinson's disease are missing cells in the substantia nigra, cells that normally send their axons to the putamen. Therefore the chemical anatomy of the substantia nigra and putamen

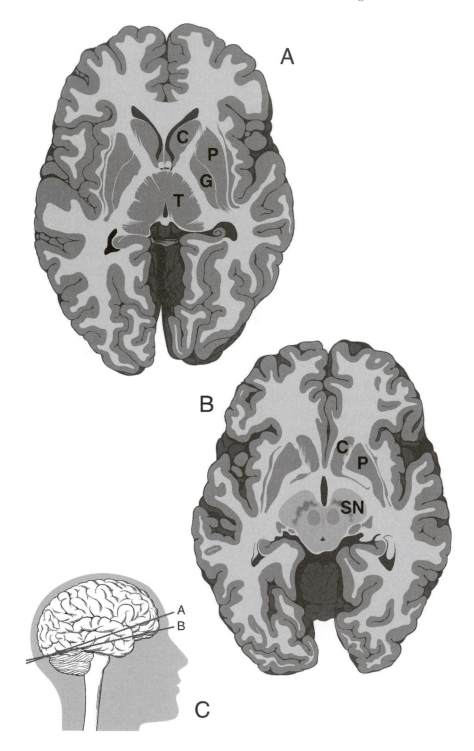

in patients with Parkinson's disease is particularly interesting. Patients with Parkinson's disease have only about one-fifth the normal content of dopamine in their putamen. The more cells they have lost from their substantia nigra, the less dopamine they have in their putamen.[10,11]

The new fluorescent stains for dopamine let us actually look through a microscope and see details of the synapse. The dopamine concentrates in small circular structures inside the nerve cell axon that forms part of the synapse. The axon side is called the presynaptic side; the other side is called the postsynaptic side; the gap between the two cells is the synaptic cleft. Therefore the circular packets containing the dopamine are located in the presynaptic region.

The puzzle of neurotransmission has been slowly unraveled using animal and laboratory experiments, starting with simple systems of peripheral nerves and muscles before studying the brain and applying new techniques like electron microscopy, microelectrodes, fluorescent stains, and radioactive labeling. The clinical benefits for treating human disease are often unknown while investigators gradually reveal the secrets of biological systems. The evolving, improving models of the synapse exemplify the progress of basic biological research.

FIGURE 2.3: The structures important to understanding Parkinson's disease are deep in the brain. (*A*) A slice of normal brain, viewed looking from above, showing the caudate (C) and putamen (P), the destination of most of the axons from the dopamine neurons that originate in the midbrain. Other important structures in the circuitry of Parkinson's disease are the thalamus (T), globus pallidus (G), subthalamic nucleus (not shown), and cerebral cortex. (*B*) A slice of normal brain showing the substantia nigra (SN) in the midbrain, and surrounding structures. (*C*) Side view of the brain showing the orientation of slices *A* and *B*. (Drawn by Douglas Katagiri.)

CHAPTER THREE

Is There an Epidemic of Parkinson's Disease?

Epidemiology of Parkinson's Disease

Each person with Parkinson's disease has a unique story, but Dad is hardly unique in having Parkinson's disease. The disease is endemic, which means that it occurs relatively consistently worldwide, in contrast to epidemic diseases, which break out suddenly in one spot. Throughout the world, Parkinson's disease affects men more frequently than women. On average, it is recognized at about age 60 years, and the prevalence of the disease increases with age. There are as many as a million people in the United States with Parkinson's, based on estimates that between 1 in 300 and 1 in 1000 Americans have it. The prevalence of the disease is 57 per 100,000 population in Libya, compared to 182 per 100,000 population in Iceland.[1] The prevalence elsewhere falls between these extremes.

These differences around the world are not due solely to different ages in the populations. Variations in diagnostic criteria, culture of disease recognition or reporting, quality of medical care, genetic backgrounds of the populations, or environmental factors all can change the prevalence.

These problems in explaining disease prevalence are evident at the Manor, the assisted-living facility to which my parents moved in 2002. A year later, my mother-in-law moved to the Manor from the east coast. She had been living independently in an apartment outside New York

City and spending her winters in her own home in Florida, but she wanted to be closer to us. She did not need the assistance required by many other residents of the Manor, but as long as she was moving, it made sense for her to live where she could get more help if she ever needed it. She saw my parents each day and was quite aware of Dad's progressive problems. She noted that others in the Manor were as shaky as Dad. She saw many of her new neighbors moving slowly and using walkers or canes. She asked me if the Manor was having an epidemic of Parkinson's. In the east she had never seen this many people with the disease.

I doubt that she realized that she was asking a very hard question; she should have asked an epidemiologist. Epidemiology is a scientific discipline that studies disease in populations, not just in individuals, and can provide useful clues to the cause and prevention of illness. It is worth digressing from Parkinson's disease to see some fascinating triumphs of epidemiology, investigating illnesses as varied as cancer, mad cow disease, or simple diarrhea. For these illnesses, epidemiologists can provide only part of the answer, generating hypotheses that must be tested in basic science experiments. Even for Parkinson's disease, epidemiologists have offered useful clues about its cause.

Epidemics, outbreaks of one illness in many people in a community, have undoubtedly occurred as long as man has existed. In fact, animal epidemics must have preceded human history. Epidemics, like the plague in fourteenth-century Europe or the smallpox brought to Native Americans by European settlers, changed history. Today, epidemic infection with HIV, the virus that causes AIDS, is causing heartbreaking misery worldwide. In addition to infections, other causes of epidemics include environmental toxins, nutritional deficiencies, and diet. Today, the techniques developed to study epidemics are being applied to endemic diseases like Parkinson's disease.

John Snow—The Father of Epidemiology

The study of epidemics was pioneered by John Snow, an English physician who made a major scientific advance after an outbreak of cholera in London. Cholera causes severe diarrhea, so severe that death can result quickly from dehydration. Today, intravenous fluids or special drinks that replace not only water, but also vital minerals prevent many cholera deaths. In Snow's time, cholera was often fatal. In 1855 he wrote, "The most terrible outbreak of cholera which ever occurred in this kingdom, is probably that which took place in Broad Street, Golden Square, and the adjoining streets a few weeks ago.... The mortality in this limited area probably equals any that was ever caused in this country, even by the plague; and it was much more sudden, as the greater number of cases terminated in a few hours." Snow's original description of his investigations[2] is much easier to read than the writing in most modern medical journals; scientific journals today demand a style and organization, including a full description of methods and results, that would exclude a paper like Snow's, regardless of its scientific merit.

Over 500 people died within 10 days in the Broad Street epidemic. Snow charted the residences of the dead on a map and noted the clustering of cases near a pump on Broad Street. Of course, at that time, there was no indoor plumbing with running water, and most people in a neighborhood got their daily water from a common pump. Snow found a few cases of cholera that affected people who lived farther from this pump. He questioned families of the victims and found answers that confirmed his suspicions about the Broad Street pump. In some instances the cholera victims who lived at a distance sought water from Broad Street because they preferred its taste. Some children who died of cholera did not live near the pump but went to school near it and drank water from it during the school day. In contrast, there was a brewery near the pump, but none of the brewers contracted fatal cholera. Snow interviewed the brewery owner and found that the brewery had its own well; anyway, most of the 70 brewery workers drank the brewer's malt liquor rather than water.

Snow concluded that water from the Broad Street pump caused the epidemic and arranged for removal of the pump handle. The epidemic ended shortly thereafter. Some say that the epidemic was already ending before the handle was removed, but the story of the pump handle is firmly entrenched in the mythic history of epidemiology. Snow is sometimes called the "father of epidemiology" because of this systematic investigation of an outbreak of illness.

After I told Snow's story to a class of high school students, one of the students went to Mexico on vacation with his family. When he returned, he told me that he had become an epidemiologist. Many of his travel companions developed diarrhea. By carefully questioning each of the travelers about food intake, the student determined that only those who had eaten guacamole got sick. He warned his family about the suspected food contamination, and the small epidemic ended.

Today, epidemiologists from the Centers for Disease Control and health departments in each state investigate clusters of illness. If they had been asked to look into the Mexican diarrhea, they would have questioned food intake and other exposures, just as my student did. Once the guacamole was identified as the probable or hypothetical culprit, they would want to confirm the hypothesis with nonepidemiological techniques.

Snow examined the Broad Street water and found it relatively free of visible impurities. In 1854 the role of bacteria and other microorganisms as causes of disease was not yet known. Microscopic examination of the water with staining for bacteria was not an available technique at the time.

Koch's Postulates

In the late nineteenth century, the understanding of the spread of infectious diseases blossomed. Innovative investigators like Pasteur and Lister saved countless lives. We honor them when we speak of pasteurized milk or Listerine mouthwash. Robert Koch was a particularly important investigator from this era because he described a framework for deciding whether a microorganism actually causes disease. He suggested that four experiments in the microbiology laboratory were needed to prove that an organism was the cause of an illness:

1. the organism should be found in every individual with the illness
2. the organism from an infected, ill individual should be grown in pure culture
3. organisms taken from the culture and injected into an animal should make the animal ill with a version of the disease
4. the organism should be found in the ill animals.

Koch isolated bacteria called *Vibrio cholera* from the feces of those with cholera. On the basis of his postulates, Koch showed that this bacteria causes cholera. Now, the diagnosis of cholera can be confirmed by cultures from infected people. Koch's four steps do not need to be repeated for each individual case.

Today, we know that cholera is caused by intestinal *Vibrio cholera* infection and is spread by eating food or drinking water that is contaminated by infected feces. Cholera does not normally occur in communities with modern plumbing and water systems but is still an important problem in some developing countries, particularly if war or natural disaster disrupts the usual water supply.

Epidemiology is a powerful method, but the hypotheses generated by epidemiological research must be tested for biological explanations. This truth is emphasized by the aphorism "epidemiology never proved anything, except that life is frustrating." Epidemiologists need to collaborate, in this instance, with microbiologists. If epidemiologists and microbiologists had investigated the Mexican diarrhea that affected my student and his family, they might have taken cultures from the guacamole and from the sick travelers. In fact, formal bacteriologic studies of restaurants in Mexico have confirmed that guacamole is a common source of infectious traveler's diarrhea. Fortunately, the infections that cause traveler's diarrhea are usually much milder than cholera infections.

Investigating Clusters of Parkinson's Disease

Infrequently, Parkinson's disease does occur in a cluster or group of people living or working together. About 2001, researchers learned that three people who had worked with Michael J. Fox on a TV show in Vancouver, British Columbia, in the late 1970s had also developed Parkinson's disease.[3,4] There were about 125 people working on the show. The cases of Parkinson's disease were diagnosed 7 to 13 years after the group worked together. Of course, this intersection in the lives of four patients with Parkinson's disease could be a coincidence. Most of us in our lifetimes will meet many more than three people who later develop Parkinson's disease. However, Fox developed Parkinson's at a relatively early age and worked closely with the other three, so epidemiologists are looking carefully to see if this cluster of cases of Parkinson's disease has a common cause.

To explore the cause of the Parkinson's disease experienced by Michael J. Fox and his three coworkers, epidemiologists ask questions about the workers' diet, environment, and other experiences, searching for a common exposure that was not shared by other workers who remained well. They are challenged to locate and question a representative sample of the 125 people who worked together over 20 years ago. Assessing who was exposed to what so long ago will tax most memories. They have found that all four worked for at least five years in underground TV studios. The studios were poorly ventilated, so poorly that the air contained high amounts of carbon dioxide. We do not believe that exposure to excess carbon dioxide causes Parkinson's disease, but the poor ventilation could mean that the workers were exposed to other toxins or were more prone to share infections.

Researchers have also identified other small clusters of Parkinson's disease, one among teachers at a college who taught in a portable classroom that had been placed over a filled-in waste dump and one among office workers at a small garment manufacturing company. Given the known incidence of Parkinson's disease, statisticians estimated the chance of any of theses clusters occurring by chance, rather than because of some common factor, at less than one in a million. One in a million is clearly a long shot, but Fox and his coworkers should be considered in the larger context of many other workers and many other workplaces. If we could examine all Canadians, we do not know how many other instances we would find, but in a country of more than 32 million people, we can reasonably expect to find some other one-in-a-million clusters.

The abundance of Parkinson's disease that my mother-in-law found at the Manor undoubtedly has explanations other than a local infectious or environmental cause. Most residents of the Manor have reached the age when Parkinson's is common, regardless of where you live. Furthermore, many of those moving slowly or shaking have other reasons, such as strokes, for their infirmities.

Kuru and Creutzfeldt-Jakob Disease

A less ambiguous example of the role of epidemiology in neurological research is the story of Creutzfeldt-Jakob disease, a neurological degenerative disease that shares some characteristics with Parkinson's disease. Like Parkinson's, it causes a relentlessly progressive loss of specific neurological functions and causes specific pathologic changes in localized parts of the brain. However, as shown in Table 3.1, Creutzfeldt-Jakob disease has many characteristics that clearly distinguish it from Parkinson's disease.

An unusual infection is the cause of many cases of Creutzfeldt-Jakob disease. The fascinating story of this disease includes the discovery of a unique infectious agent, called a prion, for which Stanley Pruisner won the Nobel Prize in 1997, and the appearance of a variant of Creutzfeldt-Jakob disease, known now as mad cow disease. The proof that Creutzfeldt-Jakob disease can be infectious started with epidemiology and proceeded with the use of Koch's postulates.

Understanding the cause of infectious Creutzfeldt-Jakob disease began with investigations of a similar disease, called kuru, that occurred in the Fore tribe inhabiting a small area of the highlands of Papua New Guinea.[5] Carlton Gajdusek visited this area of New Guinea to investigate the disease, which causes incoordination, abnormal shivering tremors (*kuru* means "shivering" in Fore), and progressive neurological deterioration. Early symptoms of kuru are incoordination, difficulty

TABLE 3.1: Comparison of Parkinson's Disease and Creutzfeldt-Jakob Disease

Feature	Parkinson's disease	Creutzfeldt-Jakob disease
Clinical findings	Tremor, bradykinesia, rigidity, postural instability	Dementia, movement disorders, weakness
Pathology	Lewy body	Spongy microscopic holes in brain tissue
Area of brain involved	Substantia nigra	Cerebral cortex
Rate of progression	Slow	Rapid (death usually within two years of onset)

walking, or trouble with balance. Patients develop writhing arm movements and slurred speech. As the disease progresses, the patients eventually are unable to walk. On average, kuru causes death within one year once symptoms begin.

The prevalence and incidence of kuru were both about one percent of the population. To epidemiologists, incidence and prevalence have very different specific meanings. The annual incidence of an illness is the number of cases that newly appear in the population within a year. The prevalence is the total portion of the population that has an illness. The prevalence and annual incidence for an illness are rarely the same; this occurs only for an illness that lasts a year. A brief repetitive illness like a cold might have an incidence far in excess of its prevalence. A chronic illness like multiple sclerosis or diabetes has a prevalence that is much higher than its incidence.

Gajdusek drew detailed epidemiological maps, similar to Snow's. Kuru affected boys, girls, and adult women, but rarely adult men. Gajdusek found that the Fore women traditionally prepared the dead for burial and ate their brains, including the brains of those who died with kuru. The women touched the children of either sex with their dirty hands. Gajdusek hypothesized that the disease was contagious and spread by this contact. The adult men were less likely to be infected because they ate the muscles, rather than the brains. When the Fore gave up cannibalism, the effect was like removing the Broad Street pump handle; the disease nearly disappeared.

Gajdusek's epidemiological research in New Guinea set the stage for laboratory experiments. He and his colleagues injected the brain tissue from kuru victims into chimpanzees and caused a fatal disease in the chimps, with microscopic changes in their brains that looked like the changes of kuru. Injection of other tissues, such as blood, from kuru victims into the chimps was much less likely to transmit the disease. Brain tissue from infected chimps could be injected into other chimps, further transmitting the disease. For kuru, Koch's postulates were not strictly met because Gajdusek did not succeed in isolating the organism in a culture medium, but the transmission from man to chimp to chimp is strong evidence that kuru is infectious.

Kuru occurs only in limited areas of Papua New Guinea, but Creutzfeldt-Jakob disease causes very similar microscopic changes in the brain. On the basis of this similarity, Gajdusek injected brain tissue from some patients who died with Creutzfeldt-Jakob disease into chimps, reproduced the disease in chimps, and established that some cases of Creutzfeldt-Jakob disease are infectious.

If chimps are injected with brain tissue from patients who died with Parkinson's disease, the chimps suffer no ill effects. Of course, this experiment alone does not exclude infection as a possible cause of Parkinson's disease. For example, theoretically, an infection could damage the brain, then disappear from the body, so that the infectious organism is no longer in the body years later, when the neurological symptoms develop. However, many additional studies confirm that Parkinson's disease is rarely caused by infection. We must look elsewhere for its causes, and epidemiology is helpful in the search.

Does Smoking Cause Parkinson's Disease?

My father began smoking cigarettes in medical school. In the army he switched to the more mature, sophisticated look of a pipe. When I was a child, he often relaxed with a cigar. In 1975, when his first grand-child was born, he threw his cigars and pipes away and never smoked again. Today, we have no doubt that nearly 40 years of smoking caused his throat cancer, even though he stopped smoking more than a decade before the cancer was found.

Recognition that smoking is a cause of lung and throat cancer came from using epidemiology to study endemic diseases. In the 1950s, lung cancer was becoming more common, especially in men. Many investigators favored the hypothesis that smoking causes lung cancer; however, that smoking causes illness could not be proven using Koch's postulates. All smokers do not develop lung cancer, and many people develop lung cancer without ever touching tobacco. Smoke cannot be isolated from a cancer victim the way *V. cholera* is isolated from the cholera sufferer.

In later chapters, when we review treatment of Parkinson's disease, we shall review drug trials and the desirability of prospective randomized double-blind controlled studies to see how a chemical affects the human body. However, with a potential toxin like cigarette smoke, no one would contemplate a controlled trial, assigning people randomly to smoke or not to smoke. Thus epidemiological studies comparing smokers to nonsmokers are extremely important research tools to check the relationship between smoking and disease.

In the 1950s Richard Doll and Austin Hill used epidemiology to study men who had died with lung cancer. For controls they found an equal number of men without cancer. The cancer cases and the controls were matched for age, sex, socioeconomic status, and site of hospitalization. Hence this type of epidemiology is called a case-control study. Case-control studies are retrospective, which means that they look back in time, trying to discover what caused an illness. Case-control studies are particularly useful for examining effects that develop slowly over years or that affect only a small fraction of the population. Doll and Hill found that lung cancer victims were nearly 10 times more likely than the controls to be smokers. This was one of the studies that began to establish the relationship between smoking and lung cancer. In the 1950s, at least five other case-controlled retrospective studies found similar results. This confirmation from multiple studies makes the finding more important because it decreases the chance that the smoking–cancer association is limited to a specific population or is a freak of chance, like flipping a coin and getting heads five times in a row. The chance of getting five heads in a row is 1 in 32; most epidemiological studies are considered statistically significant if the probability of a statistical fluke is less than 1 in 20. The similarity of findings from study to study is called consistency of association.

These studies of lung cancer and smoking elicited much criticism, not only from tobacco companies, but also from professional statisticians. A particular issue was whether the controls truly matched the cases in genetic background and life experiences, other than smoking, that might cause cancer. Another kind of epidemiological study, a prospective cohort study, avoids this problem of case-control studies. A cohort is simply a group of people. For example, everyone in a school class might form a cohort. In a prospective cohort study, investigators observe a large group of people over time. Cohort studies of smoking looked at who in the cohort would develop lung cancer. Over and over again, prospective cohort studies showed an association between smoking and the development of lung cancer. The prospective studies showed that the more one smoked, the more likely one was to develop lung cancer, a so-called dose-response relationship: As the amount of exposure increases, the probability of an effect also increases.

Cohort studies can be critiqued. For example, the diagnostic criteria and methods to measure amount of smoking must be determined in advance, and a cohort study should always be examined to see how well those in the cohort represent the general population. Although critics could find fault with each epidemiological study, the nature of the faults differed, and the consistency of association of multiple studies made it more likely that the association was real, rather than the result of methodological errors.

Causation versus Association—The Hill Criteria

Epidemiologists find associations, but a basic principle is that associations do not prove causation. A trivial illustration shows this: Most murderers drink milk during childhood, but this does not prove that drinking milk causes homicide. We need a rigorous analysis to decide if an association is a clue to the cause of a disease. For epidemiological studies Hill[6] listed the criteria necessary to support causation:

1. a strong and consistent statistical correlation between the reputed cause (such as smoking) and the reputed effect (such as lung cancer)

2. a dose-response relation between reputed cause and effect
3. a temporal relation between reputed cause and effect (innumerable statistical associations would be unconvincing if the smokers did not start smoking until after they developed cancer).

Using these criteria, epidemiological statistics can support causation, but statistics never prove causation. Even if each of the first three criteria is met, many alternative hypotheses can explain the statistical findings. We know now that smoking causes cancer, but by the statistics alone, we cannot reject other explanations. Could some genetic defect or childhood experience predispose people to smoke and predispose to cancer? Could people with a few cancer cells starting in their lungs have an increased urge to smoke? Hypotheses are always cheap; the possible explanations for a statistical association are endless.

Hill added another key criterion:

4. biological plausibility supporting the causal nature of the association.

For infectious disease the biologic plausibility might come from use of Koch's postulates. For toxins, like cigarette smoke, the biologic evidence might come from experiments exposing animals or tissue cultures to the toxin and be supplemented by biochemical studies documenting the mechanism of toxicity. We are now convinced that smoking is a cause of lung cancer because of the combined work of many epidemiologists and of laboratory and clinical investigators who have confirmed the disease causation in varied settings. This is a typical story of real life science: studies and experiments, criticism, improvement and refinement, all made possible by the interaction and collaboration of different disciplines.

If smoking caused Dad's throat cancer, could it also be the cause of his Parkinson's disease? If the contents of cigarette smoke are toxic to lung cells, could they also be toxic to brain cells?

Epidemiology of Smoking and Parkinson's Disease

If I have a hundred patients with Parkinson's disease in my practices, why don't I question them all about smoking, find some control patients for comparison, and begin my own retrospective case-control study to answer the question? I can imagine the newspaper headline when I report the results: NEUROLOGIST LINKS SMOKING TO PARKINSON'S DISEASE.

Researchers at the Mayo Clinic did just that. They found 196 patients who had Parkinson's disease and compared them to age- and sex-matched controls living in the same county.[7] Their task was eased because the Clinic has a superb record-keeping system, both for its own patients and for residents of Olmstead County, Minnesota, where the Clinic is located.

Amazingly, in the Mayo study, the controls were more likely than the people with Parkinson's disease to be smokers! Could smoking actually prevent Parkinson's disease? This surprising result raises many questions. Is difference in smoking between the two groups simply by chance rather than a true biological effect of smoking? In this particular study, statistical analysis showed that the difference between the two groups might be by chance alone. However, a number of other case-control studies have found a similar association: Patients destined to develop Parkinson's disease seem less likely than their peers to smoke. The studies of smoking and cancer and the studies of smoking and Parkinson's disease both show consistent associations, even though for Parkinson's disease, smoking appears protective rather than pathogenic.

The Mayo Clinic case-control study of Parkinson's disease and smoking was retrospective. Therefore information about an individual's smoking history for both patients and controls chiefly came from old medical records. The retrospective design can bias an epidemiological study. Statistically speaking, a bias is an error that leads to misinterpretation of the study results.

A good research paper examines potential biases and otherwise critiques itself in its discussion section. The authors of the Mayo Clinic paper on epidemiology of Parkinson's disease mention a number of potential biases. For example, there is exposure suspicion bias: The investigator going through medical records to find the smoking history might have looked more or less hard for smoking in one group based on preconceived notions of what the study might find. Second, there is misclassification bias: If old medical records are incomplete or unreliable, smokers might be called nonsmokers, or vice versa. Third, there is ascertainment bias: Since patients with Parkinson's disease might have more extensive medical records than do controls without chronic diseases, the Parkinson's disease patients might have more extensive histories of habits such as smoking. Of course, in this instance, ascertainment bias would increase the chance of knowing that a patient with Parkinson's disease had smoked and so would make the study less likely to show that nonsmokers were more prone to Parkinson's disease.

Another bias that needs consideration when evaluating case-control studies is selection bias. Possibly, those who come to the Mayo Clinic for care of Parkinson's disease are not representative of all those with the disease. If the patients and controls had actually been interviewed about their smoking habits, recall bias would be an issue: Ill patients might be more or less likely than controls to remember how much they smoked. We could list other sources of bias, but the point is that every epidemiological study has biases; it is impossible to design a bias-free study.

Prospective cohort studies have also shown that smokers are less likely than nonsmokers to get Parkinson's disease. These studies need to track thousands of people for many years. For example, the Nurses' Health Survey has followed 121,700 women since 1976, and the Health Professionals Follow-Up Study has included over 50,000 men since 1986.[8] In these cohorts the incidence of Parkinson's disease was 60 percent lower among current smokers. Furthermore, there was evidence of a dose-response effect: The risk of Parkinson's disease decreased as the number of cigarettes smoked increased. Among those who had stopped smoking, the incidence of Parkinson's disease increased as the number of years since quitting increased.

This article on the prospective studies critiques its own findings. Naturally, it discusses potential biases and introduces two other issues relevant to all epidemiological studies: confounders and reverse causation.

Confounders are factors that might influence the studied groups (such as smokers and nonsmokers) differently. In most studies, investigators control for common confounders like age and sex. They often try to control for possible confounders, like socioeconomic status; however, some confounders can be difficult to define or measure. There are always potential confounders, like unknown genetic or environmental causes of Parkinson's disease, that cannot be identified at the time of a study.

Reverse causation means that an association is real, but the cause is the opposite of the initial hypothesis. For example, before developing tremor or other classic manifestations of Parkinson's disease, someone destined to develop the disease might have early or "preclinical" effects that decrease the predilection to smoke. Since patients with Parkinson's disease frequently lose their sense of smell early in the disease, could they be less likely to smoke because they stop enjoying the smell of tobacco?

The final sentences of the paper on the these two prospective cohort studies bear repeating:

> Of course any public health benefits of smoking derived from a potential reduction of the incidence of Parkinson's disease would be overwhelmed by its detrimental effects on conditions such as cancer and cardiovascular disease. The chief interest of elucidating the role of smoking on Parkinson's disease is to enhance our understanding of the pathogenesis of the disease, which may lead to preventive or therapeutic advancements.

The inverse association between smoking and the risk of developing Parkinson's disease has inspired laboratory research for possible cellular, molecular, and genetic mechanisms.

Pesticides, Head Trauma, and Parkinson's Disease

Epidemiologists have looked at many factors besides smoking for associations with Parkinson's disease. In contrast to the inverse association between smoking and Parkinson's, studies have shown a positive association between exposure to pesticides and the risk of developing Parkinson's disease. For example, in one case-control study, patients with Parkinson's disease were about four times more likely than control subjects to have worked with pesticides.[9] Most patients with Parkinson's disease do not have a history of much pesticide exposure, but this association for some patients is another clue to possible toxins for basic scientists to pursue.

Epidemiologists have also studied whether head trauma causes Parkinson's disease. Muhammad Ali, the former heavyweight-boxing champion, developed Parkinson's when he was still in his early forties. In his youth he had been famous for his quick footwork. Years later, his public appearances, such as at the 2000 Atlanta Olympic Games , when he shuffled to the podium carrying the Olympic torch, have increased public awareness of the ravages of Parkinson's. Did his boxing career cause him to develop Parkinson's disease at a relatively young age?

In a few instances, trauma to the brain has clearly caused parkinsonism. In the best-documented cases the head trauma has been severe enough to cause loss of consciousness, brain scan images have shown localized damage in parts of the brain that are central to Parkinson's disease, and parkinsonism emerged within days, or at most, months, after the trauma. These convincing cases of posttraumatic parkinsonism are quite rare, and the vast majority of people who are hit in the head, even those who are hit hard enough to be knocked out or to have amnesia for the blow, do not develop parkinsonism. Neurologists have long hypothesized that boxers, jockeys, and others who are likely to experience multiple blows to their heads are at higher risk for developing Parkinson's disease; this hypothesis is best tested with epidemiological studies.

Both retrospective case-control studies and prospective cohort studies have checked whether head trauma is a risk factor for developing Parkinson's disease. A prospective cohort study followed 821 people who had had head trauma severe enough to cause loss of consciousness, amnesia, skull fracture, or abnormal neurological examinations.[10] The study did not find that these people were at increased risk of developing Parkinson's disease. However, these 821 people might have been too few to show the effect of the head trauma. In contrast, a number of retrospective case-control studies do show that patients with Parkinson's disease are more likely than controls to have been hit on the head severely enough to cause loss of consciousness, amnesia, or other acute evidence of neurological injury. The retrospective studies suggest that there is some increased risk of developing Parkinson's disease among those who have had mild head trauma; combined, the retrospective and prospective studies show that this risk is small. For example, a case-control study of 196 patients with Parkinson's disease in Olmstead, Minnesota, found that head trauma preceded the onset of Parkinson's disease in only five percent of the cases, but patients with Parkinson's disease were about four times more likely than the matched controls to have had a concussion that was severe enough to knock them out.[11]

These epidemiological studies of individuals after a single concussion clearly do not include boxers whose heads are routinely pummeled and who therefore might have a greater tendency to develop parkinsonism. For an individual former boxer who develops parkinsonism, proving that trauma is the cause may be impossible without studying the brain after death. We can suspect, but not prove, that Ali's illness is a result of his career in the ring.

Parkinson's at the Manor

Let's return to my imaginary headline: NEUROLOGIST LINKS SMOKING TO PARKINSON'S DISEASE. The headline would be true: The link is that smokers are less likely than nonsmokers to get Parkinson's disease; however, a newspaper reader would need to look carefully beyond the headline, aware that inverse associations, biases, confounders, and competing hypotheses all influence the meaning of the link. Epidemiology provides a powerful tool for studying disease, but like every powerful tool, it is dangerous or misleading if misused.

How would an epidemiologist approach the question of an epidemic of Parkinson's disease at the Manor? If the investigators did a case-control study of those with Parkinson's disease in an assisted-living home, would my mother-in-law's former neighbors living independently in Florida or New Jersey be the appropriate controls? At the very least, the investigators would need to do careful matching for age. Furthermore, the very act of moving to assisted living creates a selection bias because those with slow movement and postural instability are more likely to need assistance. Because they are looking carefully for a particular disease, the researchers might have an ascertainment bias, making the diagnosis too readily. They would need to avoid misclassification bias: How many people were using walkers for reasons other than Parkinson's disease?

We are all prone to misperceiving associations or epidemics. A friend asked me if Parkinson's disease is more common now than it was a generation ago. I do not know the answer, but I do know how easily the disease can seem to be everywhere. Weekly, there is news about it in the science sections of the newspapers. Patients like Michael J. Fox talk about it publicly and urge Congress to spend more on research.

TABLE 3.2: Epidemiological Concepts and Terms

Case-control study

Consistency of association

Prospective cohort study

Dose-response relationship

Exposure suspicion bias

Misclassification bias

Ascertainment bias

Selection bias

Recall bias

Reverse causation

Confounding

Organizations like the Parkinson's Action Network, the Parkinson's Disease Foundation, the National Parkinson Foundation, and the American Parkinson Disease Association catch our attention while advocating research and good patient care. We all need some familiarity with the basics of epidemiology, like the concepts listed in Table 3.2, just to keep up with the news.

CHAPTER FOUR

Causes of Parkinson's Disease

Most people who get Parkinson's disease naturally want to know what caused their illness. They ask questions like, Is there anything that I could avoid so that the disease will not worsen? Are my children likely to inherit the disease? Do I need to worry about my friends catching it from me? Physicians still do not know the cause of most cases of Parkinson's disease, but there are a few instances where a cause is known, and these give important clues for future research. We are learning that most cases of Parkinson's disease are due to an interaction of genes and the environment.

Does an Infection Cause Parkinson's Disease?

When I was a second-year medical student, we were invited to many evening seminars given by different specialists to help us choose our areas of interest. I was drawn to the neurology and psychiatry talks. One evening, Dr. David Poskanzer gave the neurology seminar. He was an animated, imaginative speaker who attracted students to neurology. He challenged us with creative ideas; sometimes I was not sure whether he really believed his own theories.

That evening, he spoke on Parkinson's disease, offering his own hypothesis about the cause. He had observed that the average age of his patients with Parkinson's disease was increasing. He explained that in any medical practice, patients often find a young physician and then

remain patients in the practice for years, so many physicians find that
their patients get older as they themselves age. Poskanzer believed that
the ages of the patients who were consulting him about Parkinson's
disease were increasing even faster than the ages of his other patients.
He thought that this observation provided a clue to the elusive cause of
idiopathic Parkinson's disease.

Poskanzer's idea was that a brain infection caused all, or at least
most, cases of Parkinson's. He thought that the infection was by the
same virus that caused encephalitis lethargica, a devastating illness that
spread as an epidemic between 1916 and the mid-1920s. *Encephalitis* simply means "brain inflammation"; there are many causes of encephalitis,
especially different viral infections. In 1916 Dr. Constantin von
Economo in Vienna began seeing patients with a form of encephalitis
that he had not previously encountered.[1] This form of encephalitis was
called lethargica because it caused severe sleepiness; it was a so-called
sleeping sickness. Those with this illness developed nonspecific symptoms like headache, fever, and nausea, and then within days would
become irresistibly drowsy. They would fall asleep eating or in strange
positions. Many developed double vision due to difficulty moving their
eyes in tandem. Some would become comatose and die. Those who
died had brain inflammation that was most pronounced in and around
the substantia nigra, the same area where cell loss occurs in Parkinson's
disease. The double vision occurred because areas near the substantia
nigra control eye movements.

Within the next decade, thousands of people had encephalitis
lethargica. About 40 percent of those who developed this sleeping sickness died; a few recovered completely, but nearly one-half of the victims
recovered only partially and were often left with neurological problems
very much like Parkinson's disease. Poskanzer was especially interested
that some of those who initially seemed to recover completely developed
parkinsonism months or years later. Parkinsonism that develops after
encephalitis lethargica is called postencephalitic Parkinson's disease.

The epidemic of encephalitis lethargica overlapped with a much
larger pandemic of influenza. A pandemic is an illness that is everywhere. "Just had the flu" hardly describes what occurred during the
influenza pandemic of 1918. All over the world, millions of people were
infected by the worst flu infections ever recorded. More people died
of this flu than had been killed in battle in World War I. The death
toll from this infection reached 20 to 40 million people, and for every
death, there were perhaps 40 people with milder infections. Many of
those with nonlethal flu had headaches and fever. Could some of them
have had mild encephalitis?

I asked my parents, who were young children during the flu pandemic,
if they had memories of the flu. My mother-in-law was told that she had

had it as an infant, having caught it from her mother. For both of them the flu was a mild illness, and they developed neither encephalitis nor parkinsonism. My father and mother do not remember if they had the flu as children. Dad said, "If I did have it, at least the doctor would have made a house call and treated me with a mustard plaster. They do not make doctors like that today."

Poskanzer suggested that for every patient who was known to have had encephalitis lethargica followed by postencephalitic Parkinson's disease, there might be many more patients who had had a much milder flu-like illness between 1918 and the early 1920s, had not realized that the virus had also infected their brains, and then had developed Parkinson's disease as a late effect of this infection from their youth.

When an investigator offers a hypothesis, it should make some sense based on what we know of biology. Poskanzer argued that other viruses damage the nervous system of a fraction of those infected, even though most people infected by the same virus are free of neurological illness. He described the effects of poliovirus as an excellent example.

The varied forms of poliovirus infection illustrate that a virus can cause different illnesses in different victims. Most people infected with this virus have a mild illness that causes only diarrhea or upset stomach. Only a small fraction of those infected by the poliovirus develop a neurological illness, which, like encephalitis lethargica, often begins with fever and headache. In contrast to the virus of encephalitis lethargica that targets brain cells near the substantia nigra, poliovirus kills different nerve cells, especially cells in the spinal cord that control muscles. The full name of the neurological illness is polio encephalomyelitis. *Encephalo-* refers to the brain, *-myel-* refers to the spinal cord, *-itis* means "inflammation," and *polio* means "gray." Polio encephalomyelitis is a viral infection of the gray matter of the brain and spinal cord. Many polio victims are left with localized muscle weakness and muscle shrinkage or atrophy.

Polio and encephalitis lethargica share the ability to disturb the nervous system in ways that first become apparent years after the initial infection. Just as some patients recover from encephalitis lethargica but develop Parkinson's disease years later, some patients recover from polio with little weakness but develop progressive muscle weakness and atrophy in later decades.

In 1954, when I was in the second grade, I was one of 600,000 American schoolchildren who participated in the large Salk polio vaccine trials. Acute poliomyelitis was so dreaded that our parents gladly allowed us to receive the experimental injections. The Salk vaccine, and later, the Sabin oral vaccine, have nearly eliminated acute poliovirus infections in the United States. Unfortunately, the disease still occurs in areas of India and Africa, where the vaccination programs are not yet complete.

As an American neurologist, I have never seen anyone with acute polio. Nonetheless, patients in their fifties and older still come to my office with progressive weakness due to polio that they had in their youth. It would be extraordinary for an American under 50 years old, born after the vaccine nearly eliminated the disease, to see me for this effect of polio. In a generation or so, neurologists will almost never see progressive weakness due to a poliovirus infection that had occurred long ago.

When Prophecy Fails

Poskanzer and his colleague, Robert Schwab, hypothesized that most cases of Parkinson's disease were late effects of the virus or viruses that caused encephalitis lethargica and the influenza pandemic of 1918. For unknown reasons these infections disappeared in the 1920s, so by the 1960s, the number of people who had been exposed to these viruses in their youth was decreasing. In the early 1960s Poskanzer and Schwab tested their hypothesis by surveying all the patients who had been treated for Parkinson's disease at their hospital, the Massachusetts General Hospital, over an 86-year span.[2] The average age of these patients was increasing, as Poskanzer had predicted it would. On the basis of these results, he made another prediction: Parkinson's disease would disappear by the late 1980s.

I remember when Poskanzer treated a number of medical students to an expensive dinner at the famous Boston restaurant, Locke-Ober. His extravagances and hypomanic enthusiasms made him a mythic favorite of the medical students, even though he was hardly the most famous neurologist on a celebrated faculty. He was a superb teacher who had taught us enough neurology that we understood the weaknesses of his theory.

Even before Poskanzer and Schwab surveyed the ages of their patients, many neurologists doubted their hypothesis. Although postencephalitic Parkinson's disease does resemble idiopathic Parkinson's disease, the two conditions also have clear clinical and pathologic differences. For example, the eye movement difficulties that are common in postencephalitic disease are not typical of idiopathic disease. Furthermore, the brain of someone who has had encephalitis lethargica usually shows extensive loss of nerve cells rather than loss localized to the substantia nigra. Lewy bodies are not usually found in the brains of those with postencephalitic Parkinson's disease.[3]

The events of the end of the twentieth century have disproved Poskanzer's hypothesis. We know now that the prevalence of Parkinson's disease has not fallen in the last 40 years. In retrospect, scientists can read the Poskanzer and Schwab report from 1963 and find defects in the statistical methods that led them to an incorrect conclusion.

Nonscientists are often frustrated when scientists cannot seem to keep the facts straight. We read in the newspaper one day about how much cholesterol is best for our health or what hormones to take or when to have tests for cancer. It seems that we can be certain that next year, we will read new and different conclusions.

A book called *When Prophecy Fails*[4] tells of a cult that was awaiting a visit from aliens to the earth. The group leader predicted the date of the visit. When the predicted visit did not occur, the cultists held strongly to their beliefs, despite this strong contradictory evidence.

What happens in science when prophecy fails? Clearly, the prediction by Poskanzer and Schwab did not come true. In the United States today, there are hundreds of thousands of people with Parkinson's disease who were born long after the encephalitis lethargica outbreak ended. When a scientific paper is in error, the errors often generate new hypotheses or prompt researchers to turn their energies in new directions. For example, Poskanzer and Schwab later helped discover a new medication for Parkinson's disease.[5] Investigators have pursued many other avenues of Parkinson's research in the last 40 years.

When a hypothesis is disproved, the investigator uses the knowledge of error to plan further investigations. In one sense, scientists share the tenacity of the cult members; we cling to some beliefs, specifically to our faith in the scientific method as a source of increasing knowledge. We learn from disproved hypotheses.

There are two interesting postscripts to the story of Parkinson's disease and infection. Even though encephalitis lethargica does not cause most cases of Parkinson's disease, it still accounts for some instances of the disease. Oliver Sacks's book *Awakenings*[6] tells an eloquent story of postencephalitic parkinsonism. In the movie based on the book, Robin Williams plays a physician, resembling Dr. Sacks, who cares for patients with postencephalitic Parkinson's disease in a chronic disease hospital. Many of these patients are so rigid and slow that they can barely talk or move. Many of those caring for these patients did not realize that the mute sufferers could still think.

In the movie Robert De Niro plays Leonard, a stage name for one of Sacks's actual patients. Leonard was born in 1920, five years after my father. As a child, Leonard caught acute sleeping sickness. Although he largely recovered, he was withdrawn and bookish. When he was 15 years old, his right hand gradually stiffened. He was able to continue his education and graduated from Harvard College, but his stiffness immobilized him more and more. By the time he was in his thirties, he was hospitalized for chronic care. When Sacks met him in 1966, Leonard was speechless and could move his right hand only minimally. With slight hand movements he spelled out messages on a message board. His body was frozen, masking his active mind.

By the late 1960s, Sacks was able to offer Leonard and other patients a remarkable new treatment for their immobility. In the chapters on treatment we will return to the *Awakenings* story.

The second postscript is the twenty-first-century story of West Nile virus, a virus that is quite different from the viruses that cause polio, influenza, or encephalitis lethargic. West Nile virus has been spread widely in the United States by mosquitoes. Most people infected by the virus have a mild, nonneurological illness, but a few develop encephalitis. Of all those with encephalitis, a fraction develop neurological illnesses that resemble the weakness of poliovirus infection, while another small fraction get postencephalitic parkinsonism. Even though encephalitis lethargica and polio are now diseases of the past, neurologists still need to understand viral-induced parkinsonism. If Poskanzer were alive today, West Nile virus would inspire his imagination.

Do Toxins Cause Parkinson's Disease? An Answer from the Frozen Addicts

In July 1982, six patients appeared at hospitals in the San Francisco Bay area with very unusual illnesses. Four of these patients were described in a landmark paper that heralded a new focus for research in Parkinson's disease:

> The patient group consisted of one female and three males, whose ages ranged from 26 to 42 years. Each patient had a history of previous heroin abuse (3 months to 14 years). Patients 1 and 2 obtained a "new heroin" sample in San Jose, California, about 3 weeks earlier. Dosages ranged from 5 grams over 4 days (cases 1 and 2) to 20 grams over 5 to 8 days (cases 3 and 4). All patients became symptomatic within a week after starting to use the new drug. First symptoms included almost immediate visual hallucinations (one patient), jerking of limbs (two patients), and stiffness (one patient). Generalized slowing and difficulty moving occurred within 4 to 14 days after the initial use of the substance. In at least one patient, symptoms continued to evolve over a period of 3 to 5 days after the drug was stopped.[7]

This paragraph of case histories comes from a dry research paper, but the story is expanded in an engaging book, *The Case of the Frozen Addicts,*[8] which is the source of many of the anecdotes in this chapter. The police brought George Carillo, 42 years old, to the Santa Clara Valley Medical Center Emergency Room in early July 1982. He had been in the county jail for a few days and then was taken to the emergency room because he was mute, stiff, and walked with a very slow shuffle. The doctors in the emergency room considered possibilities. Could he be faking symptoms to get transferred from the jail to the more comfortable hospital? Could he be intoxicated or overmedicated with tranquilizers like chlorpromazine? Could he have a mental illness? He was sent to the psychiatric ward, where the physicians diagnosed catatonic schizophrenia, a variety of schizophrenia characterized by severe rigidity.

Carillo did not improve on the psychiatric ward, and many days later, the neurology resident, Phillip Ballard, and the attending neurologist, William Langston, were asked to see him in consultation. They recognized that his face was masked like that of a patient with Parkinson's disease. He was bradykinetic and had postural instability. Checking the tone in Carillo's arms, Dr. Langston felt the characteristic cogwheel rigidity of Parkinson's disease. Carillo did not have tremor, but otherwise, his physical examination was characteristic of someone who had idiopathic Parkinson's disease.

Carillo was unable to talk. He was like Leonard, Oliver Sacks's patient with postencephalitic Parkinson's disease: Unless you made special efforts to communicate with him, you might believe that he could not think. But Carillo could slowly answer questions in writing. He offered an important clue: He had injected himself with a "new heroin" shortly before his symptoms started. Over the ensuing weeks Langston learned of five other heroin addicts nearby who had problems similar to Carillo's. Carillo was younger than most patients with Parkinson's disease, and the other addicts were even younger. Even more unusual, their illnesses all began suddenly within a few days of each other.

Bill Langston and I were residents together at Stanford University in the early 1970s. By 1982, our paths had diverged. I was busy in my clinical neurological practice. Langston was a junior member of the Stanford Medical School faculty. In his book Dr. Langston modestly describes his research career as mired in teaching and patient care. He was doing little investigation. However, his original insights and observations about Carillo and the other Frozen Addicts changed the direction of research on Parkinson's disease and redirected his career so that he has devoted himself to investigation of Parkinson's, written hundreds of papers, and founded the Parkinson's Institute in Sunnyvale, California. *The Case of the Frozen Addicts* is a lesson for young investigators, not only about progress in understanding Parkinson's disease, but also about how serendipity can change knowledge and change a career, when good luck is coupled with skillful observation and dedicated experimentation.

In 1982, drug dealers near San Francisco were selling synthetic drugs that were meant to have the same effects as heroin. Heroin is made from opium, the natural product of opium poppies *(Papaver somniferum).* Opium has been smoked, ingested, or injected for centuries because it can induce a carefree stupor and relieve pain. About 1805, morphine was isolated from opium and found to be its most powerful ingredient. It was named after Morpheus, a Latin god of dreams.

Late in the nineteenth century, chemists synthesized heroin from morphine. Thus heroin is a semisynthetic drug, modified by chemical processes from a naturally occurring compound. Initially, heroin was meant to be a treatment for morphine addiction, but it is actually more potent and addicting than morphine. (How these drugs affect brain cells and neurotransmitters is discussed in Tables 4.1 and 4.2.) Laws now ban heroin use and strictly control prescription, possession, and use of morphine and other narcotics derived from opium. In the United States the Drug Enforcement Administration (DEA) oversees use of these substances. Every physician who wishes to prescribe narcotics must register with the DEA and get a registration number that is then written on each prescription of a controlled drug.

TABLE 4.1: Opiate Receptors

The story of morphine and opiate receptors has many similarities to that of dopamine, the most important neurotransmitter in Parkinson's disease. Morphine and other opiates bind to specific cells of the brain. The outer membranes of these cells contain receptors for the morphine molecule. These opiate receptors were some of the first neurotransmitter receptors identified using a technique called autoradiography. Chemists made opiate molecules containing a radioactive isotope. If the radiolabeled opiate is spread on a slice of brain tissue and then washed off, the radioactive molecules remain attached to specific parts of the brain. The identified areas of opiate binding merit investigation for their role in pain control and other functions affected by opiates.

This method identifies molecules on the membranes of certain nerve cells that bind the opiates. These molecules are the opiate receptors. The receptor molecules are located near synapses and are most abundant on the postsynaptic membrane.

After investigators identified the opiate receptors, they were able to find molecules in the brain, now called encephalins and endorphins, that bind to the opiate receptors. These encephalins and endorphins are neurotransmitters, just like dopamine, but work on different nerve cells than dopamine does. The receptors are called opiate receptors because they were discovered using radiolabeled opiates. If the order of research had been a little different, we might be calling them endorphin receptors or enkephalin receptors.

Another outcome of opiate research has been the identification of opiate antagonists, chemicals that bind to the opiate receptor and block opiates from activating the receptor. Examples are naloxone and naltrexone. If someone arrives in an emergency room comatose and breathing poorly from a heroin overdose, emergency treatment is intravenous injection of naloxone. The naloxone goes to opiate receptors in the brain and displaces the heroin, and the patient will quickly awaken if the treatment is begun in time to prevent brain damage caused by lack of oxygen.

This model of neurotransmitter, receptors, agonists, and antagonists applies to other neurotransmitters, like dopamine or acetylcholine (see Table 4.2).

Morphine and heroin are obtained by chemically processing the opium poppy. Synthetic narcotics, like meperidine (Demerol), can be made from chemicals rather than from poppy extracts yet have effects on the body like the drugs made from opium. In the early 1980s, synthetic drugs were popular because they could be made in relatively simple makeshift labs, using chemicals that were ordered legally from chemical supply companies. Although meperidine was controlled by the DEA, the law in the early 1980s had not yet been expanded to control some of the newer synthetic narcotics, the so-called designer drugs.

Illicit drug makers, who supplied Carillo and other Bay Area addicts, were trying to make a relative of meperidine called MPPP. Langston's research team obtained samples of the powder that the Frozen Addicts had injected. They analyzed the powder and identified its contents. The "new heroin" injected by George Carillo and the other Frozen Addicts had high concentrations of a related drug called MPTP (Figure 4.1). Langston and his colleagues found a prior report of similar toxicity[9] in a user of MPPP. In that instance a graduate student had been making and using MPPP for months. Apparently, at least once, the synthesis went awry, contaminating the product with MPTP. The young student developed findings of Parkinson's disease. Two years later, after he died of a drug overdose, pathological examination of his brain showed destruction and loss of blackness in the substantia nigra and one area

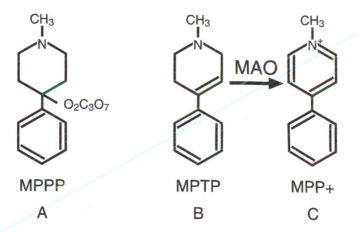

FIGURE 4.1: (*A*) The chemical structure of MPPP, the synthetic "new heroin." (*B*) The chemical structure of MPTP (methylphenyltetrahydropyridine), the accidental byproduct of making MPPP that caused parkinsonism in the Frozen Addicts. (*C*) The chemical structure of MPP+, which forms in the brain when MPTP is broken down by the enzyme MAO. MPTP is not directly toxic to brain cells, so MPP+ causes the damage that leads to parkinsonism. (Drawn by Douglas Katagiri.)

TABLE 4.2: Receptor Agonists and Antagonists

	Opiates	Dopamine
Neurotransmitter	Encephalins, endorphins	Dopamine
Postsynaptic receptor	Opiate receptor	Dopamine receptor
Receptor stimulators (agonists)	Opiates	Bromocriptine, pergolide, ropinirole, pramipexole
Receptor blockers (antagonists)	Naloxone, naltrexone	Chlorpromazine and others

resembling a Lewy body, reminiscent of the characteristic pathology of Parkinson's disease.

Langston and his colleagues treated the Frozen Addicts with the strongest medications for Parkinson's disease, and all of them improved. Whenever the Frozen Addicts stopped taking the medication, the parkinsonian findings returned. Two of the patients were treated with other drugs for Parkinson's disease and improved even more.

Langston and his colleagues were excited by the very unusual, possibly revolutionary implications of their patients. They wanted to publish their observations as soon as possible in a peer-reviewed journal that would reach the widest possible audience. Peer review is the process that journals use to check the quality of research papers. When a scientific article is submitted to the journal, the editor sends copies to other scientists for their assessment. On the basis of these assessments, an article may be accepted for publication, rejected, or sent back to the authors for revisions. Journals that do not use the peer-review system are held in less esteem in the scientific community, and journals have reputations for being more or less rigorous in the quality of their peer review.

Langston knew that some of his important observations had already been hinted at by Davis and colleagues in 1979, but that article had attracted little attention, at least in part because it had been published in a new journal with small circulation. Davis first submitted the article to the *New England Journal of Medicine,* one of the most widely read and prestigious medical journals. The *New England Journal* rejected the article with a note saying that it did not accept case reports (see Table 4.3 for a discussion of case reports and other types of scientific papers). Davis next sent the article to another widely distributed journal, *JAMA, The Journal of the American Medical Association. JAMA* accepted the article on the condition that the list of authors would be pruned from seven to six. Davis and his colleagues were unwilling to do this and turned down the acceptance. They finally published the article in a new journal, *Psychiatric Research,* one of whose editors was part of the Davis research team.

Langston and his colleagues decided to submit their paper to *Science. Science* is a great journal for those wanting to stay current with many aspects of research. It publishes relatively brief reports of new or unusual work in a wide variety of scientific fields. It also has well-written reviews and science news. When Harvard College recently revised its science curriculum for undergraduate nonscientists, one goal was that all students should be able to read and understand the review and news articles in journals like *Science.*

TABLE 4.3: Publication Types

A case report is a paper describing an unusual patient. It rarely contains hypothesis-driven research and is held in low regard by the most competitive journals. A paper describing a group or series of patients, often without formal controls or formal checking of hypotheses, is slightly higher in the perceived order of scientific quality. Though it is tempting to dismiss these clinical reports as lacking scientific rigor, case reports can generate new hypotheses and encourage future, well-controlled studies. Parkinson's 1817 essay reported only six patients, and the initial reports of the AIDS epidemic were of small series of patients with unusual immunodeficiency.

There are many other types of papers in peer-reviewed journals, including meta-analyses, editorials, letters, reviews, randomized controlled trials, and practice guidelines. A review is a discussion of previous research papers, criticizing, comparing, and offering conclusions. A review is usually an excellent place to start exploring a new subject.

An editorial is a brief review. Many journals highlight what they consider their most noteworthy articles by asking authorities other than the authors to write an editorial that places the article in context.

A meta-analysis is a review that analyzes a group of papers for methodological quality and bases conclusions on the strongest papers or uses statistical techniques to combine results of papers with compatible methods.

A randomized controlled trial is an important type of treatment trial that we will discuss in more detail in the chapters on treatment of Parkinson's disease.

Letters to the editor are often responses to recently published articles. I am repeatedly astonished by how often a letter writer will identify a weakness in or implication of a paper that both the peer reviewers and I have overlooked.

A practice guideline is a set of suggestions for good medical practice in a certain area. For example, the American Academy of Neurology has published a set of Practice Parameters for Parkinson's Disease, which evaluates the scientific evidence about diagnosis, prognosis, and treatment. These are listed in the appendix.

Understanding Parkinson's Disease

When the Frozen Addicts were described in *Science* in 1983, the report attracted wide attention. Soon Langston was receiving invitations to travel and describe his work and was meeting new potential collaborators.

The Langston group emphasized three implications of their observations. First, what they learned about MPTP-induced parkinsonism allowed them to warn addicts about the dangers of "new heroin" and other designer drugs and to treat future victims of MPTP. Second, MPTP might cause parkinsonism in animals, producing a model for testing hypotheses about causation, prevention, and treatment. Third, MPTP showed that a toxin could cause parkinsonism, and understanding its action might clarify the cause of idiopathic Parkinson's disease.

Animal models of disease are indispensable for thorough study of human illnesses. Experimentation in humans, cell cultures, test tubes, and culture dishes and analyses and simulations with computers all have a role, but some questions, such as safety of new drugs, are best tested in animals before being extended to people. Federal and state laws and rules in every research institution are designed to make this animal research as humane as possible, and scientists should always be vigilant to insure humane experimentation.

One of the earliest animal models of Parkinson's disease was created by injecting a close relative of dopamine called 6-hydroxydopamine into the brains of rats. Although dopamine and 6-hydroxydopamine are closely chemically related, the latter is strongly toxic to brain cells. The compound must be injected directly into the brain because it does not cross the blood-brain barrier, an important structure that keeps many chemicals found elsewhere in the body out of the brain. If 6-hydroxydopamine is injected at the correct dose in the right place on one side of a rat's brain, the rat will walk in circles, turning toward the injected side, and be unable to walk straight.

Shortly after discovering the toxic effects of MPTP, researchers administered it to animals, looking for a better animal model of Parkinson's disease. Rats and hamsters did not become ill when given MPTP, but monkeys developed an illness from it that had many features of Parkinson's disease. Analysis of brain tissue from these parkinsonian monkeys showed that their brains did not contain MPTP but instead contained a related substance, called MPP+. Further investigation showed that a common brain enzyme called MAO (monoamine oxidase) helped change the MPTP to MPP+.

If the monkeys were given MPTP plus an MAO-blocking chemical, then MPTP, but not MPP+, accumulated in their brains, and the monkeys did not become ill. From experiments like these, investigators deduced that MPP+ was the toxic compound, and MPTP was a nontoxic precursor. A precursor is a chemical that is changed or metabolized to make another compound. Morphine is a precursor of heroin. If

MPP+ is given to monkeys by mouth or by vein, it has no toxic ef.
on the brain because it does not cross the blood-brain barrier. If MPP
is injected into the monkey brain, it can cause monkey parkinsonism,
even if MAO-B blockers are present.

By the mid 1980s, perhaps 100 research teams were working on the
puzzle of MPTP-induced parkinsonism. The research combined animal
models of disease and basic biochemistry done in vitro, which literally
means done in laboratory glassware. We now think that MPP+ works
chiefly by getting into the mitochondria of brain cells. Mitochondria are
responsible for producing energy for cell function, and MPP+ destroys
the cells by interfering with their energy supply.

There are countless fascinating aspects of the MPTP story. Research
on how MPTP poisons nerve cells has produced new ideas for drugs to
treat Parkinson's disease. The monkeys with MPTP-induced parkinsonism
have been important research participants. Meanwhile, the Frozen
Addicts continued to need medications for Parkinson's disease to control
their symptoms. For some the parkinsonism stayed relatively mild. For
George Carillo the disease remained so disabling that he traveled, with
Dr. Langston's guidance, to Sweden for a trial of so-called brain transplantation. Frozen Addicts have also traveled to Vancouver, British Columbia, to help with research on new ways to take pictures of the parkinsonian brain. When George Carillo and William Langston met in 1982,
they had no notion of the repercussions their meeting would be having
in the twenty-first century.

Do Genes Cause Parkinson's Disease?

Could abnormal genes cause Parkinson's disease? Genes are
responsible for many neurological diseases. Huntington disease,
another neurodegenerative disease that impairs movement, is an example of classical dominant inheritance and of the new role of molecular
genetics in learning the causes of disease.

George Huntington was a physician on Long Island, as were his father
and grandfather before him. In 1872, coupling his observations with 78
years of his forbearers' experience, he described local families in which
many members developed abnormal movements and changes in mood,
thinking, and personality, usually beginning in midadulthood.

Huntington called the condition hereditary chorea. Physicians for
many years had seen a few individuals who developed abnormal movements called chorea, from the Greek word for "dance": "The disease
commonly begins by slight twitchings in the muscles of the face, which
gradually increase in violence and variety. The eyelids are kept wink-
ing, the brows are corrugated, and then elevated, the nose is screwed
first to the one side and then to the other, and the mouth is drawn

ı various directions, giving the patient the most ludicrous appearance imaginable."[10] Prior to Huntington's observations, chorea was considered a nonhereditary condition that chiefly affected children. We now know that there are many causes of chorea. There are many nonhereditary causes; there are also inherited causes of chorea, the most common of which is now called Huntington disease.

Huntington traced the hereditary chorea through multiple generations in a large family, showing that affected individuals usually had an affected parent. If a person suffered from hereditary chorea, some of his or her children usually developed the disease. However, among the children who did not develop the disease, their children (the grandchildren of the patient with chorea) were not subject to the disease. Huntington observed, "Unstable and whimsical as the disease may be in *other* respects, it never skips a generation to again manifest itself in another; once having yielded its claims, it never regains them."

Huntington was describing the pattern that we now call dominant inheritance. Gregor Mendel, the Austrian monk who pioneered the understanding of inheritance, published his famous description of the genetics of peas in German in 1866; it was not published in English until many years later, so in 1872 Huntington was probably unaware of Mendel's explanation of dominant inheritance. We now know that plants and animals, including humans, normally have two variants, or alleles, of each gene, one of which they inherit from their mothers and one of which they inherit from their fathers. An allele is dominant if the trait it controls is expressed whenever the animal has even one copy of that allele. If we consider a gene for eye color, the brown allele of the gene is dominant over the blue allele, so someone who inherits a blue-eyed gene from one parent and a brown-eyed gene from the other parent will have brown eyes. A person who has one allele for Huntington disease will develop symptoms of the disease, unless he or she dies prematurely, and, on average, will pass the allele, and with it the disease, to one-half of his or her offspring.

In the last few years, there has been an explosion of knowledge about Huntington disease, paralleling progress in Parkinson's disease. For almost every topic here—brain chemistry, brain electricity, brain imaging—we could have a similar chapter about Huntington disease. Unfortunately, treatment of Huntington disease is far less successful than treatment of Parkinson's disease.

The abundant extra movements that trouble patients with Huntington disease seem to be the opposite of the bradykinesia and rigidity experienced by those with Parkinson's disease. Interestingly, parkinsonian patients sometimes develop extra irregular movements as an adverse effect of their antiparkinsonian medications. These movements, called dyskinesias, are very similar to chorea.

Patients with Huntington disease develop atrophy of part of the brain called the caudate. This atrophy was first described after autopsy of patients with Huntington disease and now can be seen during life on MRI scans of Huntington sufferers. The cell degeneration occurs in cells in the caudate that contain a neurotransmitter called GABA (γ amino butyric acid), and patients with Huntington disease have decreased GABA in this area of the brain.

In the 1980s, powerful new techniques became available to study the chemistry of individual genes. The techniques use multiple blood samples from large families with a known pedigree. In *Mapping Fate*,[11] Alice Wexler tells the moving story of the search for the gene that causes Huntington disease. Researchers studied a large Venezuelan family affected by Huntington disease, first examining many family members to determine who had or did not have the disease, and then analyzing DNA from their blood samples. They localized the gene causing Huntington disease on the short arm of chromosome 4 in the late 1980s, knew the sequence of the gene by 1993, and a couple of years later, identified the protein made by the gene. This investigation of the molecular genetics of Huntington disease became a model for research on genetics of many neurological diseases, now including Parkinson's disease. (Table 4.4 compares Parkinson's disease and Huntington disease.)

The role of genes in Parkinson's disease is complex. About 1996, a few years after we realized that Dad had Parkinson's disease, his younger brother asked me about a mild tremor. At age 80 my uncle was vigorous, still operating as an assistant surgeon, and sculpting in his workshop, but his hands shook at times, and he wondered if this tremor might one day interfere with his work. I watched his hands trembling slightly when he held his arms outstretched. This is called postural tremor. The classic tremor of Parkinson's disease occurs with arms at rest, with the hands lying in the lap. In contrast to resting tremor, postural tremor is quite common and is usually not a sign of Parkinson's disease. However, my uncle had other subtle hints of in-

TABLE 4.4: Parkinson's Disease and Huntington Disease Compared

	Parkinson's disease	Huntington disease
Cardinal features	Tremor, rigidity, bradykinesia, postural instability	Chorea, personality change, dementia
Inheritance	Usually not familial	Dominant
Pathology	Substantia nigra degeneration, Lewy bodies	Caudate atrophy
Neurochemistry	Decreased dopamine	Decreased GABA
MRI brain scan	Normal	Caudate atrophy

coordination. He could walk briskly but hesitated for an instant when he turned around. When I took his hand and gently bent his elbow while he was trying to relax, I felt a slight intermittent resistance that is called cogwheeling. I wondered if my uncle might have the initial signs of Parkinson's disease.

Shaking, incoordination, and just slowing down often happen as we age. Postural tremor occurs in about one-sixth of people by age 74, one-fifth by age 84, and one-quarter of those over 85 years old.[12] Hesitant steps while turning can be seen in nearly one-third of people by age 75. My 80-year-old uncle's findings were not unusual for a man his age and certainly not proof of Parkinson's disease.

I told him that he had postural tremor, rather than Parkinson's disease, and that I should recheck him in about a year. I knew that even if he had very early parkinsonism, there was no reason for him to take medications for it when his motor problems were so subtle. In the future, when we develop medication to prevent Parkinson's disease, the physician's response to a patient like my uncle, who has suggestive but equivocal findings, may be much more aggressive.

Within a couple years my uncle was walking more slowly, stooped slightly, and had less facial expression. His hands shook when he rested his arms in his lap. Now, he clearly had Parkinson's disease. Why have both my father and his only sibling developed the same form of brain degeneration? Could this simply be coincidence? Perhaps one-half of people have some indications of parkinsonism by age 85, so for a pair of octogenarian brothers both to have Parkinson's could be due to chance rather than to genetics.

Following the mainstream of neurological opinion in 1997, I initially dismissed any concern that my uncle and my father might have inherited the disease. About this time, Dr. Langston wrote, summarizing his work with MPTP, "To many neuroscientists ... the conclusion seemed inescapable: Parkinson's did not seem to be primarily a genetic disease. It had to be caused by something in the environment."[13]

Even the best scientists cannot predict the future. Shortly after Langston stressed the importance of environmental factors, exciting discoveries rekindled interest in the genetics of Parkinson's disease.

Each person's genome is his or her total genetic collection of DNA molecules. Genes control all aspects of our bodies, from our eye and hair color, to our metabolism, to our propensity to develop disease. The Human Genome Project is identifying the molecular structure of all human genes. Rapid genetic advances are changing scientific understanding of almost every disease. Progress in Parkinson's disease is a prime example of the power of molecular genetics.

Before the era of molecular genetics, investigators studied inheritance by looking at families, clinically and epidemiologically. They found that you are more likely to develop Parkinson's if you have a relative with Parkinson's disease. Up to a quarter of patients with Parkinson's know a relative with the same disease. Perhaps one-sixth of patients with Parkinson's disease have an affected parent or sibling. Are these observations explained by genes, by environment, or by statistical bias? Initial interpretation of these familial associations, concentrating on studies of twins, pointed away from genetic explanations.

Genes do not directly explain all familial disease. Environmental exposures run in families. Siblings usually live in the same house during childhood, often go to the same schools, and may pursue similar hobbies or vocations. If toxic or environmental factors cause Parkinson's disease, these might explain some of the familial aggregations of the disease.

The distinction between genes and environment is not always clearcut. Muhammad Ali has Parkinson's disease; therefore, statistically, his daughter has increased risk for developing the disease. This risk might be due to environment rather than to a familial gene for Parkinson's disease. Like her father, Laila Ali is a professional boxer, likely to suffer repeated blows to her head, which can cause parkinsonism. The environment of the boxing ring would be the source of her risk.

Arguably, Ms. Ali's risk is genetic in a larger sense. Did she inherit genes from her father for strength, agility, or aggressiveness, for "floating like a butterfly and stinging like a bee"? Her hypothetical boxing genes might foster her success in the ring but increase her chance of repeated head trauma. If we consider all the genetic factors that determine how we interact with our environment, every disease has genetic causes.

Just like epidemiological studies of smoking and Parkinson's, these family studies are prone to ascertainment bias. If you have a relative with Parkinson's disease, you might be more aware of and anxious about the disease and hence be more likely to self-diagnose the illness or seek medical attention for it. Similarly, a physician, aware that a patient's relative had Parkinson's disease, might be more likely to make the diagnosis or to overinterpret subtle findings on physical examination as evidence of Parkinson's disease. The best studies try to avoid ascertainment bias by carefully examining the subjects and using well-defined diagnostic criteria. A family tree is likely to be more accurate if a neurologist examines each family member and less accurate if the diagnosis is based solely on family lore.

When I see a patient in my office with a familial disease, I usually cannot examine all the family members; some are dead, others live far away. This can be a particular problem in patients with Huntington disease because the mental deterioration that accompanies the disease often leads sufferers to move away from their families. The patient and I will often write to obtain old medical records of these kin to make the family tree as accurate as possible.

Surveys of twins are a common approach to separating environmental and genetic influences on familial diseases. Twins are more likely than their nontwin siblings to have a similar environment in their mother's womb and in childhood. Identical twins have identical genes on their chromosomes, whereas fraternal twins have the same mix of paternal and maternal chromosomes that any pair of siblings have. If Parkinson's disease is inherited and if one identical twin has it, then the other twin is very likely to have it, but the association should not be as tight for fraternal twins. In fact, repeated surveys in the 1980s of twins with Parkinson's disease found that most identical twins are no more likely than fraternal twins to develop typical Parkinson's disease.[14,15] These surveys implied that heredity is not a major cause of most cases of Parkinson's disease.

The results of the twin studies reinforced the perception that genes were not important in Parkinson's disease. However, on close reading, these studies did hint at a role for genes in the disease. Some atypical cases of Parkinson's disease contradicted the general conclusion. Among twins who develop Parkinson's disease before age 50, identical twins are more likely to share the disease.

When both identical twins do develop Parkinson's disease, environment and genes undoubtedly interact. We know that environment plays a role because the Parkinson's disease in one twin usually develops years after the Parkinson's disease in the other. Differences in exposures like head trauma, cigarette smoking, or unknown toxins could account for these differences in age of onset of disease. This gap in age of onset also means that twin studies might overlook occurrence of the disease in both twins if the studies do not examine the twins over many years or do not look for subtle signs of disease. In a later chapter we will review how new imaging techniques have identified "preclinical Parkinson's disease" and changed the interpretation of the twin studies.

In contrast to Huntington disease, which is always associated with a dominant gene, Parkinson's disease is usually not caused by a single gene. However, a few families belie the traditional teaching that Parkinson's disease is not inherited. Molecular study of these families may provide important clues about the cause of idiopathic Parkinson's disease.

In Contursi, a small town near Salerno in southern Italy, researchers found a large family in which typical Parkinson's disease affected some members of five successive generations (Figure 4.2A). In this family, now called the Contursi kindred, the disease has an average age of onset of 47 years, a bit earlier than the usual onset for idiopathic Parkinson's disease, but otherwise has typical parkinsonian clinical features, including improvement after treatment with L-dopa. In the few instances in which the brains of patients from this family have been examined after death, the substantia nigra lacked black pigment and contained Lewy bodies, matching the pathological findings in patients with noninherited Parkinson's disease.[16,17]

The Contursi kindred show the typical features of dominant inheritance:

1. the disease appears in successive generations
2. men and women are equally affected
3. about one-half of the offspring of an affected individual develop the disease.

However, if you look closely at the pedigree (Figure 4.2A), you will see that some family members developed Parkinson's disease even though the disease was not diagnosed in their parents. For example, we strongly suspect that the man represented by a gray circle in Figure 4.2A carried the bad gene for developing Parkinson's disease because both his mother and many of his sons were parkinsonian. When some of those who have an allele for a dominantly inherited disease do not develop the disease, we say that the gene has variable penetrance. The variable penetrance might be due to premature death, incomplete detection of the disease, or to other environmental or genetic factors that protect the gene carrier from developing symptoms of the disease.

We all have 48 chromosomes, either an XX for women or an XY for men, plus 23 pairs, numbered 1 through 23. On each chromosome the locations of many genes are already known. To identify the gene causing parkinsonism in the Contursi kindred, investigators started from the locations of known genes to find which chromosome contained the parkinsonian gene. The technique relies on blood samples from multiple family members, each clearly identified as having or not having Parkinson's disease. The gene was localized to the long arm of chromosome 4.[18] Eventually, investigators showed that the gene of interest on chromosome 4 coded for a protein called α-synuclein.[19]

Everyone has a gene on chromosome 4 that controls formation of the α-synuclein protein. The individuals in the Contursi kindred who have Parkinson's have a variant allele so that α-synuclein made in their cells is abnormal. The inheritance in this family is dominant, which means that one bad allele for the protein is sufficient to cause parkinsonism, even if a person also has one normal allele for α-synuclein. The α-synuclein gene was the first gene shown to cause Parkinson's disease and is now named PARK1.

For the Contursi kindred the time between identification of the family and identification of the disease-causing abnormal protein was less than a decade. If you compare this to identification of the Huntington gene, which occurred over a century after George Huntington described the disease, you have a sense of the remarkable acceleration of modern genetic research.

In 1999, geneticists described six generations of a large family in Iowa with autosomal dominant Parkinson's disease.[20] The family members who developed Parkinson's disease usually were symptomatic as relatively young adults, just like members of the Contursi kindred. Their Parkinson's disease otherwise matched the idiopathic disease. Their symptoms improved if they took L-dopa. Those who died had Lewy bodies in their brains, characteristic of Parkinson's disease. Of course, the investigators checked the family for the α-synuclein mutation. None of the family members made any mutant α-synuclein protein.

Gene localization studies, which can have molecular and mathematical pitfalls, were a bit uncertain in the Iowa family. Early reports suggested that the family had an abnormality on chromosome 4, probably on the short arm, whereas the α-synuclein gene is on the long arm. Without knowing the exact genetic abnormality, geneticists hypothesized another gene for Parkinson's disease that they called PARK4.

The mystery of the Iowa family was clarified in 2003 when investigators discovered that the affected family members had extra copies of the α-synuclein gene on chromosome 4. All the α-synuclein in their cells was normal; they just made too much of it. For the Contursi kindred, abnormal α-synuclein causes Parkinson's disease; for the Iowa kindred, excess normal α-synuclein seems to be the culprit.

In a third family with dominantly inherited Parkinson's disease, a different gene, the gene for an enzyme called UCH-L1 (ubiquitin carboxy-terminal hydrolase L1) seems to cause the disease.[21] The abnormal UCH-L1 gene is now designated PARK5. These different genes, each causing autosomal dominant Parkinson's disease, illustrate an important genetic principle: Different abnormal genes can cause clinically identical disease. Therefore, even if we identify a number of genetic causes of Parkinson's disease, there may be more unidentified genetic causes of the disease.

In contrast to the Contursi kindred and other instances of dominantly inherited Parkinson's disease, investigators have found families in which Parkinson's is inherited in a recessive pattern. For recessively inherited traits, both alleles of a gene pair must be abnormal for the trait or disease to develop. The affected individual inherits one disease allele from each parent. Each parent usually has one disease allele and one normal allele, so neither parent has the disease.

A recessively inherited disease might occur in many members of the same generation, whereas the disease has not occurred in their parents (Figure 4.2B). On average, one child in four will inherit the disease if each parent has one disease allele and one normal allele. In a number of families, Parkinson's disease shows this recessive pattern and has distinctive characteristics of early onset (typically, before age 45), variations in severity during the day with improvement following sleep, responsiveness to L-dopa therapy, and high incidence of abnormal movements (dyskinesias) as an adverse effect of the L-dopa. In many of these kindreds the abnormal gene, now called PARK2, is on the long arm of chromosome 6. Investigators identified the gene using techniques similar to those used to find the α-synuclein gene. After investigators identified the gene, they were able to find the protein made by the gene and named it parkin. There are many different alleles of the parkin gene; each allele represents a separate mutation. This gene accounts for many, but not all, cases of familial early-onset Parkinson's. As expected for a recessive gene, an occasional person with Parkinson's who has no family history of the disease turns out to have two abnormal copies of the parkin gene. Abnormal parkin genes are fairly common in individuals with early-onset Parkinson's but quite unusual in those who first develop Parkinson's after age 45. Other recessive genes can also cause early-onset Parkinson's.

Clinical clues, like early onset and improvement after sleep, suggest that illness associated with abnormal parkin genes is a bit different from classical Parkinson's disease. The neuropathology of patients with early-onset, parkin-associated parkinsonism also shows differences from classic Parkinson's disease. Like patients with Parkinson's disease, parkin-mutation patients lose pigmentation from the substantia nigra; however, they have areas of cell loss elsewhere in the brain in a pattern uncharacteristic of Parkinson's disease and lack the Lewy bodies that are seen both in classic Parkinson's disease and in Parkinson's disease associated with the α-synuclein mutation.

Where do Dad and his brother fit in this wealth of new genetic information? Should I be concerned that I might inherit the disease? The proven genetic causes of Parkinson's disease, like α-synuclein and parkin, usually cause early-onset disease. However, one member of the Contursi kindred was not diagnosed with Parkinson's disease until he was 85 years old. My grandparents remained healthy well into their eighties and never showed clues to Parkinson's disease, so my father and uncle are unlikely to have dominantly inherited Parkinson's disease. My father and my uncle have been interviewed and have donated blood for genetic research studies. Blood samples can now be screened for thousands of genes, and these studies hint that some familial cases of late-onset Parkinson's disease might be due to mutations on chromosome 1; others might be due to possessing a single allele for some parkin mutations. A number of other genes have possible associations with Parkinson's disease; nonetheless, most families with late-onset Parkinson's disease do not have known mutations.

My father and uncle's shared illness might still represent coincidence given the high prevalence of Parkinson's disease in octogenarians. I also speculate about a possible familial environmental factor leading to their disease. When they were teenagers, their father owned a gas station, where they worked regularly after school. The gas pumps were the old-fashioned kind that had to be physically pumped to deliver a tank of

A

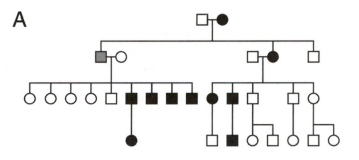

B

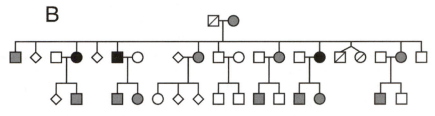

FIGURE 4.2: (*A*) A portion of the family tree of the Contursi kindred with dominantly inherited Parkinson's disease (adapted from Golbe LI, Di Iorio G, Sanges G, et al. Clinical genetic analysis of Parkinson's disease in the Contursi kindred. *Ann Neurol.* 1996;40:767–775, Figure 1). The circles represent women; the squares represent men. The black symbols represent those with Parkinson's disease. The gray square indicates a man without Parkinson's disease who is suspected of carrying the abnormal gene for the disease because his mother and many of his sons are parkinsonian. (*B*) A portion of the family tree of a family with recessively inherited Parkinson's disease due to the parkin mutation (adapted from Terreni L, et al. New mutation (R42P) of the parkin gene in the ubiquitinlike domain associated with parkinsonism. *Neurology.* 2001;56:463–466, Figure 1). The three black symbols represent the only family members known to have Parkinson's disease, all of whom had two copies of the mutant parkin gene. The gray symbols represent individuals who had one copy of the mutant gene. Family members who were deceased at the time of the study have diagonal lines through their symbols. Some members of the family could not be checked for the gene and are indicated by diamonds. (Drawn by Douglas Katagiri.)

gas. They both served in the U.S. Army in Europe and North Africa during World War II. They both were weekend gardeners who occasionally used pesticides. Could they both have been exposed in their youth to some toxin, starting the pathologic process that made them tremulous over half a century later? So far, this is an unanswerable question.

Genes and environment constantly interact. The epidemiologists have found that some of those exposed to pesticides develop Parkinson's disease, while others do not. This is not explicable solely by the amount of exposure. One explanation is that people inherit genes that determine how easily their bodies get rid of toxins like pesticides. According to some studies, people might develop Parkinson's disease only if they are exposed to toxins and also lack the genes to protect themselves from them.

The molecular changes found in those rare cases of Parkinson's disease that are clearly inherited have provided some tantalizing clues to the causes of idiopathic Parkinson's disease. I am following this exciting research with natural self-interest. As I age, every year, I have an increasing risk for developing the disease. Does my genetic makeup increase my risk? Should I be worried every time I stumble? Can I blame my illegible handwriting solely on being a physician? The future will be interesting.

All Disease Is Genetic Disease

I have suggested that in some sense, all disease is genetic, and gave the example that Muhammad Ali's daughter might develop posttraumatic Parkinson's disease because of her inherited prowess as a boxer. With accelerating advances in genetics and continued interest in gene therapy, I am thinking about whether my brothers, our children, and I will soon want to have our DNA screened for genetic risks of developing Parkinson's disease.

Geneticists report new wrinkles on genetic diseases every week. In late 2004 a report linked Parkinson's disease to another gene, one for an enzyme called glucocerebrosidase. Suddenly, my father, his brother, and maybe our whole family were right at a new frontier of research on the genetics of Parkinson's disease.

The story of glucocerebrosidase goes back to at least 1882, when Pierre Gaucher, in his doctoral thesis, published in Paris, described an illness that now bears his name. The most common variant, now called Gaucher's disease, Type I, is usually first symptomatic late in childhood or in early adulthood. The disease causes enlargement of the liver and spleen, anemia and other blood abnormalities, skin pigmentation, and skeletal changes. For years, physicians believed that Type I Gaucher's did not damage the brain.

Roscoe Brady at the National Institutes of Health identified the chemical cause of Gaucher's disease by the mid-1960s. Deficiency of the glucocerebrosidase enzyme causes the disease; the deficiency is inherited in an autosomal recessive pattern so that it occurs in those who have mutations for both of their alleles for the glucocerebrosidase gene. By the traditional Mendelian genetic rules, those who are heterozygotes, who have one good allele for the enzyme and one bad allele for the enzyme, still make the enzyme in their bodies and have no symptoms. Those who are homozygous for the bad allele cannot make the enzyme normally and develop symptoms of Gaucher's disease.

More than 20,000 Americans have Gaucher's disease. About two-thirds of these are Ashkenazic Jews. Ashkenazic Jews are those whose ancestors were from Germany and Eastern Europe, including countries like Latvia, Lithuania, Poland, Hungary, Ukraine, Czechoslovakia, and Austria. I have Ashkenazic genes from both Dad's and Mom's sides of the family. Dad's parents were born in Kupl, a small town somewhere near the border of Hungary and the Ukraine, and immigrated to the United States in the early years of the twentieth century. Among the Ashkenazim, about 1 person in 17 is a Gaucher heterozygote, carrying an allele that miscodes for the enzyme; in comparison, about 1 in 100 of other Americans possess a bad allele for this gene.

Gaucher's disease is just one of a number of inherited diseases that are unusually common in Ashkenazic Jews (Table 4.5). Interestingly, four of these—Gaucher's disease, Tay-Sachs disease, Niemann-Pick disease, and Mucolipidosis IV—are due to related chemical abnormalities. Furthermore, more than one mutation in the glucocerebrosidase gene is unusually prevalent among Ashkenazim. There are many other examples of genetic diseases clustering in specific groups of people. Another variant of Gaucher's disease, Type III, is more common in certain Swedes. Sickle cell anemia, another recessively inherited disease, is more common in blacks.

In the 1990s, clinicians in various countries described individuals with Gaucher's disease who also developed Parkinson's disease. Initially, these were dismissed as randomly coincident occurrences of two fairly

TABLE 4.5: A Few of the Genetic Diseases More Common in Ashkenazic Jews

Mendelian disorders	Disease predisposition genes
Cystic fibrosis	
Factor XI deficiency	Breast cancer (BRCA1 and BRCA2)
Familial dysautonomia (Riley-Day syndrome)	Familial colon cancer
Fanconi anemia	Parkinson's disease (possibly glucocerebrosidase and LRRK2)
Gaucher's disease	
Mucolipidosis IV	
Niemann-Pick disease	
Tay-Sachs disease	
Torsion dystonia	

A resource for more information is the Chicago Center for Jewish Genetics (http://www.jewishgeneticscenter.org).

common illnesses. More recently, clusters of patients with both diseases were reported. For example, an Italian center that cared for 58 patients with Gaucher's found that 4 of them also had Parkinson's disease.[22] This is not a controlled study, but if the prevalence of Parkinson's disease in the general population is about 1 in 100, the prevalence in Gaucher's patients of 4 in 58 deserves more investigation.

Gaucher described his disease over a century ago. Why is its association with Parkinson's disease just now being noticed? In the early 1990s, physicians were finally able to provide replacement enzymes to those deficient in glucocerebrosidase. The enzyme is given by vein and can prevent at least some aspects of Gaucher's disease. I can offer some hypotheses on how this leads to the recognition of combined Parkinson's disease and Gaucher's disease. Perhaps those receiving enzyme replacement therapy are living longer so that the parkinsonian part of their illness finally becomes evident. Those with both illnesses often develop the parkinsonism when they are in their forties or fifties, a bit earlier than the norm for idiopathic Parkinson's disease. Perhaps the enzyme replacement therapy protects most of the body from enzyme deficiency but does not protect brain cells because the injected enzyme cannot cross the blood-brain barrier. Perhaps the new enzyme treatment is leading physicians to treat groups of patients with Gaucher's. If I have one patient with Gaucher's and Parkinson's diseases, I might dismiss this as coincidence. If I run a clinic where I treat many patients with enzyme replacement, I can observe enough patients to notice unusual associations.

A group of Israeli investigators, prompted by the observations about Parkinson's and Gaucher's diseases, checked the genes of Ashkenazic patients with Parkinson's disease or Alzheimer's disease and compared them to the general population (Table 4.6).[23] Over 30 percent of the patients with Parkinson's disease had abnormal copies of the Gaucher's gene. This was about five times the prevalence of the gene in the healthy

TABLE 4.6: Rates of Carrying an Abnormal Copy of the Gaucher's Disease Allele among Ashkenazic Israeli Jews

Population	Number tested	Percent carrying an abnormal Gaucher's allele
Parkinson's disease	99	31
Alzheimer's disease	74	4
Healthy controls	1543	6

Data from Aharon-Peretz J, Rosenbaum H, Gershoni-Baruch R. Mutations in the glucocerebrosidase gene and Parkinson's disease in Ashkenazi Jews. *N Engl J Med.* 2004;351:1972–1977.

Ashkenazic population. Those with Alzheimer's disease did not have an increased prevalence of the Gaucher's gene.

Among the patients with Parkinson's disease in this study, three actually had Gaucher's disease due to inheriting two copies of a Gaucher's allele. The other 28 patients with Parkinson's disease had only one copy of the allele. Prior to seeing these results, I believed that carrying one copy of the Gaucher's allele had no clinical effect on the body; now it appears that this allele sometimes contributes to brain pathology.

Let's review how a single bad allele can affect the body.

1. A single bad allele can always cause disease. This is the pattern of autosomal dominant inheritance exemplified by Huntington disease.
2. A single bad allele can usually cause disease. This is called dominant inheritance with variable penetrance. We saw this pattern for the α-synuclein gene for Parkinson's disease when we reviewed the family tree for the Contursi kindred.
3. A single bad allele can increase the risk for developing a disease. If we assume that the prevalence of Parkinson's disease in Israel is about one percent, we can very roughly estimate that about five percent of those carrying a single copy of the Gaucher's allele eventually develop Parkinson's disease. While the Gaucher's allele somewhat increases the risk of getting Parkinson's disease, the disease develops only in the minority who are also exposed to other genetic or environmental risk factors. When I say that all disease is at least partially genetic, I am emphasizing the myriad risk factor genes, many yet unknown, that we all possess.
4. A single "bad" allele can have no effect on the body. The allele is only bad when the individual possesses two copies of the allele and inherits recessive disease.
5. A single "bad" allele can actually have both bad and good effects on the body. The classic example is the gene for sickle cell anemia. Two copies of the gene lead to serious disease, but those who are born with one copy of the gene have inherited some protection against getting malaria, a survival advantage in large parts of the world.

People have wondered why so many disease alleles are more common among Ashkenazic Jews. There are two competing theories. One theory is called the founder effect. The ancestors of many modern Ashkenazim were probably a few thousand people or less who left the Middle East and moved to middle Europe shortly after the destruction of the Second Temple in Jerusalem in 70 A.D. The population intermarried and grew for more than a millennium and then, in the Middle Ages, was decimated by violence, like anti-Semitic rampages by the Crusaders, and disease, like the Black Plague. When the size of the group was smallest, whether in 70 or about 1350, a mutation might appear in one person and then, over generations, persist in thousands of his or her descendants. At times, cousins, both carrying the disease allele, would marry and have children who inherited Gaucher's or one of the other genetic diseases.

A mutation in another gene called LRRK2 is associated with autosomal dominant Parkinson's disease and has increased prevalence in both Ashkenazic and North African Arab populations.[24,25] Genetic analysis suggests that in each population a single ancestor developed the mutation and spread it through succeeding generations. Perhaps the mutation was already in the Ashkenazic gene pool before the emigration from the Middle East 2000 years ago.

The second theory about disease genes prevalent in Ashkenazic Jews is that at least some of the genes might have survival value. Just as one copy of the sickle cell anemia gene protects against malaria, could one copy of the Gaucher's gene protect against tuberculosis or other infectious diseases that were endemic in the poor, crowded, poorly ventilated living conditions that many Ashkenazim endured in Eastern Europe? A numerical analysis[26] suggests that a single founder mutation about 2000 years ago is sufficient to explain the current prevalence of the Gaucher's gene, but these theories are still being compared, debated, and investigated.

I live in a much different environment than my ancestors. Even if the Gaucher's allele had some survival value for them, I would be very surprised if it has survival value in twenty-first-century America.

Before I decide whether I need genetic testing for Parkinson's disease, I want to reconsider where some of the other recessive Parkinson's disease genes fit in this scheme. Parkin is the best studied of these, clearly responsible for many cases of early-onset Parkinson's disease in those who inherit two disease alleles. If I inherited one parkin allele, would it have a good, bad, or indifferent effect on my body? The answer is still uncertain, in part because there are so many different mutations in the parkin gene. Many of these mutations cause recessive early-onset parkinsonism when an individual inherits two copies of the mutation; however, the effect of inheriting one copy of the mutation might vary. For now, it looks like inheriting a single copy of at least some parkin mutations does increase the risk of developing late-onset Parkinson's disease.

If I do get genetic testing, maybe for the Gaucher's gene, maybe for LRRK2, maybe for all of the genes now associated with Parkinson's disease, how will the results affect my life? If I carry none of the abnormal genes, I remain at risk to develop Parkinson's disease. Taking all the known risk genes together, we have discovered the cause of only a small fraction of all cases of Parkinson's disease. There is much to learn about environmental and other genetic risk factors.

If my genome does include the Gaucher's allele or another gene for Parkinson's disease, I face some hard decisions. I could start taking coenzyme Q_{10}, hoping that it would decrease my risk of developing Parkinson's disease. But, for now, we are not even certain that it helps people with early Parkinson's disease, let alone those with asymptomatic bad genes. I might spend a couple thousand dollars a year for CoQ_{10} and then learn in a decade about long-term side effects of overdosing on the vitamin.

If I were known to carry the Gaucher's allele, would my health and life insurance carriers want to charge me higher premiums? Would my family, colleagues, and friends treat me differently? Would my children want to get tested for the gene, and then think about prenatal genetic screening before they had children? Would I become depressed or worry that I might spend my retirement years shaking like my father and uncle? I can comfortably muse about these questions, but for children in families with more ominous diseases like Huntington disease, deciding on genetic testing is frightening. When families of my patients consider genetic testing, I urge them to consult genetic and psychological specialists to help with this difficult decision.

For now the disadvantages of learning which genes I carry far exceed any advantages. Year by year, the balance will change. When we have neuroprotective treatments for Parkinson's disease and when we can tailor these treatments to match each person's genetic risks, genetic testing will be much more routine.

CHAPTER FIVE

Medications for Parkinson's Disease

In 2005, shortly after his 90th birthday, I asked Dad what he had been taught in medical school, 67 years earlier, about treatment of Parkinson's disease. His memory was no longer phenomenal, so he often forgot the names of his own daily pills, but he recalled without hesitation, "Tincture of belladonna, 10 drops, three times a day." Now, the drugs available to treat Parkinson's disease are much more varied and effective (Table 5.1). Our pharmacopoeia is now so extensive that we sometimes call it a "pharmacopia," a horn of plenty brimming with powerful medications. The power of new medications to help or to hurt is often big news. Drugs like Vioxx (rofecoxib) stir debate not only in doctors' offices, but also in the news media, the FDA, and the courts. For each prescription drug, there are at least three levels of decision making for medicating an individual patient. First, the FDA has to approve the drug for sale in the United States. Second, the physician has to advise the patient on the optimal drug regimen and write a prescription. Third, the patient has to accept the physician's advice, fill the prescription, and actually take the drug. Each decision maker, whether the FDA, the physician, or the patient, needs reliable information about a drug's benefits and possible ill effects. As I review some of the drugs that I prescribe for Parkinson's disease, I am going to emphasize how scientific studies test these drugs for efficacy and toxicity.

TABLE 5.1: Drugs for Treatment of Parkinson's Disease

Class of drugs	Generic name	Trade name
Levodopa	Levodopa (L-dopa)	Dopar
Anticholinergic	Benztropine	Cogentin
	Trihexyphenidyl	Artane
	Parsidol	
	Others	
Dopamine agonist	Bromocriptine	Parlodel
	Pergolide	Permax
	Pramipexole	Mirapex
	Ropinirole	Requip
	Apomorphine	Apokyn
Amantadine	Amantadine	Symmetrel
DOPA decarboxylase inhibitor	Carbidopa	Lodosyn
MAO inhibitor	Selegiline	Eldepryl
	Rasagiline	Agilect
COMT inhibitor	Entacapone	Comtan
	Tolcapone	Tasmar
Combinations	Carbidopa/levodopa	Sinemet, Parcopa
	Carbidopa/levodopa/ entacapone	Stalevo

The Herbal Tradition

In the mid-1990s Dad's tremor gradually troubled him more and more, but he remained fairly steady on his feet and enjoyed daily walks on gentle trails near his home. One day, he was strolling in the woods when he passed a vigorous young hiker. The man turned to him and said, "You have Parkinson's disease. I know because I am a physical therapist. I hope you are eating tahini every day." My father thanked him for his advice and walked home. He was intrigued by the willingness of a stranger to offer a diagnosis and treatment advice so spontaneously. When he had been a practicing physician, he would never have made a diagnosis so casually nor prescribed a treatment without thorough examination and careful consideration. Later, he asked me why I had not suggested tahini to him.

I knew that tahini was a product of nature, a paste made from sesame seeds, a Middle Eastern version of peanut butter, used in various dishes such as hummus. I had never heard that tahini had any medicinal value, so I did a PubMed search on "Parkinson's disease AND tahini." PubMed, a free service of the National Library of Medicine, is an excellent way to carefully search peer-reviewed medical literature.[1] I could not find one scientific article on the use of tahini as treatment for Parkinson's disease; I could not find one article on the use of tahini for treatment of anything. I tried searching "Parkinson's disease AND sesame" and again did not find a single article. I found no published experiments suggesting that tahini had any value for those with Parkinson's disease.

I did a Google search on Parkinson's disease and tahini; I got 167 hits! For example, one site claimed that regularly eating sesame products had numerous health benefits, including preventing cataracts and decreasing the risks of developing diabetes, Alzheimer's disease, and Parkinson's disease. Tahini is rich in vitamin E and in other nutrients. According to the Web site, its vegetable proteins contain an unusually high percentage of the amino acid tryptophan. A hypothesis that vitamin E, tryptophan, or some other chemical in tahini is beneficial for patients with Parkinson's disease is not absurd; however, all the information that I could find about the health benefits of tahini was based on conjecture rather than on experiment.

Herbal and natural remedies are very fashionable now, but the medicinal power of plants is hardly a new concept. The opium poppy is the original source of narcotics, like morphine, codeine, and heroin. If I made tea from the bark of the willow tree growing in my garden, I could make a drink rich in salicylic acid, closely related to aspirin, to ease my aches and pains. But why is there such widespread faith that natural products are healthier than manufactured pharmaceuticals? My local organic grocery sells tahini but refuses to carry aspartame (Nutrasweet) because it is synthetic. Scientifically, the issue is not organic versus synthetic, but fanciful or hypothetical versus tested and retested by experiment.

Physicians are often accused of being too cynical about natural medicine, of thoughtlessly rejecting natural cures. Actually, every physician is taught the wealth of pharmaceuticals that we owe to nature. My father lived through a golden age, when scientists refined and perfected natural products for medicinal use. Insulin was discovered in 1922, and physicians saved the lives of diabetics using this protein extracted from pig and cow pancreases. When he was treating war wounds during World War II, penicillin, made from a common mold, was a new tool that allowed him to cure infections that he had learned in medical school were incurable. While training at the Mayo Clinic, he worked with Phillip Hench, who won the Nobel Prize for development of cortisone, a steroid derived from the adrenal gland.

In medical school Dad learned to prescribe digitalis leaf, made from foxglove plants, to treat heart failure. Foxglove grows in my garden and wild along the Oregon roadsides. From its leaves I could make a powder that is a powerful heart stimulant but can also have fatal, toxic effects. William Withering tested the effects of foxglove in the mid-eighteenth century. The plant was known to be potentially deadly, yet also helpful for some forms of dropsy, an old term for the body swelling that can occur with heart failure. The scientific name for foxglove is *Digitalis purpura,* so the drugs made from it have been named digitalis. Twentieth-century drug makers purified digitalis leaf to specific molecules, such as digoxin. One advantage of the purified, synthetic digoxin over foxglove leaves is that we can give the purified material as an exact known dose. Dried leaves vary in drug content from one batch to the next. Each vintage in each vineyard produces a different wine because of subtle variations in chemical contents of the grape; this variation is pleasurable for wine drinkers, but slight variations in powerful, potent drugs can be dangerous.

Once the active ingredients of an herbal drug have been identified and purified, pharmacological researchers study how the body uses the drug. How much gets from the stomach to the blood? Does it move from the blood through the blood-brain barrier into the brain? How fast does it leave the body? How does the body remove or break down the drug? When these facts are known, drug doses and dose scheduling can be much more rational. Another advantage of purified digoxin is that we can measure the amount of digoxin in a patient's blood and then adjust the dose to maximize therapeutic effect and minimize toxic risks. Physicians now routinely measure levels of many drugs in the blood to facilitate dosage adjustment and maintain drug levels that are most likely to be helpful and least likely to be toxic.

Some proponents of herbal therapy believe that the impurity of herbs is beneficial. Each herb contains many different chemicals that may have combined effects superior to those of a single purified compound. This is a reasonable hypothesis. No pharmacologist can produce a fine wine just by mixing chemicals together, yet the wine gives pleasure to the drinker far more than a cocktail of synthetic chemicals would. Those who wish to prove that a specific herbal remedy is better medicine than its purified chemical components need to do clinical trials comparing the herb to an inactive control substance, like a sugar pill, and to the purified substance. Controlled evaluation of efficacy and safety of herbs is rare, despite this scientific imperative.

Herbal Treatment of Parkinson's Disease

When the physical therapist suggested tahini to my father, Dad was not skeptical that a plant product could help him. During much of his medical career, prior to 1967, the only treatments that he had for his patients with Parkinson's disease were plant derivatives. Plant therapy of Parkinson's disease has a history reaching back thousands of years.

In India a medical system called Ayurveda developed over 3000 years ago. Ayurvedic physicians were familiar with a disease that they called *kampavata,* which in Sanskrit means "tremor and lack of muscular movement." The symptoms of kampavata are slow movement, drooling, reptilian stare, tremor, constant somnolence, rigidity, and dementia, strongly suggesting that kampavata is another name for Parkinson's disease. The Ayurvedic treatment of kampavata included a bean called atmagupta, which grows on the vine *Mucuna pruriens.* Chemical analysis shows that atmagupta beans contain L-dopa.[2] In controlled clinical experiments, patients with Parkinson's disease improve when they take atmagupta.[3] Both L-dopa, the strongest medication for Parkinson's, and atmagupta can have side effects, like headache, abnormal muscle postures, fatigue, increased tremor, fainting, and thirst. Adjusting doses of either drug for maximum effect and minimum side effects is very challenging for some patients with Parkinson's disease and for their physicians. The modern synthetic drug is safer and more effective to use than its ancient organic predecessor because a pure, measured dose of L-dopa pills can be prescribed precisely, whereas the chemical content of beans varies from crop to crop, and even from plant to plant.

The presence of L-dopa in some kinds of bean can have ill effects for patients with Parkinson's disease. The broad or fava bean is another herbal source of L-dopa. Eating these beans, with their small dose of L-dopa, has little effect on a healthy nervous system, but some patients with Parkinson's disease are supersensitive to slight variations in L-dopa content of their blood and can develop adverse effects by eating fava beans.

In the late nineteenth century the great French neurologist Charcot was superb at examining patients and diagnosing neurological disease; however, he had very limited ability to treat, although he had a name for the disease, knew its prognosis, and might even have known its pathology. He prescribed ergot and belladonna for Parkinson's disease, realizing that these herbal drugs might decrease some symptoms without curing the disease. Ergot, a fungus that affects rye, had been used as a treatment for paralysis agitans and other tremors even before Charcot. Ergot is the source of the dopamine receptor agonist drugs, bromocriptine and pergolide, that are now used as effective treatments for Parkinson's disease; however, we do not know if the ergot preparations used in the nineteenth century would pass modern drug evaluations. Charcot was unable to purify, improve, and test these the way that pharmacologists do today.

The story of belladonna exemplifies how a traditional herbal remedy evolved to scientifically proven, effective drugs. Belladonna comes from plants in the family of the deadly nightshade *Atropa belladonna.* In midsummer I often see a member of the nightshade family with delicate, purple, inverted sepals and prominent yellow anthers growing as a weed along the roads. The chemicals derived from these plants are called belladonna alkaloids and include atropine, scopolamine, and hyoscyamine, all of which are now available as purified drugs. For example, scopolamine is the active ingredient in the patches that can be taped behind the ear to prevent seasickness.

Bella donna means "beautiful lady" in Italian. Long ago, Italian women used extracts of the deadly nightshade plant on their eyes to dilate their pupils because large pupils were considered beautiful. The "deadly" part of the name refers to the long-known toxic effects of these plants. Medical students learn the mnemonic "*hot* as a hare, *blind* as a bat, *dry* as a bone, *red* as a beet, and *mad* as a hatter" to memorize the results of atropine poisoning. Relatives of the nightshade in the *Datura* genus have been used as hallucinogens since antiquity. A recent journal article described a teenager who tried to get high with Jimson weed *(Datura stramonium)*; his mother brought him to the emergency room when she found him hallucinating:

> The patient was restless, pacing incessantly, and shaking. He was awake, alert, and oriented to name but not to place or time. Vital signs included oral temperature 99.3°F (37.4°C) [hot], blood pressure 117/72 mmHg, heart rate 103 beats/min, and respiratory rate 24 breaths/min. Pupils were dilated to 8 mm, symmetric, and minimally reactive to light [not fully blind, but unable to focus]. Mucous membranes were *dry* [emphasis added], and bowel sounds were decreased. The extremities were warm to the touch but were not hot [probably red]. Neurologic examination showed that the patient was confused and mumbling, cranial nerves were intact, and both motor strength and reflexes were within normal limits. During the examination, the patient reached into the air as if trying to catch a nonexistent object [mad].[4]

By studying how atropine and its relatives affect the body, physicians have learned to treat deadly nightshade poisoning. Atropine disrupts the nervous system by blocking chemical messengers called neurotransmitters that relay information from nerve to nerve. In fact, atropine played an important role in the first discovery of a neurotransmitter.

Information travels along a nerve electrically, crosses the gap of the synapse chemically, and then proceeds along the next nerve again electrically. In about 1921 Otto Loewi first showed the central role of chemicals in the process.

Otto Loewi was born in Germany in 1873. In medical school he often skipped lectures and preferred to study philosophy. He barely passed his first major medical examination but shortly thereafter began to study medicine enthusiastically. The poor results of early-twentieth–century treatment of illnesses like tuberculosis and pneumonia discouraged him from practicing clinical medicine. He found his niche in pharmacological research.

Loewi wanted to investigate how nerves communicate across synapses. Experiments on a frog heart seem unlikely to illuminate understanding of the human brain, but Loewi recognized that studying the difficult question of neurotransmission would need a model less complex than a whole animal. Like Galvani, who in the eighteenth century did the famous experiments of making a frog leg twitch by shocking its nerve, Loewi chose to use an isolated preparation of frog nerve and muscle (in this case, heart muscle).

Loewi conceived a groundbreaking experiment on a nerve called the vagus. The vagus nerve originates in the lower brain stem and travels out of the skull and through the neck, sending fibers to the heart, stomach, and intestines. The vagus nerve slowing the heart rate is a simple example of the idea that sometimes, stimulating a nerve can turn nerves or muscles off, rather than on.

Loewi was one of many scientists who were interested in the role of chemicals in neurotransmission. His contemporaries had not found the right experiment to prove that chemicals were important in passing messages from cell to cell. Loewi claimed that one night, he dreamt of the experimental design. He awoke, made notes of his dream, and then slept the rest of the night. In the morning he was distraught because he could neither remember the experimental plan nor read his own notes. The next night, he had the same dream. In the middle of the night he rushed from his bed to his laboratory and did the experiment before he could forget it again. Within hours he had the first experimental proof of chemical neurotransmission.

Loewi dissected the nerve and heart from the frog and kept the heart in liquid. Next, he electrically stimulated the nerve attached to the heart; as expected, the heart rate slowed. He transferred the liquid from the first heart to a second heart. The second heart slowed just as the first heart had slowed, showing that the liquid from the first heart contained a chemical that caused the slowing of heart rate. Liquid from the first heart did not slow the second heart unless the vagus nerve was stimulated.

Loewi deduced that stimulating the vagus nerve released a heart rate–slowing substance into the liquid. In German he called this substance *vagusstoff*. This experiment was the first proof that nerves communicate by releasing chemicals.

Loewi did further experiments to identify the *vagusstoff*. He found that its action disappeared quickly from the fluid. He found substances that blocked or enhanced its effects on the heart. Eventually, acetylcholine was identified as the active chemical in *vagusstoff*. Acetylcholine is therefore the first proven neurotransmitter. A neurotransmitter is a chemical that is released when a nerve is stimulated; the neurotransmitter carries messages from the nerve across the synapse to adjoining tissue. Now, we know that acetylcholine is the neurotransmitter of the vagus nerve, and one of its actions is slowing the heart rate. Acetylcholine is a very important neurotransmitter, with different actions at numerous synapses.

Loewi's experiments not only taught about neurotransmission but also clarified the biological mechanisms for the action of belladonna and its derivatives. He found that the acetylcholine did not slow the heart if atropine was added to the liquid bathing the heart. Atropine acts by antagonizing or blocking some receptors for acetylcholine, Otto Loewi's *vagusstoff.* A few examples of what acetylcholine does and how atropine affects it are shown in Table 5.2.

Charcot was correct that belladonna helps some patients with Parkinson's disease. Long before Charcot, Ayurvedic physicians included herbs containing hyoscyamine, a derivative of belladonna, in their treatment of the disease. Before L-dopa was introduced to treat the disease, drugs in the atropine family were the best available treatment, but they were not very good. We still use them at times because they often suppress parkinsonian tremor better than the newer drugs, but we use them very cautiously for fear of side effects, particularly of brain toxicity, such as decreased memory and hallucinations. Examples of acetylcholine-blocking drugs currently used to treat Parkinson's disease include trihexyphenidyl (Artane), benztropine (Cogentin), and parsidol.

In the late nineteenth and early twentieth centuries, chemists identified the chemicals in many medicinal plants. They extracted morphine from opium poppies, cocaine from coca leaves, and banisterine from a vine that was used by Amazonian natives to make *ayahuasca,* a powerful hallucinogenic drink. In addition to hallucinations, banisterine could cause tremors and unnatural movements, so physicians began

TABLE 5.2: Some Actions of the Neurotransmitter Acetylcholine and of Blockage of the Acetylcholine Receptors by Atropine

Location of acetylcholine action	Atropine effect
Nerve endings on the heart that slow the heart rate	Atropine blocks acetylcholine effect and increases the heart rate.
Nerve endings on the smooth muscles of the intestine that aid digestion	Atropine blocks acetylcholine effect; at times it is used to treat nausea or diarrhea.
Nerve endings on skeletal muscles	Atropine has little effect on this connection because the acetylcholine receptors on muscles are different than those elsewhere in the body.
Brain synapses, especially in the frontal lobes	Overdose of atropine can cause drowsiness, memory loss, and hallucinations.

experimentally giving it to patients with abnormal movements, including those with Parkinson's disease. In about 1929 the experimenters reported that banisterine improved the slow movements of Parkinson's disease but did not help the tremors. At medical meetings they showed movies of patients injected with banisterine, then moving with unexpected speed and agility. Banisterine was briefly hailed as a miracle drug but did not live up to the initial hype because of a disappointing balance between benefits and toxic effects, like hallucinations and nausea. By the time my father was in medical school, banisterine was no longer used. Chemical study of banisterine continued. Now, we know that one action of banisterine is to inhibit the enzyme known as MAO (monoamine oxidase), which has an important role in the chemistry of Parkinson's disease.

Each of the herbal derivatives, atmagupta, belladonna, ergot, and banisterine, did partially treat the symptoms of Parkinson's disease. Over the years, scientists have purified active ingredients, elucidated their mechanisms of action, and developed pure drugs that are more effective than their herbal predecessors (Table 5.3). Controlled clinical trials have proven the value of the modern drugs. The U.S. Food and Drug Administration (FDA) has approved the purified drugs for sale based on extensive investigation of efficacy and of adverse effects and carefully monitors their manufacture and marketing.

Herbal remedies are just one form of the so-called complementary and alternative therapies that attract many disease sufferers. About 40 percent of Americans use therapies such as herbal medicines, massage, megavitamins, self-help gurus, folk remedies, energy healing, and homeopathy.[5] In 1997 Americans paid about $27 billion for alternative therapies. The National Institutes of Health now has a National Center for Complementary and Alternative Medicine. A survey of patients with Parkinson's disease found that about 40 percent of them were using some form of alternative therapy.[6] They commonly used vitamins, herbs, acupuncture, or massage to complement the care and medications offered by their traditional physicians. For example,

TABLE 5.3: From Herbal Remedies to Modern Antiparkinsonian Drugs

Herbal derivative	Mechanism of action	Modern drug
Atmagupta	Precursor for dopamine	L-dopa
Belladonna	Acetylcholine receptor antagonist	Trihexyphenidyl and others
Ergot	Dopamine receptor agonist	Bromocriptine, pergolide
Banisterine	Monoamine oxidase inhibitor	Selegiline, rasagiline

one woman was taking coenzyme Q_{10}, NADH, N-acetylcysteine, acetyl L-carnitine, selenium, zinc, multivitamins, *Ginkgo biloba*, glutathione, S-adenosyl methionine, lipoic acid, milk thistle, folic acids from fish oil concentrate, and hormone replacement therapy in addition to her two prescribed, FDA-approved antiparkinsonian medications. Those using alternative therapies were apt to be younger and better educated than those not using these therapies. The use of alternative therapies did not seem to be influenced by the severity of a person's Parkinson's disease.

Alternative therapies are so common that physicians routinely ask their patients about use of herbal, nontraditional, or folk remedies, and many are dismayed at or dismissive of what their patients are taking. One concern is that alternative therapies can be toxic. Traditional physicians point to increasing reports of toxic effects of herbal preparations, whereas proponents of herbal remedies retort that the adverse effects and even deaths caused by prescribed medications are much more common than those caused by alternative therapies. The same lesson applies to herbal and synthetic medications: Any substance that is used as a medication or remedy inevitably has adverse effects for some users. Even sugar pills have side effects, and adverse consequences are apt to be more severe and more common for those herbs or medications that are more powerful or have stronger beneficial effects.

A second concern is drug interactions. Each additional medicinal substance that a person takes increases the chance that the substances will interfere with each other. For example, when a patient is taking L-dopa, movement of the drug from the stomach to the blood can be partially blocked if proteins and L-dopa are in the stomach at the same time. The blockage is due to competition for absorption of certain amino acids, especially L-dopa, phenylalanine, tyrosine, and tryptophan; tahini has a relatively high concentration of tryptophan, so a patient taking tahini might be blocking absorption of L-dopa. Competition between tahini and L-dopa for absorption from the stomach is a hypothetical drug-herbal interaction, but it is not far-fetched because interference with L-dopa absorption by high-protein foods does occur. If patients with Parkinson's disease were actually using tahini and L-dopa together, it would be important to evaluate this hypothesis experimentally and, if the interaction did occur, to measure its effect. Many drug interactions are known, but not all of them have important effects on a patient's health. In other words, just as only experiments can determine if tahini is beneficial to patients with Parkinson's disease, only experiments can show if it is detrimental.

Third, physicians are worried about quality control of herbal preparations. As illustrated by digitalis in foxglove leaf or L-dopa in at-magupta beans, the patient never knows the purity or concentration of varied chemicals in an herbal remedy. For example, one-fifth of

Ayurvedic herbal medications easily purchased in stores in Boston contained potentially toxic amounts of lead, mercury, or arsenic.[7] The FDA does not monitor herbal quality with the same care that it checks drugs for purity, concentration, and manufacturing process.

A fourth issue is resources: Why do patients spend their time and money on unproven therapies? Surveys suggest that most patients using these remedies also seek care from traditional physicians; for many, their decision to use alternative therapies, in addition, reflects their spiritual or philosophical beliefs about holistic health. Today, both prescription drugs and alternative therapies can be expensive, and patients need to carefully consider how to spend their health care dollars for maximum benefit.

Many patients believe that their alternative therapies make them healthier. Isn't this sufficient reason to take them? Although all FDA-approved medications for Parkinson's disease do decrease symptoms, not one is proven to slow progression of the underlying brain degeneration. If I offer my patients prescriptions for L-dopa, some will prefer no medication. They may have heard about adverse effects, dislike taking medication, or find their symptoms too mild to bother. I rarely urge them to change their minds because the drugs that I can prescribe only relieve symptoms, and the patients know best how their own symptoms feel. With this philosophy, why should I object if the patient who has rejected my offer of a prescription returns a few months later on a tahini diet?

Alternative therapies provide hope to many. In fact, sustaining an illusion of hope is part of the sales pitch. According to one herbal remedy marketer, "When I train salespeople, I say to them, 'Do you know what people are calling you for? It isn't the pill. They are calling you for hope. That is really what they want from you.'"[8]

If I have forthrightly told patients that the drugs that I can prescribe are not proven to prevent disease progression, how can I begrudge them a belief that tahini is protecting them from future troubles? Vitamin E, a popular alternative therapy for Parkinson's disease, illustrates the dilemma. Unfortunately, vitamin E seems not to slow the progression of Parkinson's disease. In a careful, randomized, double-blind controlled study, it did not show benefit. Should I confront the patient with this evidence about vitamin E or let him or her continue hopeful daily use of the vitamin pill? For years the issue seemed moot since vitamin E appeared harmless at usual doses and may have other health benefits. In late 2004, however, investigators reported that taking a relatively low dose of vitamin E might increase the risk of heart disease. This report is still being debated and investigated, but it emphasizes that any chemical entering the body, no matter how natural, can do good or harm and merits scientific study.

Hope is vital. A patient with chronic illness has much to hope for: that the diagnosis is wrong, that the disease will have a slow and benign course, that research will find a cure, that a miracle will happen, that his or her family will stay well and prosper. As a physician, I believe that I can always foster hope without relying on irrational therapies or misleading my patients.

The key issue in treatment with herbs or drugs should not be natural versus synthetic or available by prescription only versus readily available in health food stores. The scientist and the patient should both care about the power, purity, potency, and possible toxicity of everything that enters the body, and the only way to establish these is through well-designed experiments. The story of tahini, all hype and hypothesis, is so different from the story of L-dopa, which was introduced based on years of extensive basic science investigations, then proved beneficial through carefully controlled human drug trials. I believe that the FDA should require all herbal or alternative remedies to pass the same standards of quality and purity and the same experimental verification of safety and benefit that it now requires for prescription drugs. Congress and the President set the duties of the FDA. We should urge them to improve current laws and regulations, which do not protect Americans from dangerous or useless herbal or alternative remedies.

"There is no alternative medicine. There is only scientifically proven, evidence-based medicine supported by solid data or unproven medicine, for which scientific evidence is lacking."[9] This sets a high standard for scientific medicine. In practice, every physician mixes proven with unproven therapies, as the following chapters illustrate.

Rational scientific inquiry continues to advance our treatment and understanding of Parkinson's disease. Still, even the most rational and informed among us has hopes, dreams, and unproven beliefs. My mother read the first draft of this chapter and asked, "Why don't you give your father some tahini?"

Awakenings—L-Dopa Therapy

In 1967 I was just starting medical school when L-dopa therapy was established as a treatment for Parkinson's disease. I do not have personal clinical experiences from that era, but Oliver Sacks has eloquently described how therapy, prognosis, and scientific understanding of the disease suddenly improved.

In *Awakenings*, Sacks tells the stories of patients with postencephalitic Parkinson's disease. The title of the book and movie comes from the remarkable improvement that Sacks observed in 1969, when he gave L-dopa to some of these patients. In the body, enzymes change L-dopa to dopamine (Figure 5.1). Sacks chose L-dopa to treat his patients based on unprecedented experimental results described two years earlier by George Cotzias and colleagues.[10] Cotzias conceived these experiments, which revolutionized treatment of Parkinson's disease, by understanding the chemistry of the nervous system, particularly from work like that of Arvid Carlsson on dopamine in the brain.

If patients who have Parkinson's disease lack dopamine in the brain, will pills or injections of dopamine cure them? The answer is no because dopamine in the blood does not get into the brain. There is a crucial structure, known as the blood-brain barrier, that separates the brain from circulating blood. Some chemicals, like sugar, cross this barrier relatively easily; many others, like dopamine, do not. If a patient swallowed a dopamine pill, it could affect the peripheral nerves, but the dopamine would not reach the brain cells and so could not benefit patients with Parkinson's disease.

To help patients with Parkinson's disease, scientists needed to get more dopamine into the brain, even though dopamine could not cross the blood-brain barrier. Direct injection of dopamine into the brain could be dangerous and would not work. The trick is to administer a chemical that does cross the blood-brain barrier and, once in the brain, increases the brain content of dopamine. The trickster is L-dopa.

In theory, dopa, which the body changes to dopamine, can cross the blood-brain barrier. (For more on the chemistry of dopa and dopamine, see Table 5.4.) After noting dopamine deficiency in the brains of patients who had Parkinson's disease, scientists tried giving the patients dopa. One report suggested some success with this treatment, but other attempts at dopa therapy failed. Cotzias hypothesized that dopa therapy initially failed because the patients were not given enough of it. He

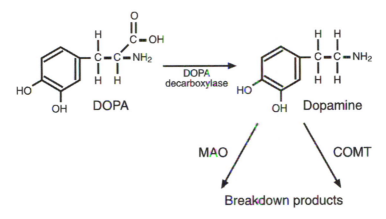

FIGURE 5.1: Chemical structure of L-dopa (L-dihyroxyphenyl-alanine). L-dopa is converted in the brain into dopamine by the enzyme dopa decarboxylase. The enzymes MAO and COMT break down dopamine. (Drawn by Douglas Katagiri.)

thought that higher doses might be needed to get enough drug across the blood-brain barrier and into nerve cells.

The chance of dopa passing from the mouth into the brain and then changing to dopamine stored in a nerve cell is like the chance of survival of a young salmon swimming downriver to the sea, successfully growing for years in the open ocean, and then swimming back upriver as an adult to spawn. Countless salmon eggs are laid and fertilized to enable one salmon, escaping disease, dams, and predators, to return years later to the spawning ground. From the time it enters the mouth, dopa can be lost or destroyed at many steps along its path to the brain cells. Only part of an oral dose is absorbed from the intestines into the blood. Enzymes in the blood destroy much of the dopa before it gets to the blood-brain barrier. The transport mechanism in the blood-brain barrier carries only a fraction of the blood dopa into the brain. In patients who have Parkinson's disease, the nerve cells have impaired conversion of the dopa to dopamine. Cotzias guessed that a lot of dopa was needed to cause a small increase in brain cell content of dopamine. Even he did not fully appreciate all the barriers to dopa in its journey to become brain dopamine.

Cotzias planned a clinical experiment. In prescribing treatments I depend on experiments like Cotzias's to tell whether a treatment is truly good for my patients. I need to understand the experimental methods and results so that I can decide whether, when, and for whom to prescribe the medication. Fortunately, these clinical experiments are also assessed very critically by journal editors and by experts with the FDA to help physicians choose safe and beneficial therapies.

Physician-investigators who do clinical experiments have challenges and responsibilities that exceed those of basic science investigators and of nonexperimental physicians. Humans, particularly ill humans, are much more biologically complex than a simple preparation of frog nerve and muscle or than a colony of experimental animals bred for

---

TABLE 5.4: Chemistry of L-Dopa and Dopamine

The theory of using L-dopa to increase brain dopamine comes from basic biochemistry. Dopa (dihyroxyphenylalanine) is an aromatic amino acid. Look at its structure in Figure 5.1. The molecule can be made a left-handed shape (L-dopa) or a right-handed shape (D-dopa). Every amino acid has an amino group (NH_2) and an acid carboxyl group (COOH) as part of its structure. Aromatic amino acids all have a ring group as well. The body has a special chemical transport system that carries aromatic amino acids across the blood-brain barrier. Dopamine is formed when the carboxyl group is removed from dopa by an enzyme called dopa decarboxylase. Dopamine is not an amino acid because it does not have a carboxyl group, so the aromatic amino acid transport system will not help it cross the blood-brain barrier.

---

genetic homogeneity. A clinical experiment needs to be controlled so that variations in individual biology or in the natural history of disease are not mistaken for effects of treatment. Furthermore, human experiments must be very carefully designed for the safety of the participants. And, of course, human experimentation is fraught with difficult ethical issues.

Cotzias used pink capsules containing 100, 200, or 500 mg (milligrams) of dopa. A teaspoon of water weighs 5000 mg, so the largest capsules contained drug that weighed as much as one-tenth a teaspoon of water. The investigators prepared identical capsules containing lactose, the sugar found in milk, to serve as a control, a treatment that has no known direct therapeutic effect on the body. When the patients were given the pink capsules, they were not told whether they were getting lactose or dopa; they were blind as to whether or not they were receiving the active drug.

Cotzias started treating patients with a few hundred milligrams of dopa and gradually increased the dose until the patients either benefited from the treatment or could not tolerate the treatment because of adverse drug effects. He treated some patients with over 10,000 mg of dopa each day.

Some simple calculations, based on basic science experiments with dopamine, can show whether Cotzias achieved his goal of providing massive amounts of dopa. In the parts of the brain with the most dopamine, each gram of brain tissue contains less than 5 mcg (micrograms, or millionths of a gram) of dopamine. A normal brain weighs about 1500 gm (a bit more than three pounds). Therefore the total dopamine in a normal brain is much less than 7.5 mg (5 mcg in a gram of brain tissue times 1500 gm of brain tissue = 7500 mcg = 7.5 mg). This means that less than one-thousandth of the dopa that the patients swallowed needed to be converted into brain dopamine for the experiment to succeed.

Twice a day, while the patients were getting the pink capsules, the study team examined the patients' handwriting, walking speed, and other aspects of their mobility and agility. Each patient received sugar pills on some days and dopa on other days, but no patient was told which days were which. Day by day, the investigators compared the effects of dopa and the effects of sugar pills in each patient. There was not one group of treated patients and a separate group of untreated patients. Instead, each patient acted as his own control.

There were 16 patients in the study. Eight of them showed marked improvement in their parkinsonism while they were receiving dopa. They had improvement in tremor, cogwheel rigidity, facial masking, and speed of movement. Because the patients gradually took higher and higher doses of dopa, Cotzias could compare the effects of lower and higher doses. Rigidity improved at lower doses; tremor did not improve until the dose was higher. When dopa treatment was stopped, the findings of Parkinson's disease returned to pretreatment severity. The patients improved within two or three hours of taking a high enough dose of dopa; when dopa was stopped, the patients maintained the improvement for 4 to 14 days before returning to their pretreatment status.

With such dramatic responses, why did the investigators bother with the sugar pills? The part of the answer is that every patient with Parkinson's disease has daily variations of the disease, often for unknown reasons. Sometimes, with urging, a patient can move quickly for a while; in contrast, at times of anxiety or fatigue, symptoms can worsen. One role of the sugar pills was to help distinguish the natural fluctuations of the disease from the effects of the dopa.

In the movie *Awakenings,* there is a particularly striking, realistic example of sudden improvement of a patient with Parkinson's. Long before she was given dopa, a woman with postencephalitic Parkinson's disease stood frozen in place like a statue. She was immobile, unable to move on her own or when asked to do so. Suddenly, the physician tossed a ball to her; to the astonishment of those around her and of movie viewers, she just as suddenly reached up and caught it with hands that moments before had seemed paralyzed. The movie actress portrayed something that actually happens to some patients with Parkinson's disease. This unexpected, paradoxical movement is most likely to occur when emergency action is automatic, like running out of a burning building. A classic anecdote tells of a parkinsonian man sitting frozen in a beach chair. Suddenly, he saw his grandson struggling to stay afloat in the ocean. He charged out of the chair, swam out, and saved the boy, then again froze to his prior immobility and needed to be helped back to his chair. This surge of movement occurs unpredictably and beyond the patient's conscious control, showing that dramatic, seemingly miraculous movements by a patient with Parkinson's disease are not always attributable to drug treatment.

The use of a control pill in a drug trial is done with blinding, which means the patient is not supposed to know whether the treatment being given is active drug or the control pill. If the drug is very effective, the blinding is lost as soon as the drug takes effect. Blinding can also be lost if the drug has adverse effects, whereas the control pill does not. Blinded drug trials have confirmed that sometimes patients will have objective improvement in their parkinsonian findings after taking control pills. Blinded controlled trials are needed to assess any Parkinson's disease treatment, be it with drugs or surgery or alternative therapies.

If people were getting grams of dopa, but only milligrams were needed by their brains, what was the rest of the drug doing in the body? Every drug hurts some of the people who take it. The most common adverse effects of the dopa therapy were nausea, faintness, and occasional vomiting. More worrisome, one-quarter of the patients developed partial loss of their white blood cells while taking the drug. White blood cells are essential to the immune system, so the loss of white cells was potentially dangerous. Could the adverse effects be avoided if the dose of dopa were decreased?

Three of the eight patients who benefited from dopa developed excessive or extra movements while taking the drug. One patient had exaggerated facial movements and gesticulations while talking; the drug not only abolished the facial impassivity typical of Parkinson's disease, but also went further to cause excessive facial movements. Another patient had intermittent writhing movements of his tongue. A woman showed writhing movements of all four limbs. These three patients had the extra movements just when the therapeutic response to dopa was most impressive. Cotzias mentioned these extra movements in the paper but did not characterize them as adverse effects. Now, we call these excessive movements dyskinesias, contrasting them to the slow movements, or bradykinesia, of Parkinson's disease. Dyskinesias are now recognized as one of the more troubling ill effects of treatment of Parkinson's disease. Understanding, treating, and avoiding dyskinesias is currently a major topic in the clinical care of patients with Parkinson's disease.

Cotzias's report of dopa therapy was a turning point in the treatment of Parkinson's disease. Published in 1967 in the *New England Journal of Medicine,* the most widely read medical journal, the article spread a new concept: treatment of a neurodegenerative disease using a precursor of a deficient neurotransmitter. Dopa promised more powerful therapy for hundreds of thousands of patients. Cotzias was not the first to successfully treat Parkinson's disease with dopa; five years earlier, a patient with Parkinson's disease had improved briefly after receiving some dopa by vein.[11] The important advances by Cotzias were oral treatment, use of unusually high doses, and sustained benefit with continued treatment.

Cotzias and his colleagues published a further report on their results in 1969.[12] They had changed treatment from dopa to L-dopa. Many chemicals in the body can have alternative structures called "D" and "L" forms. The "D" and "L" stand for *dextro* and *levo,* indicating right- and left-handed versions of a molecule. The two forms are mirror images of each other, but body enzymes and receptors often work on only one of the forms. The dopa joins the enzyme or receptor like a key inserts into a lock; unless a key has exact symmetry, a mirror image of the key will not work in the lock.

Cotzias's first experiments had been done with equal parts of D-dopa and L-dopa. By purifying the treatment drug to L-dopa (also called levodopa) alone, he was able to treat patients with one-half the previous dose because the patients were no longer receiving the ineffective D-dopa. A major benefit of this change was that the patients treated with L-dopa did not lose white blood cells. The blood cell toxicity had been caused by D-dopa; however, the other toxic effects were still present with L-dopa treatment.

The L-dopa trial published in 1969 had a better experimental design: double blinding. Now, neither the patient nor the examiner knew whether the pink capsules contained L-dopa or the lactose. Why is it important to blind the examiner? Every experimenter has hopes for success and preconceived notions of what an experiment will show. These hopes and preconceptions must not influence how the examiners rate subjective clinical findings, like degree of rigidity or amount of facial expression. Furthermore, an enthusiastic, unblinded examiner might bias results by unwittingly charging the patients with enthusiasm for the new treatment. In the L-dopa trial the double-blind assessment confirmed the exceptional therapeutic effect of the new treatment.

By 1969, Cotzias had added another refinement to the dopa therapy. He treated some patients with L-dopa and simultaneously with a drug that inhibited the enzyme dopa decarboxylase (see Table 5.4 for details of how the enzyme works). This enzyme is present both in blood and in brain, but the inhibitor drug did not cross the blood-brain barrier. Patients who took the two drugs together did not break down L-dopa in the blood, allowing more L-dopa to reach the brain. In other words, parkinsonism improves after a lower dose of L-dopa if it is given together with the enzyme inhibitor. Today, this combination is a mainstay of treatment of Parkinson's disease. Nearly all L-dopa is now sold in combination with a dopa decarboxylase inhibitor called carbidopa.

The combination is sold as carbidopa/levodopa (brand name Sinemet) in sizes like 10/100, 25/100, or 25/250. The first number (10 or 25) indicates the milligrams of carbidopa in the pills. The second number (100 or 250) is the number of milligrams of L-dopa in the pills. A patient who takes carbidopa/L-dopa 25/100 can improve as much as one who takes 500 or 1000 mg of L-dopa without carbidopa.

The combination of L-dopa and carbidopa decreases some adverse effects, like nausea and vomiting, but does not prevent other adverse effects, like dyskinesia. This is because the nausea and vomiting are due to dopa effects in the blood, not in the brain with its protective blood-brain barrier, and the carbidopa/L-dopa combination keeps the amount of L-dopa in the blood relatively low. The dyskinesias occur when too much L-dopa crosses the blood-brain barrier and enters the brain. Extra L-dopa in the brain can cause dyskinesia regardless of whether a patient takes high doses of L-dopa alone or lower, but still excessive, doses of L-dopa augmented by carbidopa.

Oliver Sacks knew Cotzias's work. Indeed, many of Sacks's patients had heard about dopa in 1967 and begged him to treat them with it. Sacks delayed for two years before starting them on L-dopa, in part because the drug was very expensive, until the price decreased in 1969, and in part because he was concerned that patients who had postencephalitic

Parkinson's disease might respond differently than those whom Cotzias had treated for idiopathic Parkinson's disease. When Sacks did give his patients L-dopa, he observed them keenly and kept careful treatment records. They were engaged in a therapeutic trial, not an experiment with controls or blinding.

Sacks treated about 50 patients with L-dopa. In his book Sacks described the responses of many of them, but the movie of *Awakenings* focused on Leonard L., who was born in 1920. In childhood, Leonard developed an acute sleeping sickness (encephalitis lethargic). He seemed to recover well but was a withdrawn, bookish teenager. When he was about 15 years old, he noted stiffness in his right hand. Over the years his stiffness increased so that he was hospitalized at age 30. When Sacks first began caring for him, Leonard was in his late forties and had severe bradykinesia.

Under Sacks's guidance, Leonard began taking L-dopa and gradually increased the dose to 5 g (grams) daily. After two weeks of treatment, he suddenly improved. "The rigidity vanished from all his limbs, and he felt filled with an access [*sic*] of energy and power; he became able to write and type once again, to rise from his chair, to walk with some assistance, and to speak in a loud and clear voice" for the first time in nearly 24 years.[13] Leonard and Sacks lyrically described Leonard's excitement, joy, and energy during his first few weeks of taking L-dopa.

Unfortunately, the era of unencumbered improvement lasted for only a few weeks. Leonard began to have unwanted effects of the medication, including manic energy, trouble concentrating, hallucinations, extra dyskinetic movements (similar to the extra movements experienced by some of Cotzias's patients), and sudden loss of effect of the medication so that Leonard would be active one minute and frozen the next. Sacks tried decreasing Leonard's dose of L-dopa, but even with the dose decreased from 5 g daily to 50 mg daily, the ill effects persisted. Within months Leonard was no longer taking L-dopa because of these effects, and within days of stopping the medication he had returned to his prior mute, barely mobile state.

The FDA released L-dopa for sale in the United States in 1970. Most patients with Parkinson's disease who took it quickly showed improved mobility and decreased rigidity. Epidemiologists have estimated that the average life-span of a patient with Parkinson's disease increased by about five years after L-dopa was widely prescribed.

Unfortunately, some of the adverse effects of L-dopa described by Cotzias and Sacks continue to bedevil patients with Parkinson's disease. Fortunately, unless the dose is too high, patients with idiopathic Parkinson's disease, unlike Leonard, often take the drug for years without serious ill effects. Eventually, after perhaps three to five years of L-dopa therapy, treatment becomes much more challenging. Many patients begin to experience abnormal movements (dyskinesias), gradual variations of drug efficacy during the day (called "wearing-off"), sudden motor freezing (called "on-off"), and behavioral and cognitive problems, including agitation, hallucinations, and psychosis. Patients with idiopathic Parkinson's disease develop these dopa problems after years of therapy, whereas Sacks's patients with postencephalitic Parkinson's developed them within weeks, possibly because the encephalitis had caused much more severe and diffuse brain damage than that seen in idiopathic Parkinson's disease. Understanding and treating these L-dopa effects are still major research and clinical problems.

When Dad first learned that he had Parkinson's disease, he and his neurologist agreed not to treat him with L-dopa. They had three reasons for this decision. First, tremor is a parkinsonian symptom that is more resistant to L-dopa, and tremor was Dad's most troublesome symptom, so they suspected that L-dopa would not make him feel much better. Second, they knew that he would be vulnerable to problems like wearing-off and dyskinesia after taking L-dopa for a few years, and they hoped to delay these adverse effects. Neurologists are still debating whether this rationale for delaying L-dopa therapy is valid. Finally, while L-dopa can decrease the symptoms of Parkinson's disease, it probably does not slow the progression of the disease, so there is no imperative to take it when symptoms are relatively mild.

Dopamine and Schizophrenia—The Dopamine Receptor

Neurology and psychiatry are both about the brain. Sigmund Freud studied with Charcot and was a neurologist before he invented psychoanalysis. My brother Howard, who is a psychiatrist, and I are both board certified by the American Board of Neurology and Psychiatry. We both think of ourselves as intellectual great-grandchildren of Charcot. Some of my teachers might have known people who had studied with Charcot; many of my brother's teachers knew Freud. To become board certified, Howard and I spent years in postgraduate residency training and then both passed examinations, assessing neurological and psychiatric patients. For years, however, neurologists and psychiatrists took divergent approaches to their patients. The neurologists concentrate on careful physical examination of their patients. In the tradition of Charcot, we try to understand physical impairments in relation to pathology in parts of the brain. In the tradition of Freud the psychiatrists talk with their patients, both to make diagnoses and to treat them. Howard took extra training in psychoanalysis, the much-debated talking cure. Recently, however, the two specialties are reuniting, realizing how important brain chemistry is to both neurological and psychiatric illness.

Drug therapy of schizophrenia, a devastating brain disorder that affects nearly one percent of the population all over the world, advanced in the last half of the twentieth century from a combination of clinical and basic science research. Fortunately, this research has improved the lives not only of schizophrenics, but also of those with Parkinson's disease.[14]

To define some terms relevant to schizophrenia, let's start with a multiple-choice question: I firmly believe that there are invisible waves in the air that are continually distorting my body and affecting my neurotransmitters! Is this a

1. delusion (a strongly held belief that contradicts known fact)
2. fact
3. hallucination (a perception of sensation without corresponding real sensory inputs)
4. illusion (a misinterpretation of sensory inputs to the body)?

When I ask this question of my students, many answer, "Delusion." I guess they think that I am being a bit paranoid. However, the correct answer is "fact." I offer the following example as proof: When sound waves distort my eardrums, they activate the auditory nerve, sending impulses through nerve cells, releasing neurotransmitters at many sites in my brain. In fact, other sensations like touch, vision, and smell are constantly stimulating my nerves, releasing many millions of molecules of neurotransmitters in my brain every second.

Neurotransmitters play a crucial role in all our beliefs and perceptions, including delusions, illusions, and hallucinations. Delusions and hallucinations are among the symptoms of schizophrenia, a disease that differs drastically from the motor abnormalities of Parkinson's disease; however, progress in understanding and treating schizophrenia since the mid-1950s has intersected with research in Parkinson's disease in intriguing ways. At one time, research about schizophrenia concentrated on psychological issues, such as whether parents' personalities and behavior might make their children schizophrenic. Now, research on schizophrenia and research on Parkinson's disease converge to study brain circuits that are rich in dopamine. Where we once distinguished between psychiatric disease and neurological disease, we now see an exciting, unifying concept that both are due to basic brain chemistry and circuitry gone awry.

Schizophrenia and Parkinson's disease are both diseases of the brain, but whereas Parkinson's disease primarily impairs movement, schizophrenia typically impairs thinking. Schizophrenia is the type of severe mental disorder, called a psychosis, characterized by abnormal personality, poor understanding of reality, and difficulty getting along in society. The popular myth of schizophrenia as a disease of split or dual personality is incorrect; rather, it causes auditory hallucinations and delusional thinking, like paranoia. Schizophrenics also typically have disorganized thinking, impaired emotional reactions, and deficient social interactions. Even when they are not hallucinating or delusional, they have trouble maintaining intimate relationships or succeeding in a job. Unless they are in sheltered settings, they often live lonely, isolated lives.

Schizophrenia and Parkinson's disease are both chronic diseases, but whereas Parkinson's disease usually begins later in life and then inevitably worsens, schizophrenia is usually diagnosed in early adulthood. Most schizophrenics have symptoms of the illness throughout their lives, but progression is not inevitable, and some schizophrenics seem to stabilize or even improve as they age. In childhood, before their psychosis is evident, many schizophrenics exhibit mild behavioral changes that hint at their illness. Although the cause of schizophrenia is still unknown, current theories favor abnormal brain development, quite different from the course of Parkinson's, which shows progressive degeneration of a normally developed brain.

For generations, schizophrenics typically spent years of their lives in chronic psychiatric hospitals. Available treatments were imaginative, sometimes barbaric, and usually ineffective. The most infamous was prefrontal lobotomy, the surgical destruction of the front-most part of the brain.

In about 1950 French chemists developed a new drug called chlorpromazine (Thorazine), which was tried as an adjunct to surgical anesthesia.[15] The surgeons noted that it had a calming effect, so it was tried on psychotic patients, for whom it was very effective in decreasing agitation, especially in those with hallucinations and delusions. Chlorpromazine and its relatives so effectively reduced the most blatant behavioral problems of schizophrenics that by the 1960s, more and more schizophrenics were discharged from chronic psychiatric hospitals and treated (or, too often, ignored) in the community. Unfortunately, these drugs did not help many of the chronic debilitating social and emotional deficits of schizophrenics.

In the mid-1950s, shortly after physicians began prescribing chlorpromazine for treatment of psychosis, they recognized that the drug slowed the movements of some patients. Some developed signs and symptoms as if they had Parkinson's disease. Others developed acute spasms after a single dose, twisting a neck to one side or distorting a face into a fixed grimace. Some felt an irresistible need to move and would spend hours pacing aimlessly. Others took the chlorpromazine for months or years without apparent effect on their movement, but then developed facial or body twitches that persisted even after the drug was stopped.

I have already mentioned Arvid Carlsson's studies of reserpine in the rat brain that were part of the groundwork for L-dopa treatment of Parkinson's disease. Studies of the brain actions of chlorpromazine aided development of another class of antiparkinsonian drugs called dopamine agonists.

There are strong parallels between the actions of chlorpromazine and those of reserpine. Both are useful for drug treatment of psychosis. Both can cause parkinsonism. When either drug induces parkinsonism, the motor abnormalities commonly resolve after the patient stops taking the drug. However, analysis of brain chemistry shows an important difference between the two: Animals given reserpine lose dopamine from their brains; animals given chlorpromazine have normal amounts of brain dopamine.

Instead of depleting dopamine from the brain, chlorpromazine acts by blocking access of dopamine to important cellular structures called dopamine receptors. The analogy of lock and key is often used: The neurotransmitter is the key; the receptor is the lock. The key works the lock only when the structures of the key and lock are precisely matched. Just as a lock and key can open a door, the combination of neurotransmitter and receptor can open channels in the cell membrane to allow chemicals into or out of the cell; just as a lock and key can start an engine, the combination of neurotransmitter and receptor can control cellular chemical reactions.

When chlorpromazine blocks the receptors, brain cells cannot respond normally to dopamine. Cellular drug receptors are indispensable to neurotransmitter function. The dopamine receptors that are blocked by chlorpromazine are just one among many types of receptor for neurotransmitters located all over the nervous system.

Neurotransmitters have striking specificity and high potency. Specificity means that only selected cells respond to the neurotransmitter, and the response is precise and reproducible. High potency means that a miniscule amount of neurotransmitter, as little as a few molecules contacting the correct part of the correct cell, is enough to be effective. The potency and specificity are due to the receptors, which are chemical structures, mostly proteins, on the surface of the responding cell.

Our understanding of how neurotransmitters react with receptors began with Otto Loewi's experiments with acetylcholine. Atropine blocked the action of acetylcholine because atropine attached to a receptor, preventing acetylcholine from attaching to the receptor to transmit its message. We now know that a major action of chlorpromazine is blocking dopamine receptors. The chlorpromazine plugs the receptor "lock" so that the neurotransmitter "key" cannot work. Drugs that block receptors are called antagonists. Thus chlorpromazine is a dopamine receptor antagonist. When the antagonist attaches to the lock of the receptor, the neurotransmitter key either cannot fit in the lock or, once attached, cannot activate the lock. We now need to modify our model of the synapse to add the neurotransmitter receptors on the postsynaptic cell (Figure 2.2D).

One neurotransmitter often activates more than one type of receptor. To expand the key-lock analogy, the neurotransmitter is like a master key that can work in more than one lock. Evidence of this is that an antagonist often blocks only some of the actions of a given neurotransmitter. For example, atropine is an antagonist of acetylcholine at the heart receptors, but atropine does not antagonize acetylcholine at synapses between motor nerves and skeletal muscles. Where nerve synapses with skeletal muscle, curare, the famous paralyzing, Amazonian blow dart poison, is an antagonist for acetylcholine, but curare does not affect the action of acetylcholine on the heart. This difference between curare and atropine led to the definition of types of acetylcholine receptors: the acetylcholine receptor on skeletal muscle and the acetylcholine receptor on heart muscle. There are many other acetylcholine receptor types.

After the discovery of chlorpromazine, pharmacologists made and tested many similar drugs as possible treatments for schizophrenia. These drugs showed differences in their clinical dopamine-blocking effects, whether measured by their effects on psychosis or by their tendency to induce parkinsonism. In animal and in vitro models of dopamine blocking, each chemical had a unique pattern of antagonism. Analysis of these variations in blocking helped identify multiple dopamine receptors, starting with receptors named D1 and D2.

The position of dopamine receptors in the brain is visible by autoradiography, a technique that uses radioactive isotopes to visualize the location of selected molecules. Later, when we discuss brain imaging in patients with Parkinson's disease, we shall see how autoradiography can show the anatomy and function of the living human brain.

For autoradiography, chemists add radioactive isotopes to a molecule. Normally, hydrogen, composed primarily of the ^{2}H isotope, is not radioactive, but the ^{3}H hydrogen isotope, called tritium, is radioactive. Normally, fluoride (^{17}F) is not radioactive, but the ^{18}F isotope is. When a radioactive isotope is part of a molecule, the molecule is radiolabeled.

Investigators use radiolabeled antagonists to study the brain anatomy of the receptors. The technique starts by exposing a slice of brain to a solution containing the radiolabeled antagonists. Next, the brain slice is washed. In the case of dopamine, the radiolabeled dopamine antagonist molecules bind tightly to the dopamine receptors but are washed away from other areas of the brain. If the slice is then placed against a piece of photographic film, the resulting photo, called an autoradiograph, localizes the radioactive molecules. As we might expect based on the location of dopamine in the brain, autoradiographs show that the putamen and caudate are rich in both D1 and D2 dopamine receptors.

Using the techniques of molecular genetics, investigators have identified five dopamine receptors. We now know an amazing amount about these receptors, including the amino acid sequence of the receptor proteins; how they weave in and out of the cell membrane; the location and structure of their genes; and the differences among the receptors in brain locations, actions on the cell, or responsiveness to various antagonists. Investigators can breed animals that lack or overexpress the gene for a single receptor subtype or can inject chemicals into animal brains that turn off the formation of a single receptor subtype. This molecular progress has promoted further drug development aimed at selectively stimulating or blocking one type of receptor. Despite incredible molecular sophistication, researchers are still far from finding a perfect drug to treat schizophrenia or Parkinson's disease or from finding a drug that is free of adverse effects. Nonetheless, research on dopamine receptors has spawned a class of drugs known as dopamine receptor agonists that are useful for the treatment of Parkinson's disease.

Bromocriptine is a dopamine receptor agonist, meaning that it stimulates the dopamine receptors. An agonist does the opposite of what an antagonist does. An antagonist blocks the lock so that a key cannot get into it. An agonist works the lock, serving as a key slightly different from the naturally occurring neurotransmitter. By stimulating the dopamine receptors, bromocriptine partially mimics the effects of release of dopamine at the synapse. Bromocriptine taken by mouth can cross the blood-brain barrier, attach to dopamine receptors in the putamen, and decrease some symptoms of Parkinson's disease.

The history of bromocriptine goes back to the Middle Ages. It is made from ergot, a product of a fungus that grows on grain, particularly on rye. Animals or people who eat grain contaminated with the rye fungus can develop a condition called ergotism, which also has more colorful names, such as St. Anthony's fire. Epidemics of ergotism have occurred for centuries. The symptoms include loss of blood flow to the limbs, because ergot causes spasms in arteries, and neurological problems, such as seizures, delirium, and hallucinations.

Natural ergot was used for the treatment of Parkinson's disease in the mid-nineteenth century. We have little idea now whether the natural ergot was effective treatment, and we cannot assess this directly because natural products vary greatly in their chemical compositions.

Bromocriptine is only one of the many drugs derived from ergot. Relatively minor changes in drug chemical structure can greatly change the drug's effects, whether beneficial or adverse. Unlike bromocriptine, some ergot derivatives are very effective treatment for migraine headaches. Physicians carefully adjust doses of these drugs to achieve therapeutic benefit without causing ergotism. Many of the neurological toxic effects of ergot are due to overstimulation of dopamine receptors, and side effects of bromocriptine can reproduce some aspects of ergotism, like hallucinations.

In an effort to decrease ergot-type side effects, chemists have developed newer dopamine receptor agonist drugs (pramipexole, ropinirole) that are not derived from ergot. These new drugs do not cause those ergot-like side effects due to arterial spasm, but they are designed to stimulate the dopamine receptor, so excessive doses of them can cause neurological adverse effects like hallucinations.

The dopamine agonists have become very important drugs for the treatment of Parkinson's disease. Unfortunately, we have to remember the dopamine–schizophrenia connection when considering the side effects of these drugs. Just as dopamine antagonists can block some symptoms of schizophrenia, dopamine agonists can mimic some schizophrenic symptoms, causing confusion, delirium, or hallucinations, similar but not identical to those that schizophrenics experience.

In science, reality is always more complex than theory. A model never captures all the subtleties of a biological system. A theory that attempts to explain schizophrenia as a disease solely due to excessive dopamine activity is clearly wrong. For example, treatment of schizophrenia with dopamine receptor antagonist drugs can diminish hallucinations and delusions but has little or no benefit for the other manifestations of the disease, such as impaired social interactions. The auditory hallucinations that are typical of schizophrenia differ from the visual hallucinations that can occur as an adverse effect of L-dopa or dopamine agonist drugs. Nonetheless, research on dopamine does show that schizophrenia is a disease not only of thought, but also of the nerve cell.

Modern neuroscience is finding more and more that so-called mental illnesses are due to physical brain abnormalities, such as changes in neurotransmitters or nerve cell function. The basic science research of men like Carlsson and Axelrod has not only improved our treatment and understanding of schizophrenia, but has also led to drugs, like Prozac (fluoxetine), that treat depression by changing the actions of serotonin and other neurotransmitters.

Early in his career as a psychiatrist, my brother concentrated on psychoanalysis. Nearly three decades later, we have learned much about the brain chemistry of psychiatric diseases and have more and better drugs that improve brain chemistry. In 1987 an interviewer asked Axelrod if Freud was dead. The brain chemist replied, "Not for people who want to spend their money on psychoanalysis, but for the treatment of severe mental illness, yes, he is."[16] Now, my brother is increasingly a psychopharmacologist, relying more and more on medications to help his patients. However, we also know that sound activates our neurotransmitters. In other words, talk can change brain chemistry, and psychiatrists continue to study the scientific basis of talking and behavioral psychotherapies, which remain important treatments of mental illnesses.

When Parkinson described the shaking palsy, he saw the illness as a disorder of movement and completely overlooked its psychiatric aspects. We understand now that many patients with Parkinson's disease deal with depression, behavioral changes, dementia, and other psychic challenges. We will pursue these issues in later chapters.

Rational Drug Therapy—Trying to Prevent Progression of Parkinson's Disease

My fellow physicians and I proudly prescribe proven treatments for our patients. We call this rational therapy: treatment based on scientific experiments. Investigators offer a hypothesis, test it, retest it, and refine it many times to show that a treatment is reasonable, safe, and effective for human illness. Sometimes a drug derives from a traditional herbal treatment. Alternatively, a drug can spring from basic science experiments. In either case, carefully designed experiments in which people take the drugs under controlled conditions are needed to prove that the treatment is appropriate. Ironically, no matter how much we desire evidence-based treatments, we physicians can never be sure that our treatment, no matter how rational, is perfect.

A miracle is an event that contradicts our rational expectations. In the mid-twentieth century, medical science produced miracle drugs like penicillin, drugs that cured diseases previously thought incurable. When it was introduced in the late 1960s, L-dopa was a miracle drug, mobilizing patients who had thought that they would spend the rest of their lives frozen by Parkinson's disease. This illustrates the wonderful paradox that physicians are constantly aiming to prescribe rational therapy at the same time that investigators are searching for the next miracle drug that will redefine what is rational. We are still looking for the miracles that will prevent Parkinson's disease or will stop it from getting worse.

Rational drug therapy depends on testing drugs for benefit and safety, a very difficult task that in the United States is closely regulated by the FDA. Drug development starts with chemical experiments, proceeds to animal trials, and goes through three phases, labeled I, II, and III, of human experimental trials.[17] Using this process, the FDA reviewed and approved every drug that I prescribe. To illustrate, I will describe the history of a drug called selegiline, which is used to treat Parkinson's disease.

There are millions of chemicals that hypothetically might be useful as drugs, so investigators choose which chemicals to test based on their theories of disease mechanism and of drug efficacy. Hypotheses are cheap, but proof can be expensive. Typically, thousands chemicals are tested in vitro or in animals, few of which reach preliminary human trials. After the first human phase-I trials, only a fraction reach phase-II trials, and perhaps one-half of these proceed to phase III to produce one new medication that is approved by the FDA for sale to and use on humans. The cost of this process is more than one-half billion dollars for a typical new drug.

The early research on the Frozen Addicts included animal experiments to find why MPTP is toxic to the dopamine nerve cell. In rat brains the MPTP was not directly toxic until the enzyme MAO changed it to a toxic compound, MPP+. Selegiline is a drug that blocks the MAO enzyme, so investigators hypothesized that it might prevent MPTP toxicity by stopping formation of the toxin MPP+.

Before drugs are tested in people, they are routinely checked in animals for safety, efficacy, and appropriate dose. Investigators tested selegiline in both monkeys and rodents that were given MPTP to induce parkinsonism. In controlled trials, some animals received selegiline, and others received an inactive control substance. All the animals then received MPTP. As expected, the animals that got the inactive substance plus MPTP developed parkinsonism. The animals that got selegiline plus MPTP did not develop parkinsonism!

Theoretically, selegiline might be helpful for patients with Parkinson's disease in various ways. First, if MPTP, or toxins like it, cause Parkinson's disease in people, selegiline might keep these toxins from changing into their active forms. A second, related possibility is that breakdown products of dopamine might have toxic effects on nerve cells. In other words, dopamine itself might be toxic to dopamine nerve cells; in this case, selegiline might be therapeutic by decreasing the formation of toxic derivatives of dopamine. These explanations are speculative but do have some experimental support in cellular and animal experiments. If selegiline worked by one of these mechanisms, it might actually decrease cell death and slow the progression of Parkinson's disease. This type of therapeutic effect is called neuroprotective because it actually prevents brain deterioration rather than simply temporarily reversing disease symptoms. If this were indeed true, selegiline would be a remarkable advance; we currently have only symptomatic treatment, rather than ways to prevent disease progression.

Third, a different hypothesis is that selegiline could benefit patients with Parkinson's disease by decreasing their symptoms, even if it was not neuroprotective. The proposed mechanism is that selegiline might prolong the action of dopamine by blocking its breakdown. If this were the mechanism for its activity, selegiline might decrease symptoms of Parkinson's disease without preventing dopamine cell death or changing the course of the disease. However, this mechanism does not explain the ability of selegiline to prevent the toxic effect of MPTP in animals.

A phase-I clinical trial is the first test of a new drug in humans. In a phase-I trial a small number of people, usually healthy volunteers, take the drug. The dose is predicted from the animal experiments, and various doses are tried to find an optimal safe dose. Pharmacologists measure the absorption, distribution, chemical breakdown, and elimination of the drug in the body and closely watch the drug recipients for any adverse effects. Selegiline had been introduced as a mild stimulant in the mid-1960s, so it had passed phase-I evaluation long before it was tried for treatment of Parkinson's disease.

In phase-II trials, investigators treat diseased patients with the experimental drug. Again, researchers carefully evaluate patients for beneficial or ill effects. They examine patients before and after treatment, comparing the actions of the drug to other active or inactive chemicals. Objective measurement of treatment effect is important. Years ago, the FDA approved many drugs for sale based on phase-II trials. In fact, most of Cotzias's data on L-dopa came from phase-II trials.

In phase-II trials, selegiline plus L-dopa was more effective than L-dopa alone for treatment of Parkinson's disease. For example, in an uncontrolled, nonrandomized study lasting nine years, investigators tracked hundreds of patients; those who received selegiline along with L-dopa lived longer, on average, than those who received L-dopa alone.[18]

Phase-III trials compare a drug to an inactive control or to standard therapy, usually using a randomized double-blind design. An examiner who does not know which treatment the patient is receiving evaluates the patient; therefore both the patient and the examiner are blinded. Phase-III trials can treat hundreds of patients and often are collaborations among many clinics or institutions.

Two randomized double-blind controlled trials assessed selegiline as an early treatment for Parkinson's disease. Randomized means that patients were assigned by chance to receive either the selegiline or the control. The investigators chose to treat patients who had mild Parkinson's disease, thinking that if selegiline had a neuroprotective action, the protection would be easier to detect and possibly more beneficial early in the illnesses. The larger of the trials, called DATATOP, included 800 patients and tested not only selegiline, but also vitamin E as treatment options.[19] Comparing two drugs in a single trial required two control pills, one of which looked just like selegiline, while the other looked just like vitamin E. In the trial, each patient had two separate random assignments, first to selegiline or its control and second to vitamin E or its control. After randomization, one-quarter of the patients took two kinds of control, one-quarter took selegiline and control, one-quarter took vitamin E and control, and one-quarter took both vitamin E and selegiline (Table 5.5). This design is a bit cumbersome but has the advantage of testing two drugs in one trial and also checking if the two drugs together are superior to either drug alone.

Investigators checked the patients regularly over the next two years. The primary outcome measure of the trial was the number of days from the time the patient entered the trial until the patient's symptoms worsened enough that the treating physician, blind to which treatments the patient was receiving, decided that the patient should be switched to L-dopa therapy.

To review the results of the DATATOP trial, we need to digress to discuss statistical testing of hypotheses. Experiments are done to prove

TABLE 5.5: Double Randomization Using Two Drugs, Each with Its Own Control, Creates Four Treatment Groups

	Selegiline	Control S
Vitamin E	Selegiline and vitamin E	Control S and vitamin E
Control E	Selegiline and control E	Control S and control E

hypotheses. It is usually much easier to disprove something than to prove it. For instance, one counterexample might disprove a hypothesis, in contrast to the many experiments and observations needed to confirm it. Therefore an experiment often starts with a working hypothesis that it tries to disprove. For drug trials a typical initial hypothesis is that the drug is no more effective than a control treatment. This hypothesis of no difference is called the null hypothesis.

For treatment with selegiline, there are two basic, mutually exclusive hypotheses.

1. Selegiline is no better than control for the treatment of Parkinson's disease. This is the null hypothesis that there is no treatment benefit.
2. Selegiline is better than control. This is called the alternative hypothesis.

The null hypothesis is the heart of this drug trial and of many other controlled experiments. The goal of the experiment is to confirm the alternative hypothesis by proving that the null hypothesis is false. By the rules of deductive logic, the null and alternative hypotheses must be mutually exclusive; otherwise, showing that the null hypothesis is false does not establish that the alternative hypothesis is true.

Statistical analysis of drug trials can be quite complex. Investigators designing these trials routinely include professional statisticians on their teams. These statisticians, planning DATATOP or any other trial, would be very attentive to two important concepts: primary outcome measure and statistical significance.

The primary outcome measure is the result of the experiment that will be analyzed. How should the DATATOP investigators decide if the selegiline works? Ask the patients' opinions? Measure the patients' clinical status using a rating scale like the UPDRS? The list of possibilities is endless, and choice of the wrong primary outcome measure can cripple the experiment. Furthermore, the primary outcome measure must be chosen before the patients are treated in the study. Only the primary outcome measure can be used to evaluate the null hypothesis; otherwise, the statistical analysis will be inaccurate. Other results of the experimental trial can provide data for formulation of new hypotheses or for assessment of adverse effects, but these other results cannot be used for formal assessment of whether the initial null hypothesis is disproved.

In the DATATOP trial the primary outcome measure was the number of days from the time a patient entered the trial until his physician prescribed treatment with L-dopa. By choosing that primary outcome measure, the investigators essentially altered the experimental hypotheses.

1. The null hypothesis changes from selegiline is no better than control for treatment of Parkinson's disease and becomes patients treated with selegiline switch to L-dopa therapy no later than patients treated with control.
2. The alternative hypothesis, formerly selegiline is better than control, becomes patients treated with selegiline switch to L-dopa therapy later than patients treated with control.

The investigators need to ask a very important question about this new alternative hypothesis. If they successfully prove the new alternative hypothesis, will they meet the initial goal of the experiment and establish that selegiline is better than control?

The average time before a patient required L-dopa therapy was 719 days for those treated with selegiline, compared to 454 days for those treated with control. In other words, treatment with selegiline delayed the need for L-dopa therapy for about nine months.

Statisticians use mathematical tests to decide if the difference between the results for the selegiline-treated patients and the control-treated patients is statistically significant. There were 400 patients taking selegiline and 400 patients taking control. The control group took control pills for an average of 454 days before needing L-dopa. If the selegiline group had needed L-dopa within an average of 455 days, the difference of one day between the groups could easily be explained by chance variations. By how many days must the two groups differ so that the difference in days shows that selegiline is truly better than the control? The difference is statistically significant only when it is so large that it is very unlikely to be explained by chance. "Very unlikely" is often defined practically as 1 chance in 20. This is expressed in the statistical analysis as "$p < 0.05$."

In the DATATOP trial the difference between 719 days and 454 days was statistically significant. Therefore, on the basis of the primary outcome measure, the null hypothesis was not true. By rejecting the null hypothesis, the study showed that selegiline is more effective than control as treatment for Parkinson's disease.

Clinicians and statisticians can differ on the meaning of experimental results. A statistician's report that a result is statistically significant is a mathematical statement about the chance that outcomes are truly different between two groups. Clinicians may pay attention to statistics but are really interested in a separate question: Is the difference clinically significant? Here the word *significant* has the conventional connotation of "meaningful" or "important" and is no longer being used with a more restricted technical, mathematical definition.

Should Dad and others like him with Parkinson's disease care about details of the different meanings of significance? I believe so because they do not want to bother with a drug that does not have a clinically significant effect, no matter how the statisticians interpret the results. They also should not want to waste their time and money on ineffective drugs, so they want to know that a drug's benefit is proven by tests of statistical significance.

For selegiline to delay the need for L-dopa treatment by nine months is clinically important to many parkinsonian patients, so this result of the DATATOP trial was both statistically significant and clinically significant. Some treatment trial results are not as clinically meaningful, showing a statistically significant difference between experimental groups that is unimportant to patients.

Vitamin E, like selegiline, was chosen for the DATATOP trial based on nonhuman experiments that suggested it might slow the formation of toxic compounds in the brain. Vitamin E is called an antioxidant because it blocks some oxidation reactions. Oxidation is a chemical process that might form brain toxins. In the DATATOP trial, patients received 1000 IU (international units) of vitamin E twice a day. At the end of the trial the difference between the effects of vitamin E and control were not statistically significant. For vitamin E the null hypothesis was not disproved, so the alternative hypothesis that vitamin E has a treatment effect for Parkinson's disease was not proven.

The DATATOP results failed to disprove the null hypothesis about vitamin E treatment, but the results do not prove that vitamin E has no effect for patients with Parkinson's disease. There are many possible explanations for failing to disprove the null hypothesis. For example, the vitamin E effect might be smaller than the selegiline effect and would have become apparent if the DATATOP study had lasted longer or tested more patients. A vitamin E effect might have been detected if a different primary end point had been used. A different dose of vitamin E might have been effective. On the basis of the results of the DATATOP study, the strongest conclusion about vitamin E is that it has no proven benefit to patients who have Parkinson's disease. This is quite different from saying that it is proven to have no benefit.

The FDA must approve any drug that is sold in the United States. To gain FDA approval, the drug manufacturer submits extensive data to show the safety and benefit of the drug. Today, drugs are usually approved only after multiple phase-III trials including hundreds of patients. Before approving the drug, the FDA uses panels of experts to review the drug data. However, once a drug is approved and available in pharmacies for one indication, physicians can legally prescribe the drug for other indications. This is called off-label use of the drug. For example, when the DATATOP study was published, selegiline was already available in pharmacies because the FDA had approved it for use for some psychiatric conditions. FDA-approved packaging for the drug listed the conditions that might be treated with it; Parkinson's disease was not one of the listed conditions. However, any physician, acting on his own responsibility, could prescribe selegiline for treatment of Parkinson's disease. Eventually, the drug manufacturer submitted additional experimental results to the FDA, and selegiline was approved for treatment of Parkinson's disease.

The DATATOP results excited patients and physicians. Shortly after the results were published, my father's physician prescribed selegiline for him. My father began taking 10 mg of selegiline daily. The pills had no apparent adverse effects but also had no discernible benefit for his symptoms. He complained that the drug cost more than $100 each month but followed his physician's advice and took the selegiline faithfully, motivated by the promise that it might slow the progression of his illness.

On the basis of the results of the DATATOP study, many parkinsonians, like my father, began taking selegiline. However, as time passed, controversies about selegiline increased. One pivotal question was whether selegiline worked as a neuroprotective drug or simply decreased the symptoms of Parkinson's disease. If selegiline is neuroprotective, physicians should diagnose the disease as soon as possible and begin treatment as soon as the diagnosis is made. This is analogous to taking pills for high blood pressure, which are excellent neuroprotective drugs. They protect the brain against stroke rather than against Parkinson's disease. People who have high blood pressure usually cannot feel that their pressure is high and feel no better when they take drugs to drop their pressure. However, taking the drugs can be extremely beneficial for prevention of stroke, heart disease, and other conditions.

If selegiline is neuroprotective, a patient should keep taking selegiline as long as it has no adverse effects, whether or not he or she feels better on it, because the purpose of the drug is to prevent future problems rather than to treat current symptoms. In contrast, if selegiline is symptomatic, rather than neuroprotective, therapy, patients who try it and do not feel better need not waste their time and money on it.

Physicians wrote numerous articles, letters, and editorials reanalyzing and critiquing the DATATOP study. The basic conclusion of the study, that selegiline had some benefit for many patients with mild Parkinson's disease, was not in question. The debate was whether neuroprotective action or symptomatic response was the explanation for the study results. Remember, the initial null hypothesis referred only to effectiveness and not to the mechanism of the effect. Although searching for a neuroprotective drug was the rationale for experimenting with selegiline, the DATATOP results did not prove that the drug was neuroprotective.

Dad took selegiline for about a year while the neuroprotective versus symptomatic question was debated. After a year, he decided to stop taking it because it was not helping his tremor, which was his chief concern.

In the debate about neuroprotection and the DATATOP studies, investigators have discussed how to design a better study that separates neuroprotective effects from symptomatic effects. One option is to follow the patients for much longer periods of time, which is much more expensive, delays getting an answer, and can be difficult when patients are aging and deteriorating. A number of other approaches have been tried, but there is no perfect solution to this dilemma.

Many patients with Parkinson's disease are impatient with this process. From the time that basic scientists suspect that a drug might help patients until the FDA releases the drug for sale after phase-III studies, many more years than a decade pass; all this time, the patients are deteriorating. They want the FDA to streamline the process. The concentration on statistics, null hypotheses, and randomized double-blind controlled trials seems too fastidious when brain cells are dying with each passing year. Scientists agree that the drug approval process should be as efficient as possible. Unfortunately, identifying safe and effective drugs entails false positive and false negative answers; drug approval is a detection problem, just like making a diagnosis, building a burglar alarm, or finding terrorists. If the FDA starts approving drugs more readily, there will be more drugs that will turn out, years after approval, to be worthless, or even worse, dangerous. The story of Vioxx is the perfect illustration of this problem.

After a drug is used by large numbers of patients, physicians can discover adverse effects that did not bother the few patients who went through the initial drug trials. Sometimes the adverse effect is very rare and is only noted after thousands of people have taken the drug. The DATATOP study was published in 1993. A randomized controlled British study, published in 1995, compared patients treated with L-dopa to patients treated with L-dopa and selegiline.[20] The study failed to show a definite benefit from selegiline. Of greater concern, the patients who received selegiline were likely to die at an earlier age than those who received only L-dopa. The increase in death rate was slight, but this finding shifted the debate. Before the British study, many neurologists prescribed selegiline for their patients who had Parkinson's disease. As of 1993, whether selegiline was neuroprotective was arguable, but it appeared to be safe, so patients took it just in case it was neuroprotective. However, once the British study questioned the safety of selegiline, many physicians stopped prescribing it, and the sales fell dramatically. Of course, this suggestion of increased mortality from selegiline treatment was not the last word, and additional studies, reanalysis, and debate now question the results of the British study.

While this research continues, I prescribe selegiline for some patients with Parkinson's disease. A related drug, rasagiline, may be released for sale by the FDA in late 2006 or early 2007. The research helps me know the strengths and weaknesses of these drugs so that I can pick and choose when to use them.

Cynics might look at this selegiline saga and doubt the whole idea of rational therapy. There has been over a decade of research, tests of hundreds of patients, and expenditure of millions of dollars, and we still do not know exactly why selegiline helps patients with Parkinson's disease. Is this scientific process really preferable to relying on drugs that have evolved through the herbal tradition? An important part of science is being aware of the limits of our knowledge and knowing which questions to study next. Through the research on selegiline, researchers have proven that it has a clinically significant benefit for some parkinsonians and that it is generally safe, with known, possible adverse effects. The unanswered questions about selegiline are clearer than they were a decade ago and are a testimony to the power of science, rather than a sign of its impotence.

Coenzyme Q_{10}—Another Quest for Neuroprotection

In October 2002 a research team reported that a dietary supplement called coenzyme Q_{10} (CoQ_{10}) slowed the progression of Parkinson's disease. A news release from the National Institutes of Health began, "Results of the first placebo-controlled, multicenter clinical trial of the compound coenzyme Q_{10} suggest that it can slow disease progression in patients with early-stage Parkinson's disease." The results were widely touted in the media; not everyone heard the cautionary words of the lead investigator, Dr. Clifford Shults: "However, before the compound is used widely, the results need to be confirmed in a larger group of patients."[21] The next day, I was besieged with phone calls from my patients, asking a difficult question: Should they be taking CoQ_{10} for their Parkinson's disease? To answer their question, I read the research report in *Archives of Neurology*[22] and searched the Web. To learn more about CoQ_{10}, I read a number of additional articles.

Coenzyme Q_{10} is a vitamin that is naturally in our bodies and plays a role in many chemical reactions in our cells. Enzymes are proteins that aid and control body chemistry, and each coenzyme joins with specific enzymes to facilitate their actions. Among the cellular chemical reactions that use CoQ_{10}, the most important occur in the mitochondria, producing energy for the cells.

U.S. food and drug laws treat vitamins as food supplements rather than as drugs, so vitamins are easily available in pharmacies, grocery stores, health food stores, and elsewhere. Vitamin manufacturers and merchants can sell vitamins without demonstrating that they have any benefit when we take them and without passing the same purity and safety standards that apply to drugs. CoQ_{10} is usually sold in 30-mg or

100-mg capsules, often with vitamin E included, for about $1 a capsule. Many vitamin dealers advocate taking one capsule daily.

CoQ_{10} levels in our blood decrease as we get older. Low levels have been noted in some patients with cancer, so some cancer patients take CoQ_{10}. A typical ad for CoQ_{10} claims that

> coenzyme Q_{10} is essential to human life and is a crucial component in the primary energy production cycle. Research indicates that supplementation with this nutrient may support normal heart function, provide antioxidant protection and maintain the health of gums.[23]

Like many advertisements for vitamins or supplements, this ad casually makes claims about science or research without citing sources or analyzing the quality of the data. So far, there is no proof that taking extra CoQ_{10} fights cancer, helps the heart or gums, or changes the process of aging.

Everyone knows that vitamins are good. Why should scientists bother with complex experiments to test them? Why should I bother to read about the experiments? It would be easier just to tell my patients to take whatever the media and the advertisements are urging them to take. But if patients are going to take CoQ_{10}, what dose should they take? Are the 30-mg capsules that are found in most of the stores enough? Do patients need the 1200 mg daily used in research studies? Is it safe to take 1200 mg each day? After all, some vitamins are dangerous if taken in excess. If 1200 mg of CoQ_{10} costs over $6, is it worthwhile spending nearly $200 for this vitamin each month? I cannot answer these questions thoughtfully without understanding the cellular effects of CoQ_{10} and exploring the details of the experiments done with it.

Interest in giving CoQ_{10} to patients with Parkinson's disease grew from studies of how MPTP causes parkinsonism. The research inspired by the Frozen Addicts showed that MPTP itself is not a toxin. In cells, MPTP is transformed into MPP+, which is toxic by interrupting energy production in mitochondria. In the mitochondria a series of enzymes make energy for the body. MPP+ disables one of these enzymes, called complex I. These observations led investigators to check how complex I was working in patients with Parkinson's disease.

They found that patients who have died with Parkinson's disease have decreased complex I activity in parts of the brain. Brain tissue is not easily sampled in living patients, but platelets, the small blood cells that help the blood to clot, can be examined in blood drawn from a vein. In patients with Parkinson's disease so mild that they are receiving no drug treatment, platelet mitochondria lack normal activity of complex I and have below normal levels of CoQ_{10}. These observations about the blood platelets in patents with Parkinson's disease invite speculative hypotheses.

Is Parkinson's disease caused by CoQ_{10} deficiency? Probably not because many people, including the elderly and some cancer patients, have low CoQ_{10} levels but are not parkinsonian. Furthermore, when platelets from patients with Parkinson's disease are checked for complex I activity, the activity remains low, even with extra CoQ_{10} added.

Does Parkinson's disease affect mitochondria in cells all over the body, not just in the brain? If so, why are the symptoms of the disease chiefly related to brain dysfunction? Cells in the substantia nigra are among the more active nerve cells and need extra energy to fire continually, so perhaps they are more likely than other cells to be damaged if defective mitochondria are not providing enough energy.

Is Parkinson's disease a toxin-induced disease, caused by a toxin that poisons not only nerve cells, but also other cells, like platelets? So far, such a toxin has not been identified for the vast majority of parkinsonians.

Would the progression of Parkinson's disease be slowed if patients took CoQ_{10} regularly when they first showed mild evidence of the disease? The study reported in *Archives of Neurology* addresses this last hypothesis. The study, "Effects of coenzyme Q_{10} in early Parkinson's disease," was a phase-II drug trial. Phase-II trials are sometimes called dose-ranging studies because they test safety and efficacy of different drug doses. The investigators had already done a phase-I study of CoQ_{10}, giving between 200 mg and 800 mg daily for a month to a few parkinsonian patients and showing that the patients tolerated the medication. For the phase-II study, patients received varied doses of CoQ_{10}. Only 80 patients with early, untreated Parkinson's disease were in the study, divided into four groups of 20 patients each. Each group received a different dose of CoQ_{10}: 0, 300, 600, or 1200 mg daily. Each patient was expected to take the medication for 16 months or until a treating physician believed that the Parkinson's had worsened enough to require other medication.

A vital issue in planning an experiment to test a treatment is how to measure the results of the treatment. The primary outcome measure must be chosen before the study begins. A treatment experiment can be useless if its primary outcome measure does not test the effects of the treatment or does not really reflect the health of the patient. For the CoQ_{10} trial the investigators chose a rating scale called the Unified Parkinson's Disease Rating Scale (UPDRS) as the primary outcome measure. The investigators knew that in the DATATOP study of selegiline the primary outcome measure was the time until the patient began taking L-dopa. Review of the DATATOP study suggested that the UPDRS might have been a better primary outcome measure for it.

The UPDRS rates 31 different aspects of Parkinson's disease and gives a score from 0 to 4 on each item. The 31 items explore mental status, motor activity, and activities of daily living (ADLs) (Tables 5.6 and 1.4 show examples). The lowest score, 0, indicates that the patient has no abnormality; the highest score is 124 (4 times 31). At the beginning of the study, average UPDRS scores were near 23, most of which derived from motor abnormalities; this was expected for mild Parkinson's disease, a stage of the disease when mental status is minimally affected and relatively mild motor abnormalities may have little adverse effect on doing daily tasks.

I have already emphasized that the most convincing treatment trials use a randomized double-blind controlled design. The CoQ_{10} study used this design; patients were randomly assigned to one of the four treatment groups. Neither the patients nor the examining physicians knew which treatment group each patient was in. Each study participant took a wafer four times each day. The wafers that contained 300 mg of CoQ_{10} looked and tasted exactly like the control wafers. Each patient assigned to the 300 mg per day group would receive one 300-mg wafer and three control wafers each day; each patient assigned to the 1200 mg

---

TABLE 5.6: Unified Parkinson's Disease Rating Scale (UPDRS)—Sample items

---

I.   Mentation, behavior, and mood
   1.   Intellectual impairment:
      0—None.
      1—Mild. Consistent forgetfulness, with partial recollection of events and no other difficulties.
      2—Moderate memory loss, with disorientation and moderate difficulty handling complex problems. Mild but definite impairment of function at home, with need of occasional prompting.
      3—Severe memory loss, with disorientation for time and often to place. Severe impairment in handling problems.
      4—Severe memory loss, with orientation preserved to person only. Unable to make judgments or solve problems. Requires much help with personal care. Cannot be left alone at all.

II.   Activities of daily living
   5.   Speech:
      0—Normal.
      1—Mildly affected. No difficulty being understood.
      2—Moderately affected. Sometimes asked to repeat statements.
      3—Severely affected. Frequently asked to repeat statements.
      4—Unintelligible most of the time.

III. Motor examinations:
   18. Speech:
      0—Normal.
      1—Slight loss of expression, diction, and/or volume.
      2—Monotone, slurred but understandable; moderately impaired.
      3—Marked impairment, difficult to understand.
      4—Unintelligible.

The rating scales includes 4 items assessing mental status, 13 items for activities of daily living (ADL), and 14 items for motor abilities.

per day group would receive four 300-mg wafers each day; in the other groups, each patient received the appropriate mix of control and CoQ_{10} wafers.

A few patients taking CoQ_{10} reported ill effects, including joint pain, back pain, coughing, diarrhea, dizziness, upset stomach, falling, fatigue, flatulence, headache, high cholesterol, infections, muscle aches, nausea, sore throat, and sinusitis. This list is daunting at first glance. However, anyone over the course of a year or more is likely to experience many of these common symptoms, at least for a while, and the control group felt a similar incidence of these symptoms. These high doses of CoQ_{10} had no specific adverse effects.

The UPDRS scores for patients in all four treatment groups were checked before the treatment started and regularly over 16 months while taking the study drug. At the one-month evaluation the UPDRS scores had not changed significantly from baseline. This is important because it implies that the CoQ_{10} had no direct immediate therapeutic benefit on Parkinson's disease so that any effect observed after months of treatment seems likely to be due to slowing the worsening of the disease, not just to temporarily reversing the symptoms.

The study ended after 16 months for most patients, earlier for those who were switched to other treatments by their physicians. At the end of the study the average UPDRS score had increased by 12 points in the control group. This increase was expected because of the slowly progressive nature of Parkinson's disease. In the group of patients who took 1200 mg of CoQ_{10} each day, the UPDRS score had increased by less than seven points, a statistically significant improvement compared to the control group. The investigators concluded that "coenzyme Q_{10} appears to slow the progressive deterioration of function in PD, but these results need to be confirmed in a larger study."

After I read the study, I spoke with many patients to help them decide whether to take CoQ_{10}. They had a rather unusual opportunity to make independent treatment decisions. The CoQ_{10} was readily available in stores; over the Internet, for $100, patients could purchase 60 of the same brand of 300-mg CoQ_{10} wafers that were used in the study. They needed neither my permission, nor my prescription, nor approval by the FDA. This contrasts with the usual situation after a phase-II drug trial. Prior to approving a drug for prescription, the FDA will review multiple studies, phase II and phase III, testing many more than 80 patients. The FDA ultimately releases only about one-half of drugs that look beneficial and safe after a single phase-II trial.

The FDA usually requires phase-III trials to confirm and supplement the phase-II results. The phase-III trials study more patients, in more diverse settings, for longer periods of time. The phase-II trial of CoQ_{10} was limited to patients with mild Parkinson's disease who were not taking medication. A phase-III trial might be expanded to those with more severe disease. By including patients on other medications, it might investigate interactions between CoQ_{10} and standard antiparkinsonian drugs. By following more patients for longer periods of time, it might discover adverse effects that were limited to a small portion of the population or that only developed after long-term therapy. In fact, after FDA approval, a drug is still monitored for phase-IV testing that might show up effects detectable after many years of use or after giving the drug to tens of thousands of patients.

Dad's neurologist was among the investigators who did the CoQ_{10} trial and did not suggest that he begin the drug. Most of my patients told me that they were not going to take the CoQ_{10}, postponing a decision until more information was available. Many with more advanced disease were already taking multiple pills and were not willing to add a medication that had not been tested on patients at their stage of the illness. Others were reluctant to take high doses of CoQ_{10} without more assurance of its safety. For most the predominant deciding factor was cost; $200 is a lot to spend each month, and because the CoQ_{10} is unapproved and available over the counter, it is not covered by insurance plans.

My patients and I avidly await more CoQ_{10} research. Not only might we be on the brink of having a drug that prevents or slows the progression of Parkinson's disease, but also, CoQ_{10} research is likely to improve our understanding of the mechanisms of cell death and speed development of additional ways to prevent it. A number of drugs are now being considered for trials as neuroprotective agents. More patients with Parkinson's disease will need to participate in experimental trials before we know which, if any, of the drugs are worth taking.

An enthusiast for alternative medicine might be tempted look at the story of CoQ_{10} with some satisfaction. After all, here may be an exciting advance for neuroprotection of Parkinson's disease that comes from the local health food store, not from the pharmaceutical and scientific establishments. If we examine the surveys of patients using alternative therapies, many with Parkinson's disease were using CoQ_{10} long before scientists tested it in double-blind controlled trials. The irony is that traditional, alternative use of CoQ_{10} was at doses of 30 mg or 100 mg daily, much too little to be effective. It took a combination of basic and clinical scientific experiments to lead the search for a safe and beneficial dose. I repeat: "There is no alternative medicine. There is only scientifically proven, evidence-based medicine supported by solid data or unproven medicine, for which scientific evidence is lacking."

The Challenges of Taking L-Dopa

After he stopped taking selegiline, Dad tried to control his tremor with a drug named parsidol. It acts by blocking the neurotransmitter acetylcholine, just like the belladonna that Charcot was prescribing long ago. The pills helped a bit, but by the late 1990s, Dad needed something more effective. Furthermore, his physician suggested that because he was nearly 85 years old, he should be wary of ill effects caused by blocking acetylcholine, effects like decreased memory.

Dad began taking L-dopa in the late 1990s. Thirty years previously, L-dopa treatment of Parkinson's disease had introduced a new treatment era for neurological disease. Suddenly, physicians could help patients with Parkinson's disease who had been helplessly immobile or ceaselessly trembling. Suddenly, pharmacies carried a pill capable of delivering medicine into the blood, across the blood-brain barrier, and into sick nerve cells. During the L-dopa era, pharmacologists have been ingeniously improving delivery of the drug, maintaining and prolonging its actions, controlling its undesirable effects, and finding other drugs to supplement it.

Using L-dopa, Dad shook less, but some tremor persisted, which was expected because tremor is the motor symptom that is least responsive to L-dopa. Over the years he continued taking the pills, but his tremor gradually worsened, his walking slowed, and he had more trouble getting up from chairs. He began to wonder if the L-dopa was really helping.

In 2003 Dad volunteered to be part of a clinical research project and learned that L-dopa was helping much more than he had realized. The experiment was testing whether magnetic stimulation of the brain could improve tremor. The investigators, trying to minimize the variable factors in their research subjects, asked all the volunteers to come to the research laboratory after stopping their medications for a day. Dad dutifully skipped his L-dopa the day before the experiment. When he awoke the next morning, he was so slow and stiff that he could barely walk to the car for his ride to the laboratory. He was so uncomfortable that he had to resign from the experimental group after the first day. He resumed taking the L-dopa and regained the benefits of the drug.

By this time, Dad was trembling more and more. He could not type at his computer and had trouble turning the pages of a book. He usually drank through a straw because he could not hold a cup of liquid without violently spilling it. The tremor varied without a clear pattern. At lunch he might be able feed himself with little ado; at dinner he shook so much that the tablecloth around his plate became a splattered battlefield. I asked him to note how his tremor varied hour by hour after he took his L-dopa, and he discovered that there actually was a partially predictable schedule: The tremor worsened about three hours after he took the medication. He was experiencing a pattern known as wearing-off.

Almost everyone in the assisted-living facility where my parents live takes more pills than he can remember. I listened to a group of them giving advice to one of their friends who had forgotten to take a pill on time. I heard numerous bits of conflicting advice: take it now, don't bother to take it, take a double dose when the next pill is due, and so on. How do physicians advise patients when a pill dose is missed? The answer varies from drug to drug, diagnosis to diagnosis, and individual to individual, so without professional knowledge you cannot tell a friend what to do about missed meds.

Physicians answer this type of question by studying pharmacology, which includes how the body takes drugs in, distributes them, uses them, and gets rid of them. Dad recalls that when he was an intern in 1939, insulin was already used for treatment of diabetes, but blood sugar, which the insulin was given to regulate, could not be easily measured. The interns could measure the amount of sugar only in a patient's urine, which gave a rough, indirect index of whether treatment was succeeding. Today, patients with diabetes measure their blood sugar many times a day, adjust their insulin with care, and the ill effects of diabetes are lessened. Treatment of Parkinson's disease today is like treatment of diabetes was in the 1930s. We are just starting to understand treatment of the disease, and we are limited because we cannot directly measure what L-dopa is doing in brain cells.

Pharmacologists know that drug effects are often related to the amount of a drug in the blood or elsewhere in the body. For years Dad had been taking his L-dopa four times each day, and the benefit of the drug was more or less steady throughout the day, even though his blood levels of L-dopa were rising and falling. By 2004, after he had taken the medication for more than five years, the response had changed. The benefits of the drug had become very dependent on the blood levels. The tremor improved about one-half hour after he took his pills, and then worsened about three hours later, when the blood level of L-dopa dropped.

Most patients who take L-dopa have similar experiences. Initially, they have steady improvement throughout the day while taking their pills four to eight hours apart. After three to five years of using the drug, their symptoms begin to vary hour by hour. Many have wearing-off, just like my father. Others note a pattern called on-off, in which, rather than gradually losing drug benefits, they freeze up without warning.

I keep returning to the question of what is rational drug therapy. Rational therapy starts with the use of drugs that have proven benefit. Cotzias was the first to prove the benefits of L-dopa, and the FDA approved its use based on reproducible experimental evidence of its safety and efficacy. To understand and control wearing-off and other late effects of L-dopa, physicians use another form of rational therapy: adjustment of treatment based on experiments that show how the body absorbs, breaks down, reacts to, and excretes a drug. Management of L-dopa wearing-off requires a specific branch of pharmacology called pharmacokinetics. Here *kinetics* refers not to body movement, as in bradykinesia or dyskinesia, but to drug movement within the body.

When someone with Parkinson's disease first starts taking L-dopa, amazing improvement in mobility may occur within less than an hour. The delay from the time that the drug passes the lips until the improvement is due to drug movement through the body. Once the drug is swallowed, it takes many minutes to reach the intestine, pass into the blood, travel to the brain, enter the nerve cells, and be chemically changed into dopamine.

Pharmacokinetics is a complex subject. Some readers may want to skip the rest of this chapter. However, I shall try to explain it in more detail, especially for those who, like my father, are grappling with varying responses to L-dopa treatment. After a pill is swallowed, pharmacologists can measure the amount of L-dopa in the blood as time passes (Figure 5.2A). The peak blood levels of L-dopa appear as early as 30 minutes after the pill is taken and correspond roughly to the time of maximum improvement in symptoms. When a patient begins taking L-dopa, body movements do not continue to parallel the movement of the drug in the blood. The L-dopa leaves the blood nearly as rapidly as it entered so that within three or four hours of taking the pill, little L-dopa remains in the bloodstream. Even though the L-dopa does not linger in the blood, when a parkinsonian patient first takes L-dopa, improvement can last for many hours. For a patient who has never taken L-dopa the benefits of the first dose can last for days. Routinely, when patients begin L-dopa, they may take the pills three or four times each day and show sustained improvement, even though their blood levels of L-dopa are rising and falling (Figure 5.2B).

One reason for this separation between drug blood levels and the body's response is that the amount of L-dopa in the blood is much less important than the amount of L-dopa available to the dopamine nerve cells. In humans, there is no way to safely and routinely measure levels of L-dopa in the brain. This is another instance where animal experimentation is indispensable to biomedical research. Marmosets were used for one set of experiments because they are small enough to use easily in a laboratory, develop parkinsonism when given MPTP, and break down L-dopa using enzymes that are like human enzymes.[24] L-Dopa can be measured in the brains of marmosets. It reaches peak brain levels in 30 to 60 minutes, more slowly than it reaches peak levels in blood. In the brain, L-dopa levels are about two percent of the blood levels. After a single oral dose, the L-dopa disappears from the around the nerve cells over a few hours, just as it disappears from the blood. Our knowledge is still limited because this measurement of L-dopa around nerve cells measures neither dopamine inside nerve cells nor dopamine release at the synapse.

Unfortunately, the patients' initial, steady clinical response to L-dopa, apparently independent of drug levels, does not last forever. Most L-dopa users eventually develop the fluctuating motor symptoms of wearing-off, on-off, or dyskinesias.

Dyskinesias are extra involuntary movements, such as facial twitching, limb writhing, or body twisting. Dyskinetic patients may writhe, squirm, or fidget. Dyskinesias are not limited to Parkinson's disease; the dancing movements of Huntington chorea are a kind of dyskinesia. Another example is the facial twitching, called tardive dyskinesia, that can follow chronic treatment of psychosis with dopamine antagonist drugs, like Haldol or Thorazine.

A dyskinetic person looks the very opposite of the bradykinetic immobility of an untreated parkinsonian, yet dyskinesias are a major roadblock to successful treatment of Parkinson's. Experiments have shown that these dyskinesias, wearing-off, and other fluctuations occur when the brain becomes much more sensitive to blood levels of L-dopa. The most common pattern in advanced treated Parkinson's disease is for dyskinesias to appear when drug levels of L-dopa are at their peak. Many patients have both wearing-off when their blood L-dopa levels are low and dyskinesias when the levels are high.

If we were to measure blood L-dopa levels minute by minute in these patients with advanced Parkinson's disease, we would see that improvement starts a few minutes after taking L-dopa, when blood levels rise; however, dyskinesias develop a few minutes later, when L-dopa blood levels are higher (Figure 5.2C). After about an hour, the dyskinesias abate, and the patient experiences a couple hours of improved movement until drug levels drop and drug effects wear off, about three and one-half hours after the pill was swallowed. In real life, there is no fixed blood level that always leads to improvement or always leads to dyskinesia, but many patients at this stage of Parkinson's disease do go through a cycle of bradykinesia, improvement, dyskinesia, improvement, bradykinesia, repeatedly each day. By keeping his total L-dopa dose relatively low, Dad was untroubled by dyskinesias but still alternated between improvement and wearing-off.

One approach to wearing-off is to give the L-dopa pills more frequently (Figure 5.2D). The result is a trade of less off time for more time with dyskinesias. If the dyskinesias are not too violent, many patients prefer dyskinesias to bradykinesia and use this strategy of taking their L-dopa more frequently to minimize wearing-off. Another pharmacokinetic trick to decrease wearing-off is to add other drugs to block COMT, the enzyme that helps remove L-dopa from the body. By taking one of these drugs with L-dopa and blocking the COMT enzyme, the levels of L-dopa in the blood fall more slowly (Figure 5.2E). Two COMT inhibitors are entacapone (Comtan) and tolcapone (Tasmar). Stalevo is L-dopa, carbidopa, and entacapone combined into a single pill. The clinical result of adding one of these is to delay wearing-off. For example, the L-dopa might wear off after about four hours if the COMT inhibitor is included, compared to three and one-half hours if the L-dopa is given alone. Unfortunately, the trade for delaying the wearing-off can be prolonging dyskinesias.

By mid-2004, Dad was bedeviled by wearing-off many times each day. He visited his neurologist, who switched him from Sinemet to Stalevo, thereby adding entcapone to his regimen to block the COMT enzyme and prolong the effect of the L-dopa. The cautious neurologist, concerned that the entcapone might increase peak L-dopa levels and cause toxic symptoms, like dyskinesias, also told him to slightly decrease his L-dopa dose. A couple days later, Dad complained bitterly about the new medication. Rather than helping with the wearing-off, the new regimen was less effective. His tremor was worse than ever. He was unhappy with the new medication, and he was unhappy that his neurologist had not called him to check on the results of the change.

Rather than call his neurologist, who had actually given him a note reminding him to call as needed, Dad called me. I remained wary of being professionally involved in his treatment but did explain that he needed to increase his L-dopa dose a bit; his neurologist had wisely chosen to undershoot rather than overshoot in making the dosage adjustment. Too little L-dopa can be inconvenient and annoying, leading to temporary worsening of tremor, bradykinesia, and instability. Too much L-dopa can be much more destructive, causing not only dyskinesia, but also adverse mental effects, like confusion and hallucinations. With a slight dose adjustment Dad did find that the Stalevo gave him better, longer tremor control than he had with L-dopa alone. We called his neurologist to get his advice and approval of the change.

I teased Dad about his expectation that the neurologist should call to check on him after each change in medication. When he had been seeing 30 patients each day in his own practice, Dad could never have made a follow-up phone call to each of them; the calls would have added a couple hours to his long workday. We agreed that the neurologist's note, urging Dad to call as needed, was appropriate.

I went to the funeral of one of my patients who had died after a long struggle with Parkinson's disease. He had experienced many more problems than Dad, the whole gamut of wearing-off, on-off, dyskinesias, hallucinations, confusion, and more. At the funeral his wife hugged me and said, "Thank you for always promptly returning my phone calls." I was embarrassed and sad that despite all of our advances, little things like this can be among the most important care we give our patients.

During the weeks that he took Stalevo, Dad had foul-smelling urine, a bad taste in his mouth, and poor appetite. He began losing weight that he could not afford to lose. These side effects were so troubling that he gladly switched back to his old Sinemet dose, even though the Stalevo had been better at evening out his motor symptoms.

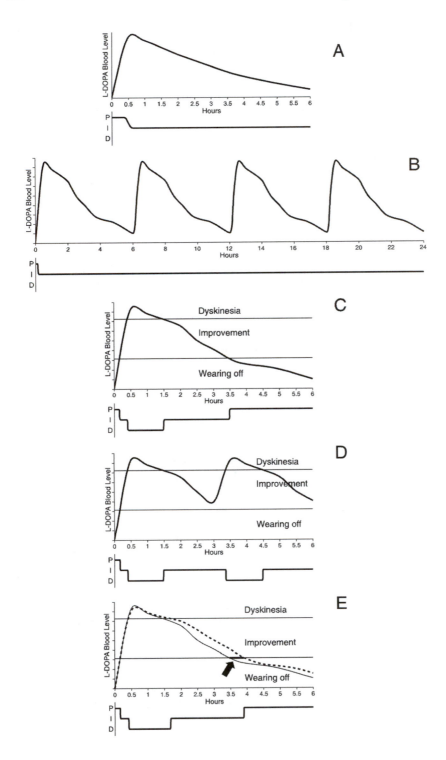

Eric Morgan, in his book, *Defending against the Enemy: Coping with Parkinson's Disease,* gives another example of fluctuating symptoms in Parkinson's disease and of fluctuating responses to medication. He had the disease for more than 20 years and cared for his wife, who also had it. He observes that his physician examined him at discrete times and so would have been unaware of how his symptoms fluctuated during the day, unless Morgan himself carefully chronicled the changes and reported them well. Despite Morgan's exceptional intelligence, knowledge, and insight about his illness, despite his communication with his physician and careful adjustment of his medication, his symptoms often waxed and waned. Sometimes he could attribute this to dietary indiscretion or emotional upset; other times, the variations were neither controllable nor easily explicable.

To help his neurologist understand the fluctuations in his symptoms, Dad decided to chart how he was changing, hour by hour. He found that one problem was that his memory was failing, and he could easily forget a dose of medication or accidentally take a double dose. Every morning, he would carefully fill the compartments of his pill container so that he could check on himself. He knew which compartment to use at 10:00 A.M., which to use at 1:00 P.M., and so on. He tried to make notes of his meal times, activities, and severity of symptoms. The hitch, however, was that his tremor was often so severe that no one could read the notes.

He made an appointment with his neurologist and brought his charts along. Even where the charts were legible, the neurologist was unsure whether Dad was experiencing increased tremor from too little

FIGURE 5.2: In each graph the top panel shows how the L-dopa blood levels change over time, whereas the bottom panel shows whether the patient remains parkinsonian (P), improves (I), or develops dyskinesia (D). (A) When a patient begins taking L-dopa pills, L-dopa blood levels peak in less than an hour and decrease to nearly zero within six hours of taking the drug. The bottom panel shows that the patient improves quickly after taking the pill and remains improved, even after the blood level drops. (B) A patient taking L-dopa four times daily will have fluctuating L-dopa blood levels but initially will have sustained improvement in movement. (C) After taking L-dopa for a few years, many patients become very sensitive to L-dopa levels. When the blood level is excessive, the patient develops dyskinesias; when the blood level is too low, the medication effect wears off, and the patient is again parkinsonian. The patient has best improvement only when the blood level is just right between too high and too low boundaries. (D) More frequent dosing can decrease wearing off but often increases dyskinesias. (E) COMT inhibitor drugs can slow L-dopa breakdown and delay wearing off. The solid line shows the L-dopa blood level when the drug is given without a COMT inhibitor. The dotted line shows the blood level when an inhibitor is added. The arrow highlights the extra improvement time gained by using the inhibitor. (Drawn by Douglas Katagiri.)

medication or increased dyskinesia from too much. He asked Dad to return to the clinic the next morning without taking his usual morning pills.

Getting to the clinic without his wake-up L-dopa was a challenge. Friends helped him into a wheelchair, drove him to the medical school, and wheeled him into the doctor's office. The doctor and his staff examined Dad before he took his first pills of the day and then every 20 or 30 minutes after his early-morning and midmorning doses. They realized that he had both tremor and dyskinesia; he could tolerate neither more nor less L-dopa. The neurologist asked him to continue his current regimen and add an anticholinergic drug in hopes of achieving a stronger antitremor effect.

Dad had first tried an anticholinergic drug very early in his illness. Dad's doctor had him stop taking it in the late 1990s because people over 80 are often very sensitive to anticholinergic ill effects, especially to memory loss. Now, the doctor was telling him to take a calculated risk. The doctor followed the clinical adage for medicating older patients, "go low, go slow," and prescribed a very small dose of the medication to start. He asked the family to watch Dad closely for side effects. If the new medicine did bother his memory, the effect would disappear as soon as the medication was stopped.

Someday, with the help of pharmacological research, we physicians will be more precise when we adjust medications. We have much to learn, such as more about L-dopa changing to dopamine in the nerve cell and the actions of dopamine at the synapse. The blood levels of L-dopa do not alter over years of use. Therefore neuroscientists have wondered about the changes that patients with Parkinson's disease experience after years of L-dopa therapy. Why do patients go from a steady response to L-dopa at the start of therapy to a cyclic pattern including dyskinesias and wearing-off? One theory is that the switch is due to the natural progression of the disease. Every year, a patient with Parkinson's disease has fewer healthy dopamine nerve cells. Eventually, few nerve cells store and use the L-dopa. Another theory is that L-dopa or dopamine has an accumulating toxic effect on nerve cells so that prolonged L-dopa therapy eventually distorts the cell response to the drug.

After many years of experiments, in cell cultures, in animal models, and in humans, neuroscientists continue to debate the relative merits of these two theories. In many cell culture experiments, L-dopa is toxic to nerve cells. However, this might be due to factors irrelevant to what occurs in the human body. Some of the cell culture experiments have used concentrations of L-dopa that far exceed those reached in the brain when a patient takes L-dopa pills. The cell cultures are grown in chemicals that can react with L-dopa to form toxic compounds; these chemicals bear little resemblance to the fluid that surrounds brain cells.

In contrast to the cell culture experiments, live animals seem not to suffer nerve cell damage when exposed to L-dopa. This difference between the results of cell culture experiments and of animal experiments shows the difficulty of translating results of basic science experiments to the treatment of people. Hypotheses can be tested and refined in the laboratory, but the human effects of treatment are never fully known without human experiments and observations.

In one randomized controlled double-blind study, investigators treated some patients with L-dopa and others with a dopamine agonist called ropinirole.[25] They treated the patients for five years; neither the patients nor the physicians knew whether the study medication was L-dopa or the dopamine agonist, but physicians had the option of prescribing extra L-dopa if the patients needed more antiparkinsonian treatment. After five years of treatment, 20 percent of those treated with dopamine agonists compared to 45 percent of those treated with L-dopa had developed dyskinesias. Patients in both drug groups had improved motor abilities and more success with activities of daily living. The higher incidence of dyskinesias in the dopa-treated patients does not resolve the debate about whether L-dopa is toxic to nerve cells. However, this study does show that many patients with mild Parkinson's disease can be successfully treated with a dopamine agonist, rather than starting early therapy with L-dopa.

Like many of my colleagues, I have been studying the ebb and flow of experimental results about possible toxic effects of L-dopa. For now I often prescribe agonist drugs early in the illness and delay L-dopa therapy until the disease becomes more advanced. However, there are some disadvantages to dopamine agonists compared to L-dopa. The agonist drugs are more expensive. In 2004 the maximum dose of ropinirole used in the study would cost $24 daily, compared to $2.50 for the dose of L-dopa with carbidopa. Furthermore, the agonist drugs are less powerful than L-dopa and have their own adverse effects, so other patients start taking L-dopa and then add dopamine agonists only if they develop wearing-off or other fluctuating symptoms.

Every month, as new journals cross my desk or when I hear about new experimental results, I learn more about the treatment of Parkinson's disease. Someday soon, new genetic findings might change my approach to choosing the right drug. Just as every illness has genetic causes, genes control every response to medication. Genetically controlled enzymes break down drugs, and many drugs act by altering intracellular enzymes or attaching to cellular receptors, also controlled by genes. Pharmacogenetics, the study of how genes control drug action, is just starting to provide information about the treatment of Parkinson's disease. Preliminary reports suggest that inherited differences in the gene for COMT, one of the enzymes that breaks down L-dopa, or in the gene for the dopamine transport protein that recycles dopamine back into nerve cells might determine how a person responds to L-dopa. In the future, studies of a patient's genes may be very helpful in choosing just the right dose of just the right drug for that person.

As a clinician, I constantly battle the imprecision of science when I choose the best treatments for my patients. I rely on the results of randomized double-blind controlled trials. When the FDA has approved a drug for a specific use, I know that results of these trials have been carefully scrutinized. For more information I use PubMed, which lists randomized trials as a separate publication type, so it is easy to find many papers on randomized trials of treatment for Parkinson's disease: Over 40 were published in 2002. However, just because a trial is randomized and controlled does not mean that it is flawless or that its results show ultimate truths. Often, many randomized trials will study a treatment issue, and the results of the trials can be compared and contrasted, a process called meta-analysis. I may read the Cochrane Database of Systematic Reviews for a good source of critical meta-analysis of randomized studies.

Clinicians carefully study pharmacology. We consider interactions with other drugs; individual patient characteristics, like allergies; intervening illnesses (such as kidney or liver failure) that change drug breakdown; pharmacogenetics; potential ill effects; and the drug costs.

Physicians and patients look at many factors before planning therapies. Ideally, we rely on randomized double-blind controlled studies to assess benefit, and we gauge safety from these controlled studies and from continued surveillance for less common adverse effects. We study the results of pharmacological experiments. Patients, however, may not match participants in studies. Physicians wish that all decisions could be based on scientific proofs, but patients often have problems that have not been researched thoroughly. For these treatment decisions the art of medicine then mixes with the science. What can the physician and patient do when evidence-based medicine provides insufficient evidence?

First, proper treatment depends on the severity of an illness. As of 2006, very early Parkinson's disease needs no treatment while investigators continue to search for a truly neuroprotective drug. In contrast, a life-threatening illness may be treated with drugs with more risk of adverse effects and at times with drugs that make scientific sense but are of unproven benefit.

Second, physicians are constantly aware of medical issues that are uncertain or not yet scientifically clarified. For one patient with an uncertain diagnosis the physician might say, "I do not know the diagnosis, but I do know you do not have a serious illness. Let me recheck you in a few months." For a second patient the advice might be "I do not know the diagnosis; please try this medication because your response to it will clarify the diagnosis or at least will help plan your treatment." We use this strategy when we give L-dopa to some patients for whom the diagnosis of Parkinson's disease is unclear. For a third patient the answer may be "I do not know the diagnosis, but you have a serious illness, and based on your findings, we should begin treatment; these are the choices, potential benefits, and adverse effects."

Finally, physicians and patients need to make treatment decisions together. The physician offers the scientific evidence. The patient needs to know the treatment rationale, benefits, costs, and adverse effects and consider personal values to participate in the decision.

CHAPTER SIX

Images of the Brain—A Picture of the Brain Is Worth a Thousand Words

Nearly every day after lunch, I walk from the hospital cafeteria to the radiology department and sit down with a brain-imaging specialist, called a neuroradiologist, to review any recent X rays or scans on my patients. The neuroradiologists sit in a darkened room all day, studying the shadows of patients created by X rays or the high-tech images from scanners like the CT, MRI, PET, and SPECT. They rarely speak to or even meet a patient, but they are masters at making diagnoses from these pictures. I rely on their skills at detecting visible abnormalities. They know much more than I do about the appearance of normal and abnormal anatomy and about the workings of modern imaging machines. They can tell me which type of scan is most likely to help solve a diagnostic puzzle. They teach me the limitations of their machines, such as when an apparent abnormality on a scan is a technical artifact.

When I view the images, I joke with the radiologists that if a picture is really worth a thousand words, their written reports are too terse. I have come to see the pictures to be sure that my patients get their money's worth. The reality behind the joke is that I usually understand a patient's problem better when I see the images. Even more important, radiology reports are like any other diagnostic test, never free of false positives and false negatives. Often, when a radiologist and I discuss a patient, the radiologist will correct false reports, improving diagnostic accuracy by a second look at the pictures and by my clinical input on where in the brain the abnormality is likely to be.

When we can see the brain, we can better comprehend its function and its diseases. Parkinson described the shaking palsy in 1817, but progress in understanding the disease was delayed for many years, until investigators began to see its pathology and anatomy. Important twentieth-century observations included the loss of black pigment from the substantia nigra by Tretiakoff in 1905, identification of the Lewy body (1912), and mapping where neurotransmitters are located in the brain in the 1950s and 1960s. These anatomical investigations were done in animals or after death. In the twenty-first century, sophisticated ways to image brain anatomy and function during life are providing new insights about Parkinson's disease. I shall describe examples from three areas of active current imaging research: diagnosis of clinical disease, evaluation of brain function before symptoms appear, and using imaging to track progression of the disease.

Imaging and Diagnosis

Understanding Parkinson's disease began with clinical observations, emphasizing the cardinal findings of tremor, bradykinesia, rigidity, and postural instability. In chapter 1, I mentioned that a study comparing clinical to pathologic diagnosis showed that even skilled clinicians are imperfect at predicting which patients have the pathologic hallmarks of Parkinson's disease, such as loss of dopamine cells from the substantia nigra of the midbrain. Naturally, then, neuroscientists have been striving for images of these pathologic changes in living patients to improve diagnostic accuracy.

Arguably, engineers and physicists rather than biologists led the greatest advances in clinical neurology in recent generations. Advances in brain imaging in the last third of the twentieth century provided invaluable information about diseases like stroke and multiple sclerosis before the images became useful in Parkinson's disease. Allan Cormack, a physicist, and Godfrey Hounsfield, an electrical engineer, won the Nobel Prize for Physiology or Medicine in 1979 for pioneering the first computed tomographic (CT) scans. There are now a host of computerized scans, such as CT, MRI, SPECT, and PET, that clarify the structure and function of the nervous system. In 2003 the chemist Paul Lauterbur and the physicist Sir Peter Mansfield received the Nobel Prize in Physiology or Medicine for developing the MRI scan.

Taking pictures of the inside of the living body began with another physicist and engineer, Wilhelm Roentgen, who discovered the X ray in 1896 and won the first Nobel Prize in Physics in 1901. Roentgen could X ray the head, revealing the bones of the skull, but was unable to show the brain tissue within the skull cavity. Before we had CT scans, the only way to image the brain itself was to inject a dye into the body to highlight specific tissues. For example, if physicians inject a dye containing iodine into arteries in the neck, the dye looks white on X rays. If an X ray is taken of the skull while the dye is flowing through the arteries, the blood vessels supplying the brain are outlined. This technique is called an angiogram (picture of blood vessels) or arteriogram (picture of arteries). An angiogram is very good at showing blockage or injury to blood vessels. It can outline bulges in blood vessels, called aneurysms. If the brain contains a tumor or swollen area, the angiogram may show that blood vessels have been pushed aside from their usual paths. However, the brain abnormalities of most neurological diseases, including Parkinson's disease, multiple sclerosis, and most strokes, are invisible on angiograms.

Another way to outline brain structures on an X ray is to inject the dye into the cerebrospinal fluid, the clear liquid that bathes the brain. Iodine-containing dye, or even a small amount of air, can provide the contrast. The dye or air outlines those parts of the brain that normally contain cerebrospinal fluid. If air is used, the technique is called a pneumoencephalogram. Pneumoencephalograms can reveal some brain tumors and other abnormalities that block or distort cerebrospinal fluid flow. They show no abnormalities in most patients who have brain diseases, certainly not in those with Parkinson's disease. They are uncomfortable and cause severe headaches. Modern computerized scans have made pneumoencephalograms almost extinct.

The CT or CAT scan was the first of the computerized scans able to display slices of anatomy as cleanly as if a brain-cutting knife filleted the brain. The CT scanner takes X rays from many different angles and then uses a computer to meld the X-ray images into pictures of slices of the brain. Sometimes dyes are injected before the CT brain scan. The invention of the CT scan in the early 1970s profoundly changed clinical neurology. Before CT scans were available, a neurological examination was the only way during life to determine what part of the brain was damaged by a stroke. After CT became available, many stroke patients had their illness diagnosed by a radiologist rather than a neurologist.

In the late 1990s Dad had his first serious fall. He tripped on a curb. Like many other patients with Parkinson's disease, he walked with a slight forward stoop and moved his arms too slowly to protect himself. He stiffly fell forward on his face, which immediately became a mass of cuts and bruises. He went to the emergency room, where his wounds were cleaned and bandaged, and the emergency room doctor ordered a CT brain scan to be sure that the trauma caused no bleeding in his brain. Fortunately, his scan showed neither blood clots in the brain nor other suggestions of brain trauma. Of course, the CT brain scan offered no hints that Dad had Parkinson's disease, which never causes visible changes on the CT scan.

CT brain scanning of stroke or trauma patients has two limitations. First, some strokes and traumatic effects are not visible on CT scans. To use the terminology of sensitivity and specificity introduced in chapter 1, the CT scan has some false negatives when used as a test for strokes. Second, the CT scan might show brain scars or abnormalities that are long standing and irrelevant to the stroke; these are false positives when the CT scan is the stroke diagnostic test. Some people thought the CT scan would make neurologists obsolete; in fact, each new scanning technology has created more work for neurologists to interpret scans in relation to patients' problems.

The MRI brain scan was invented about 1977. It uses a large magnet and radio waves instead of X rays to create the images. It provides much greater detail of most brain tissues than provided by the CT scan. Like all tests, the MRI scan has its share of false positive and false negative results. The MRI has drawbacks; some people are unable to go into the scanner because they have certain metals in their bodies or have a device, like a pacemaker, that the MRI magnet might damage; some become claustrophobic when they lie in the long magnetic tube. Also, the MRI scanner takes longer and is more expensive than the CT scanner.

Neither the CT nor MRI scans reveal the pathological changes of Parkinson's disease in the substantia nigra. The normal substantia nigra contains about one-half million nerve cells; for comparison a teaspoon of blood contains about 25 million red blood cells. Even though these nerve cells are larger than red blood cells, the presence or absence of these cells, spread across the substantia nigra, is not visible on the MRI or CT scans, partly because of their small volume, but also because on CT or MRI they look just like other brain cells.

I rarely order a CT or MRI brain scan as part of the routine evaluation and care of a patient with clear-cut Parkinson's. Some patients, however, have bradykinesia, rigidity, or postural instability but do not have all the classical parkinsonian findings. For these patients I might obtain either a CT or MRI brain scan to check for other problems, such as multiple strokes or normal pressure hydrocephalus, an abnormal accumulation of cerebrospinal fluid that can mimic Parkinson's disease.

Standard CT and MRI techniques may not be helpful for the routine diagnosis and treatment of Parkinson's disease, but investigators have developed some clever ways to visualize the anatomy and physiology of the disease during life. The trick for imaging the dopamine cells is to distinguish them visually from surrounding cells. To label a half million or so dopamine cells among 100 billion brain cells, scientists have extended a technique called autoradiography to the living human brain. For autoradiography of a slice of dead brain, the tissue is bathed in a radioactive chemical that binds only to selected tissue. For example, an unstained brain slice is washed with a molecule called dopamine transport protein. If radioactive iodine is attached to the transport protein, the resulting autoradiograph will highlight the putamen and the caudate because this molecule is concentrated in the ends of dopamine nerve cells, which are localized to this part of the brain.

A PET scanner or SPECT scanner can produce an autoradiograph of a living brain using chemicals injected intravenously. For example, a radioactive fluoride isotope, ^{18}F, can be attached to L-dopa. The radiolabeled ^{18}F-dopa crosses the blood-brain barrier and concentrates in dopamine nerve cells, just as unlabeled dopa does. The small amount of injected radioactivity causes less radiation exposure than does a skull X ray. The next challenge is obtaining images of radiolabeled brain. This is done by placing the subject in detectors like a set of Geiger counters. The detectors measure the radiation leaving the brain, and then a computer calculates the source of the radiation and creates the image.

The dopamine cells in the substantia nigra send most of their axons to the putamen and caudate. The dopamine is concentrated at the end of the axon, so the ^{18}F-dopa PET scan highlights the putamen and caudate. This area of the dopamine synapse can also be imaged by doing scans with radiolabeled haloperidol, which binds to the postsynaptic dopamine receptor, or with radiolabeled chemicals that specifically attach to the dopamine transport protein in the wall of the dopamine nerve cell. Figure 2.2D is a model of the synapse that shows the dopamine synaptic vesicles, the dopamine receptors, and the dopamine transport protein. A radioactive molecule that concentrates at any of these structures shows approximately the same PET or SPECT image in a normal individual. The sketch in Figure 6.1B represents a PET or SPECT scan of a normal brain done using one of these radioactive labels for the dopamine synapse. The comma-shaped light areas represent radioactivity in the putamen and caudate. PET or SPECT scans using these labels of the dopamine synapse clearly show that patients with Parkinson's disease lose chemical activity in the putamen, even though this area of the brain would look perfectly normal on MRI or CT scans (Figure 6.1C).

We are born with about a half million dopamine cells in the substantia nigra that send axons to the putamen and caudate. During life, a few of these cells naturally die, but most of us never develop Parkinson's disease. Perhaps one percent of the dopamine cells die routinely during each year of our adult lives. There is enough reserve and redundancy in the brain that most people can lose nearly 60 percent of these cells, yet not develop Parkinson's disease. By the time people reach age 80, about one in five has some mild parkinsonian findings by neurological examination, suggesting that for some people the natural loss of cells that occurs over a lifetime eventually leads to parkinsonism.

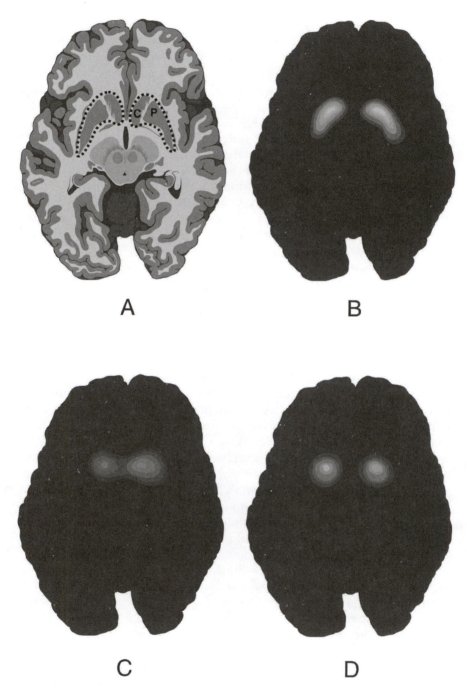

FIGURE 6.1: (*A*) Anatomical section of brain showing the areas imaged on the scans that follow. (*B*) PET or SPECT scan of normal brain using a radiolabel for the dopamine synapse, highlighting the putamen and caudate. (*C*) PET or

Those who develop Parkinson's disease, which begins, on average, in the early sixties, lose their dopamine cells prematurely. We can hypothesize various time courses of cell loss that might precede appearance of symptoms. A toxin might quickly kill a large number of nerve cells, leading to sudden onset of parkinsonism, just as MPTP injured the Frozen Addicts. Another scenario is that an insult might cause cell loss, insufficient to immediately cause parkinsonism but predisposing to later onset of the disease; this mechanism would explain why some people who had encephalitis lethargic developed Parkinson's disease years later. A third and more common pattern of cell deterioration occurs in idiopathic Parkinson's disease, which manifests, on average, around age 60, preceded by accelerated cell loss, whether due to genetic or environmental factors, reaching back over many years.

Imaging and Presymptomatic Diagnosis

The SPECT and PET scans of dopamine synapses provide insights into these hypothetical mechanisms of cell loss. If some people with an inherited or environmental predilection for Parkinson's disease lose substantia nigra cells at an accelerated rate over many years, scans might identify this cell loss before it becomes symptomatic. However, if Parkinson's disease develops shortly after sudden cell destruction, scans would be less likely to catch presymptomatic abnormalities.

Twin studies, which in the 1980s failed to detect the genetic component of Parkinson's disease, are now using scanning to provide insights into the timing of cell loss in the substantia nigra. In retrospect, one reason that the twin studies were not powerful enough to detect genetic effects was that the twins were not followed long enough. Now, investigators have used PET scans in twins to detect preclinical changes in the putamen and to show a stronger role of genetics in Parkinson's disease than previously realized.

Researchers used ^{18}F-dopa PET to scan 34 pairs of twins, each with an index twin who had Parkinson's disease and a co-twin who did not have clinical evidence of the disease.[1] The index twins, on average, developed their disease in their fifties. A family history of Parkinson's disease was positive in only 3 of the 34 families. Eighteen of the twin pairs were identical, and 16 were fraternal. All of the index twins had abnormal

SPECT brain scan of a patient with Parkinson's disease. Note the asymmetric loss of radiolabeling from the putamen. (*D*) PET scan of brain of an asymptomatic identical twin of a patient with Parkinson's disease. Even though the twin has no clinical evidence of Parkinson's, the decreased radiolabel suggests that the twin may already have pathological loss of dopamine neurons. The radiolabeling in the putamen is less than normal but not as deficient as in the parkinsonian brain. (Drawn by Douglas Katagiri.)

scans characteristic for Parkinson's disease. Three of 16 asymptomatic fraternal twins and 10 of 18 asymptomatic identical twins had loss of dopamine cell function on their scans (Figure 6.1D). The two co-twins whose ^{18}F-dopa uptake was the lowest were the first to develop clinical evidence of Parkinson's disease after the scans. Some of the co-twins with positive scans were rescanned as the years passed and showed gradual progression of their cell loss. These scanning studies of twins support the growing realization of the role of genes in causing Parkinson's disease. The loss of dopamine cell function in the co-twins, especially in the identical co-twins, implies that vulnerability of dopamine cells to destruction is genetically controlled. It also shows that loss of dopamine cells can be present for years before Parkinson's disease is clinically apparent. A third implication of these findings is that environment must interact with genes to determine the expression of Parkinson's disease; a pair of twins with identical genes usually does not show signs of Parkinson's disease simultaneously. One twin's illness is evident many years before the other twin's, so not only genes, but also environmental factors, affect development of the disease.

Many patients with Parkinson's disease, my father included, lose their sense of smell years before they experience any tremor or other motor effect of Parkinson's disease. Investigators looked at the relation between sense of smell and risk of developing Parkinson's disease. They used a radioactive label for the dopamine transport protein as the measure of dopamine cell activity and the SPECT scanner to obtain images in 48 nontwin relatives of Parkinson's disease patients.[2] About half the people had imperfect senses of smell. Of course, sense of smell can also be disturbed by a cold, nasal allergies, head trauma, or countless other events. All those with a normal sense of smell had normal scans. Among those with impaired smell, four, none of whom had any of the cardinal features of Parkinson's disease, showed loss of dopamine cell function in their putamen. Two of the four with abnormal scans developed clear-cut parkinsonism within the next year, again suggesting that scans of dopamine cells in the putamen can detect a proclivity to develop Parkinson's disease.

When we develop a true neuroprotective treatment to prevent Parkinson's disease, a treatment that decreases cell death in the substantia nigra, these imaging techniques for dopamine cell vulnerability may become extremely important. Imagine imaging all family members of patients with Parkinson's, or at least all with clinical hints like diminished sense of smell, then beginning neuroprotective therapy whenever scans identify individuals at increased risk for later developing the disease.

These findings of abnormal scans in asymptomatic individuals have important implications for the utility of scanning as a diagnostic test for Parkinson's disease. If a person has an abnormal scan for dopamine cell function but a completely normal neurological examination, that person does not have Parkinson's disease according to current diagnostic standards. Therefore the scan in that person represents a false positive result. With current technology the findings that pique our interest—detection of preclinical abnormalities and future prospects for disease prevention—also decrease the specificity of the scans as diagnostic tests for Parkinson's disease. Perhaps future, improved scans will quantify cell loss more precisely and enhance both the prognostic and diagnostic values of the scans.

I have repeated many times that we should expect all tests to have false negatives and false positives. True to this rule, the current scan techniques not only have false positives, such as the asymptomatic people I just mentioned, but also have false negatives. PET or SPECT scans of patients who have mild clinical findings of Parkinson's disease are normal at least a tenth of the time.[3] Just as the positive scans in asymptomatic people make us question how we should define Parkinson's disease, the negative scans in symptomatic people stir debate. Are the scans not sensitive enough to detect every instance of cell failure in the substantia nigra, or do these people with negative scans have a disease that is pathologically different than Parkinson's disease?

Imaging and Disease Progression

Radiolabeled scans can also document progression of Parkinson's disease. If SPECT scans are taken at different times from a single patient, using the dopamine transport protein label, the scans show progressive cell dysfunction as the months pass. Unfortunately, the changes in the scans correlate imperfectly with changes in the patients' neurological impairment.

Quantitative analysis of the rate of cell loss suggests that patients with early Parkinson's disease may annually lose one-tenth of the dopamine cells from their putamens. Many methodological issues influence these quantitative estimates, and there are less data on the rate of loss in those with preclinical cell degeneration. There are varied estimates of the time gap between accelerated loss of putamenal cells and appearance of symptoms of Parkinson's disease, but some studies suggest that this preclinical period of degeneration lasts less than five years.

These imaging studies can also assess the effects of drugs on the course of the disease. In a study comparing patients treated with L-dopa versus patients treated with the dopamine agonist pramipexole, binding of the radiolabel decreased about three to six percent per year, again demonstrating that patients with Parkinson's disease have an ongoing abnormal loss of cell function.

By scanning criteria, patients taking L-dopa seemed to lose cells faster than those taking the dopamine agonist drug. Does this mean that L-dopa accelerates cell loss, or that the dopamine agonist protects against it, or that both drugs are destructive or protective but to different degrees? One obstacle to answering this question is that the scans measure the dopamine transport protein rather than the actual number of cells. In healthy brains the concentration of transport protein is a rough measure of the number of cells, but we do not know if drug treatment or Parkinson's disease itself might somehow change the concentration or function of transport protein without actually changing the number of cells.

Studies that use scans to compare L-dopa to dopamine agonists have inspired extensive debate among physicians who treat Parkinson's disease. Some argue that these studies show that the agonists are a superior treatment. However, there are so many competing hypothetical explanations for the scan results that physicians do not all agree that these studies prove one drug is superior to the other.

CHAPTER SEVEN

A Better Model of Parkinson's Disease

So far, I have presented a relatively simple model of Parkinson's disease, repeatedly emphasizing loss of cells from the substantia nigra, where pathology includes loss of the normal black pigments and the presence of Lewy bodies. In healthy brains the axons from these substantia nigra cells travel to the putamen, where they use dopamine as a neurotransmitter to communicate with other cells. In patients with Parkinson's disease, loss of these connections causes the symptoms. This model, which evolved in the first two-thirds of the twentieth century, has been spectacularly valuable, inspiring the initial experiments with L-dopa treatment of Parkinson's disease. The success of L-dopa therapy and the later discovery of dopamine agonist drugs have reinforced credibility and utility of the model.

There was a time when you could buy a television set, take it home, plug it in, turn it on, and watch. Recently, I bought the latest model TV and spent hours fiddling with the instruction book and multiple controls. The new model was better but complex and harder to understand. Scientific models, even though they are ideas rather than objects, are similar. The aphorism "all models are wrong but some are more useful than others" is true. Even for a very useful model, like the dopamine model of Parkinson's disease, there is much to learn by examining how it is wrong or incomplete. This model fails to explain many aspects of Parkinson's disease. Examples include the following.

1. How do changes in the substantia nigra and putamen actually affect movement of muscles that are directly controlled by motor nerve cells in the spinal cord, which are in turn controlled by cells on the surface of the brain, distant from the putamen?
2. How do drugs, like relatives of belladonna, that are not converted to dopamine and are not active at dopamine receptors benefit patients with Parkinson's disease?
3. Why do many patients with Parkinson's disease have manifestations of their disease, like loss of sense of smell, separate from the well-known motor effects of the disease?
4. Why does dopamine-enhancing therapy help slow movement and rigidity much more than it helps tremor?

Basic neuroscientists have started to answer these questions and have improved models of the mechanism of Parkinson's disease. Their findings mesh with new PET, SPECT, or MRI images of the brain in action. These pictures, called functional images, show the brain at work and can give new insights into the mechanism of the symptoms of Parkinson's disease. The more we learn from these images and from basic science, the more we understand the complexities of the disease. Readers who prefer clinical to basic science can note the key points in Table 7.1 and skip to the next chapter.

Dopamine Nerve Cells Connect to Many Parts of the Brain

To understand how changes in dopamine nerve cells in the substantia nigra affect motor cells in the cerebral cortex, we need greater knowledge of nerve cell connections. The deep gray matter areas of the cerebral hemispheres are called the basal ganglia. So far, discussing Parkinson's, I have repeatedly referred to two of the basal ganglia, the caudate and putamen, and to the substantia nigra. The putamen abuts a paler region called the globus pallidus. Other important components of the basal ganglia are the thalamus and the subthalamic nucleus (Figure 2.3).

There are many kinds of nerve cells in the caudate and putamen. The axons of some cells are quite short and connect only to nearby cells. In contrast, the medium spiny nerve cells have longer axons that travel

TABLE 7.1: Toward an Improved Model of Parkinson's Disease

1. Patients with Parkinson's disease lose dopamine nerve cells from the substantia nigra that synapse in the putamen.
2. These dopamine nerve cells then connect to many parts of the brain.
3. Dopamine is only one of many neurotransmitters that are important in Parkinson's disease.
4. Patients with Parkinson's disease also lose cells from many other areas of the brain.

beyond the caudate and putamen to other structures, especially to the globus pallidus. The medium spiny nerve cells have extensive branches that synapse with axons of cells coming from other areas of the brain. Of particular import, they synapse with the axons of the dopamine cells coming from the substantia nigra and of cells coming from the motor cortex.

Tracing the complex, intersecting paths of axons as they travel through the brain is difficult. New techniques have supplemented the nineteenth-century ways of studying the brain, such as using Golgi silver stains or looking at the results of destructive lesions. For example, small amounts of radioactive amino acids can be injected near the cell bodies. The cell takes up the amino acids and uses them to make proteins, which are carried down the axon to the far reaches of the cell. Autoradiographs can outline the cell, including its long axon. Other dyes can be injected near the synapse, where they are taken up by the axon and are transported within the axon up to the cell body. Unbelievably tiny instruments can inject dyes into individual cells, outlining the extent of their connections.

Investigators also use cell electricity to study nerve cell connections and functions. They insert very small microelectrodes into nerve cells and detect cell firing. These studies are often done in monkeys, whose motor systems closely resemble those of man. The monkeys can be trained to do specific tasks while microelectrodes are in their brain cells. Some cells fire even when the animal is at rest; for example, the dopamine cells in the substantia nigra fire regularly four or five times per second. Just before or during certain movements, some cells fire more, and others fire less. One advantage of using monkeys for microelectrode studies is that function can be compared between healthy animals and monkeys that have MPTP-induced parkinsonism.

Figure 7.1A is a map of some circuits connecting the substantia nigra to the cerebral cortex. The map shows a minimum of three synapses between the putamen and the motor cortex. The map is complicated, even though I have greatly simplified it by omitting subdivisions of the basal ganglia and additional axonal pathways. An added element of complexity is that at some synapses the presynaptic nerve cell excites the postsynaptic nerve cell, whereas at other synapses the presynaptic nerve cell can inhibit firing of the postsynaptic nerve cell; other neurotransmitters change the chemistry of the postsynaptic cell rather than directly affecting electrical discharges of the cell. These connections form an interwoven control system that can refine the movements elicited by the motor cortex.

The motor abnormalities of Parkinson's disease—tremor, rigidity, postural instability, and bradykinesia—are at least partially due to errors of this control system. Figure 7.1B illustrates how the basal ganglia interactions might change in a patient with Parkinson's disease. Decreased

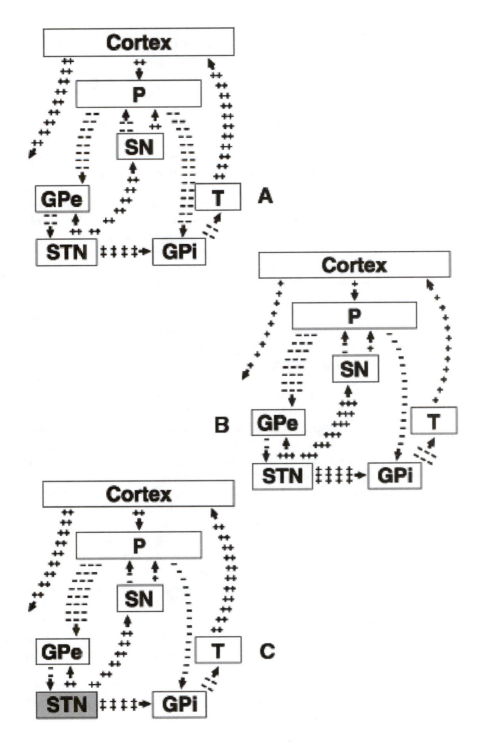

activity of substantia nigra cells causes changes at multiple synapses, increases inhibition from the globus pallidus interna, and so decreases stimulation from the thalamus to the motor cortex.

One fascinating aspect of Parkinson's disease is that slow loss of a few hundred thousand cells, accounting for less than one-thousandth of one percent of all nerve cells, can have such widespread and devastating consequences for body movement. In contrast, when a person has a stroke, the brain can lose over a million nerve cells in the first minute and millions of more cells as the stroke progresses. In Parkinson's disease the effects of the substantia nigra cells are amplified by their extensive projections and connections throughout the brain. I have already given examples of how brain scans that label the dopamine synapse can evaluate local abnormalities in the putamen. There are other scanning techniques that show nerve cell function throughout the brain and teach more about how the brain misfires in Parkinson's disease.

Each nerve cell requires energy to survive and uses extra energy when it is actively sending electrical messages down its axon. The energy comes from oxygen and sugar that are delivered to the cells by blood flowing in the arteries. Scanning techniques that measure brain blood flow, sugar, or oxygen highlight active areas of the brain.

For example, PET brain scans can use radioactivity attached to a molecule called 2-deoxyglucose, a relative of common sugar. The images highlight brain cells that are actively consuming sugar. This type of PET scan will show more activity of the motor cortex if the individual is using an arm during the scan than if the individual is just relaxing. PET scans with 2-deoxyglucose show that patients with Parkinson's disease alter sugar use in many specific parts of their brains. The loss of the dopamine nerve cells that occurs in Parkinson's disease prevents turning off areas deep in the brain. These deep areas that are not turned off show increased sugar use on the PET scan. In turn, the hyperactive deep areas send axons to specific parts of the outer gray matter, where they turn off activity in nerve cells. These areas of the outer gray matter show

---

FIGURE 7.1: (*A*) A simplified model of normal connections of the basal ganglia. Abbreviations are as follows: P, putamen; SN, substantia nigra; T, thalamus; GPe, globus pallidus externa; GPi, globus pallidus interna; STN, subthalamic nucleus. The minus signs indicate inhibitory axonal pathways; the plus signs indicate stimulatory axonal pathways. (*B*) Model of altered connections of the basal ganglia in Parkinson's disease, in which the substantia nigra has decreased in both stimulatory and inhibitory output. This leads to decreases or increases in downstream output. A single plus or minus indicates decreased output; a triple plus or minus indicates increased output. (*C*) Surgery on the subthalamic nucleus in a patient with Parkinson's disease, in theory, can counteract the effect of abnormal input and lead to normalized output so that the downstream GPi, thalamus, and cortex function more normally. (Drawn by Douglas Katagiri.)

decreased sugar use on PET images. The PET studies of patients with Parkinson's disease and in monkeys with MPTP-induced parkinsonism support the model of basal ganglia connections (Figure 7.1B) by showing that the diseased patients and animals have increased cell activity in at least part of the globus pallidus.

Special MRI techniques or PET scans using water that is labeled with radioactive oxygen can monitor brain blood flow, which is greater in areas with more active nerve cells. In a typical experiment a person reading a paragraph aloud activates specific parts of the cerebral cortex, including areas needed for vision (occipital lobes), language processing, and the motor movements of the mouth, vocal cords, and throat. A person with Parkinson's disease who reads the same paragraph will have similar activation of the occipital lobes but different changes in the areas that are needed for the motor aspects of speech.

When drugs like L-dopa help patients with Parkinson's disease, their clinical improvement is matched by a partial return to normal of the pattern seen on PET brain scans. These PET scans help understand the physiology of Parkinson's disease but are not useful as routine diagnostic tests.

Oliver Sacks describes how Robert De Niro prepared for the role of Leonard in the movie *Awakenings*.[1] De Niro spent hours carefully observing patients with Parkinson's disease and practicing for the role. During rehearsals, Sacks, illustrating for Robin Williams how a neurologist might approach a patient, examined De Niro and momentarily thought that De Niro was neurologically impaired rather than just acting. On the movie screen De Niro's immobility is movingly realistic. I wonder what functional brain images of De Niro would show while he was acting parkinsonian. His masked face and slow movement would undoubtedly show on the PET scan as decreased activity in parts of the cerebral cortex. I suspect, however, that regardless of his skill as an actor, activity deep in his brain would not match the PET changes of a true parkinsonian. To my knowledge, no one has done this experiment.

Dopamine is One of Many Neurotransmitters That Are Important in Parkinson's Disease

Another shortcoming of the dopamine model of Parkinson's disease is that it provides no explanation of why some drugs unrelated to the dopamine system can help with parkinsonian symptoms. Even Charcot knew that drugs like belladonna could suppress aspects of the disease. For some patients, drugs in the belladonna family surpass L-dopa as treatment for tremor. To explain this, we need to expand the model of Parkinson's disease to consider the role of other neurotransmitters.

In the basal ganglia, there are many neurotransmitters besides dopamine. Drugs in the belladonna family block the action of the neurotransmitter acetylcholine. Small nerve cells in the putamen have dopamine receptors and react to dopamine nerve cells from the substantia nigra, but these cells then use acetylcholine as their own neurotransmitter. Thus chemical anatomy of the putamen includes synapses where acetylcholine-blocking drugs might modify symptoms of Parkinson's disease. Of course, acetylcholine is also a neurotransmitter in many other areas of the brain, and we are unsure whether these particular small, acetylcholine-rich cells in the putamen are truly important in the genesis of tremor.

Two other neurotransmitters of particular import to Parkinson's disease are glutamate and GABA (gamma amino butyric acid). Glutamate concentrates in the putamen and is the major neurotransmitter of the nerve cells that connect the motor cortex to the medium spiny nerve cells. GABA is the major neurotransmitter of the medium spiny nerve cells. The highest concentrations of GABA are in the globus pallidus, where the medium spiny nerve cells from the putamen and caudate synapse with other nerve cells.

Microelectrode studies and other techniques show that different neurotransmitters have different functions. Some stimulate the postsynaptic cell to fire. Some, like GABA, inhibit the postsynaptic cell from firing. Neurotransmitters can also act by changing chemistry, such as formation of new proteins, inside the postsynaptic cell. The methods of molecular genetics can measure DNA and RNA activity and show which proteins are made inside a cell when conditions change.

Amantadine, another useful drug, blocks some glutamate receptors. Researchers are studying agents that manipulate glutamate, GABA, and other basal ganglia neurotransmitters as potential new drugs to treat Parkinson's disease. This research emphasizes that even if loss of dopamine function is central to the cause of Parkinson's disease, other neurotransmitter drugs can help by modifying the complex circuitry of the basal ganglia.

Patients with Parkinson's Disease Lose Cells from Many Areas of the Brain

Movement abnormalities are the cardinal features of Parkinson's disease, but the disease has other symptoms, many of which are not easily attributed to loss of cells from the substantia nigra. We know, for example, that patients with Parkinson's disease commonly have impaired sense of smell and that they can experience various disorders of thinking, mood, or behavior. Clearly, our model of Parkinson's disease needs another dimension of complexity to explain these diverse manifestations.

Lewy bodies were first found in the substantia nigra, concentrating attention on this part of the brain in Parkinson's disease. However, subsequent studies, especially those using better stains, showed that the pathological changes of Parkinson's disease are usually much more widespread and that Lewy bodies are often found in the brains of those with neurological illnesses other than Parkinson's disease. In fact, at least one-twentieth of those who die after age 60 have at least a few Lewy bodies in their brains, even though they have no clinical indications of Parkinson's disease.

A number of distinct spots in the brain show nerve cell degeneration and Lewy bodies when the brain of a patient with Parkinson's disease is studied at autopsy. The degenerating cells include some dopamine cells other than those in the substantia nigra and some nerve cells that use neurotransmitters other than dopamine. These include cells that use acetylcholine, serotonin, GABA, norepinephrine, and other neurotransmitters; to complicate matters, most cells that use these neurotransmitters do not degenerate in Parkinson's disease, and even some dopamine cells are spared from degeneration. One topic of current research interest is whether the Lewy body develops as part of the initial pathogenic process or does not appear until later, after the cell damage is well established.

Impaired sense of smell is one of the nonmotor aspects of Parkinson's disease. The deficit is selective: Parkinsonians usually can identify the odors of clove or oranges, whereas they have difficulty with other odors, including pizza, wintergreen, licorice, and pineapple. My father was aware of his impaired sense of smell even before his tremor appeared, and 70 percent or more of patients with the disease lose the sense of smell, often early in their illness. It is unsurprising, then, that in Parkinson's disease, brain pathology includes not only the substantia nigra, but also areas of the brain that mediate the sense of smell.[2] Now, neuropathological studies using improved staining methods show that in the early stages of Parkinson's disease, nerve cell losses can occur in areas of the brain that control smell, sleep, and other functions before the dopamine cells are ever disturbed in the substantia nigra.

All of the six patients described by James Parkinson had tremor. However, one can have the shaking palsy without the shaking. In fact, perhaps one-quarter of patients who meet other clinical and pathological criteria for Parkinson's disease have no tremor. This is not easily explained by a model that focuses on pathology in the substantia nigra causing deficiency of dopamine cells. Furthermore, the dopamine model does not explain why L-dopa therapy can decrease rigidity and accelerate bodily movement without dampening tremor. Some interesting brain images supplement other evidence that pathology outside the substantia nigra and neurotransmitters other than dopamine are part of the mechanism of tremor.

An area of the midbrain called the dorsal raphé nucleus is separate from the substantia nigra. In patients with Parkinson's disease, Lewy bodies are often present in the dorsal raphé, just as in the substantia nigra. The predominant nerve cells in the dorsal raphé use serotonin, rather than dopamine, as their neurotransmitter. These nerve cells send axons to a portion of the cerebral cortex where they stimulate serotonin 1A receptors. The serotonin 1A receptors are also present on the cell bodies of the dorsal raphé nerve cells. These serotonin receptors can be imaged on PET scans using a radioactive molecule called ^{11}C-WAY that binds specifically to them. The technique is analogous to using ^{18}F-haloperidol for PET scan localization of dopamine receptors. Whether a person has Parkinson's disease affects the ^{11}C-WAY PET scam. In some people with the disease, the uptake of radioactivity in the dorsal raphé is decreased. Investigators found a correlation between the loss of binding in the dorsal raphé and the severity of patients' tremors. In contrast, ^{18}F-haloperidol binding in the putamen correlates with severity of rigidity and slow movement but not with tremor. These findings are exciting not only because they provide more evidence that the pathology for Parkinson's disease extends beyond dopamine cells, but also because they suggest that drugs active at the serotonin 1A receptor might benefit parkinsonian tremor.

Neuroanatomy, neurochemistry, neuropathology, and other aspects of basic science improve the model of Parkinson's disease. An improved model offers new targets for clinical therapeutic experimentation. In the next chapter we see how an expanded model helps explain the results of surgical treatment of Parkinson's disease.

CHAPTER EIGHT

Brain Surgery for Parkinson's Disease

Can Destroying Part of the Brain Be Good?

Shortly before his 87th birthday, my father asked me whether he should have brain surgery to improve his Parkinson's disease. Neurosurgeons try to treat Parkinson's by destroying or stimulating small areas of the brain, inserting new healthy brain cells, or even improving brain genes. Unfortunately, few patients qualify for surgical treatment.

My first response to Dad's question was to urge him to ask his own neurologist. I reminded him that physicians should not treat their own families. Besides, surgical treatment of Parkinson's disease should be done only at centers where teams of neurologists and neurosurgeons have extensive experience with the surgery. My father's physicians at Oregon Health and Sciences University are part of a very fine team, expert in surgical treatment of Parkinson's disease.

To help my father make an informed decision, I told him a little about the history of surgical treatments of Parkinson's disease, a history that illustrates scientific innovation and serendipity and raises difficult issues of the ethics and regulation of human experimentation. Neurosurgeons tried a wide variety of operations for the disease throughout the twentieth century.[1] A number of these sprang from James Parkinson's initial experience with the man whose tremor improved after a stroke. The surgeons reasoned that if unintended cell destruction by a stroke could improve the tremor, a carefully planned, precise surgical destruction of the right cells would be even more therapeutic. Neurosurgeons destroyed very small groups of nerve cells in different parts of the brain. They chose the areas for destruction based on the known functions of these cells and on theoretical models of how these areas controlled movement, but no one found a place for surgery that relieved tremor without causing even more disabling weakness.

About 1939, the neurosurgical focus shifted to operating deep in the brain, destroying portions of the basal ganglia. If science were orderly, we might hope that planning this surgery began with thoughtful study of models like that shown in Figure 7.1. In fact, these models were not developed until the 1970s. As of 1939, neurologists had only a very simple understanding that the basal ganglia had something to do with movement. Russell Meyers, a neurosurgeon from the University of Iowa, began experimentally operating on different parts of the basal ganglia in patients with Parkinson's disease.[2] His first operation was on the caudate. After 12 years of human experimentation, he reported that results were best if he destroyed part of the globus pallidus, an operation that improved the tremor and rigidity for about 60 percent of his patients. However, this surgery was soon abandoned because, for some surgeons, nearly two of every five patients died from the operation.

A surgical mishap reinforced interest in making lesions in the basal ganglia. In 1953 Dr. Irving Cooper was planning to destroy part of the midbrain of a parkinsonian patient. Before he could destroy this small piece of brain, he accidentally cut one of the arteries supplying the basal ganglia. By interrupting the blood supply to these deep brain structures, he feared that he had caused a stroke, injuring the brain tissue that this artery should nourish. He stopped the operation, abandoning plans to cut into the midbrain. The next day, to the surprise of physician and patient, the patient no longer had tremor or rigidity in the arm opposite to the side of the brain that had been injured by the stroke. This experience was like that of James Parkinson's patient who had a stroke, but unlike Parkinson, Cooper knew what part of the brain had been injured by the stroke. The damage was to the globus pallidus and other portions of the basal ganglia, so he switched his operative focus for Parkinson's disease from the midbrain to these structures.

Open surgery on the basal ganglia was dangerous because surgeons might damage blood vessels and brain tissue when they cut deeply to reach their target. The danger decreased in the late 1940s when surgeons switched to stereotactic surgery. Stereotactic brain surgery is a technique for placing small instruments through the brain without seeing the target tissue directly. Before they had stereotactic techniques, surgeons operated for Parkinson's disease by removing part of the skull and dissecting to reach the target brain tissue. In contrast, in stereotactic operations the surgeon, like a pilot flying through a cloud by reading instruments, blindly guides his tools into place through a small hole in the skull without cutting the surrounding brain. The surgeon directs the tools to the desired spot using brain images and detailed knowledge of brain anatomy.

Before 1970, the images were skull X rays, angiograms, or pneumo-encephalograms. Anatomy atlases showed the relation of the deep gray matter structures to the shadows on X rays of blood vessels or cerebro-spinal fluid spaces. The stereotactic placements were approximate, and disastrous errors could occur. Perhaps the saddest and best known of these disasters affected Fuller Albright, one of the most brilliant clinical investigators of the mid-twentieth century.

Fuller Albright[3,4] was a legend when I was in medical school. He was born in 1900. As a young physician, he was a pioneer endocrinologist and described many new conditions. Physicians still study Albright's syndrome and many of his other discoveries. He first noted his own hand shaking at age 36. It was soon evident that he had Parkinson's disease.

Within a few years he could not walk steadily. Albright's wife had to shave him and cut his food. Despite progressive neurological problems, he continued experimenting, teaching, and caring for his patients. His residents and medical students would write for him, tie his shoes, and chauffer him to the hospital. By 1954, his speech was so poor that he "lectured" by silently showing written slides. As an endocrinologist, Parkinson's disease was not among his research interests. He used to joke that if he had been a neurologist, he would have found the cure to Parkinson's disease long before his illness became so advanced.

In 1956, against the advice of his own physicians, he had surgery on his right thalamus, which at that time had replaced the globus pallidus as the prime operative target. Initially, his left hand tremor improved, but on the third postoperative day, when a tube was removed from the area of surgery, he went into a coma caused by bleeding into his brain. His best recovery was to a state of mute immobility.

From 1957 until he died in 1969, Albright lay in a bed in a private room at the hospital where he had worked. During this time, he continued to require total care. There was a rumor that reverent medical students would visit his room at night to meditate. I wonder if they were dreaming of emulating his brilliant medical career, mourning his tragic illness, or thinking of a kinder medical ethic that would not conscience such a long interlude between productive, interactive life and death.

Despite sad stories like Albright's, patients with Parkinson's disease were desperate for relief and willing to take risks in the hope of improving their symptoms. By 1969, surgeons had performed nearly 40,000 stereotactic brain operations, mostly for treatment of Parkinson's disease. By this time, the risk of the surgery causing a stroke or other serious complication was probably less than 10 percent. However, the number of operations for Parkinson's disease dropped drastically in the 1970s and 1980s because of the potential for serious unintended brain injury and the introduction of L-dopa therapy.

The inventions of the CT and MRI brain scans improved the accuracy of stereotactic surgery. Today, surgeons place the patient in a frame and use MRI or CT brain scans to calculate precisely where to probe the brain, so the risk of accidental brain injury during surgery is greatly decreased.

Stereotactic surgery is usually done through a very small cut in the skull, called a burr hole, which may be as small as a dime. The surgeon can cut through the scalp, drill the burr hole, and cut the outer membranes that enclose the brain painlessly using local anesthetics. The brain itself does not have pain-sensing fibers. The surgeon places the stereotactic instruments through the brain tissue while the patient is awake. Even with modern stereotactic precision, the placement of an instrument can be slightly off. Once the instrument is near its final location, the surgeon sends a small electrical current through the instrument to stimulate the brain tissue around just the tip of the instrument. The awake patient can tell the surgeon how the stimulation feels. If the stimulation elicits unwanted effects like tingling of a limb or flashes of light, the surgeon moves the instrument slightly and repeats the test. Once the instrument is correctly in place, the surgeon sends a stronger current through it. The strong current heats the instrument just enough to kill a small area of cells very close to the tip.

The model of Parkinson's disease shown in Figure 7.1C suggests that careful surgical destruction of a few cells might improve function of other brain cells that are far from the defective substantia nigra. It would have been elegant if the experimentalists had developed the model, told the surgeons exactly where to cut, and been rewarded with marked patient improvements after surgery. Unfortunately, medical history is much messier. Neurosurgeons began operating on the basal ganglia with rather vague rationales long before neuroscientists proposed the model. In fact, one impetus for the model was scientists' efforts to explain the successes of the surgery. However, the model has inspired experiments, such as brain electrode recordings in monkeys with MPTP-induced parkinsonism, and these animal experiments have led to better understanding of how the surgery works and, more important for patients, better selection of the surgical sites.

Currently, the three main surgical targets are the thalamus, the globus pallidus, and the subthalamic nucleus. Typically, the surgery attacks brain cells at one of these locations, basing the choice on the clinical problems of the individual patient (Table 8.1). For Dad at age 87, tremor in both hands remained his worst symptom. He was having trouble sleeping because of the tremor. He was slightly slow when he got up from a chair and sometimes stumbled. He had cuts and bruises from some falls. His mind was clear, but he knew that he was not thinking as quickly as

TABLE 8.1: Modern Surgical Sites for Parkinson's Disease

Site of operation	Advantages	Disadvantages
Thalamus	Decreases tremor in opposite hand for four-fifths of patients.	Does not improve bradykinesia or postural instability.
Globus pallidus	Decreases dyskinesia caused by drug therapies. Best for patients with advanced Parkinson's disease who become less tolerant of drugs.	Improves bradykinesia and rigidity only partially and does not improve postural stability.
Subthalamic nucleus	Stimulation can improve tremor, rigidity, bradykinesia, and postural instability.	Cell destruction can cause excessive movements.

he had a few years before. His voice was a bit soft, but he was swallowing without difficulty. He was taking moderate doses of L-dopa/carbidopa and had never tried any of the dopamine agonist drugs. He was not having dyskinesias. His doctors were considering surgery on his thalamus on one side, which would have decreased the tremor in one hand, but not the other, and was unlikely to improve his slowness or unsteadiness.

Dad wanted to know how likely the surgery was to help him and the risks of the surgery. The value of surgery for Parkinson's disease is difficult to assess. There are many uncontrolled trials, but few controlled experiments. Randomized controlled surgical trials are hard to design, and double-blind trials are nearly impossible. Practitioners of evidence medicine rate the quality of evidence on which they make decisions. Table 8.2 shows a typical evidence-rating scale. Striving for the best class-I evidence is not quibbling. In reviewing rational drug therapy, we have already seen that even the results of a class-I study, like DATATOP, leave much room for differing interpretations, and lower-class studies provide less dependable evidence. Much of the evidence about surgical therapy of Parkinson's disease is only class III.[5]

TABLE 8.2: Classes of Evidence for Evaluating Clinical Studies

Class I. Evidence provided by one or more well-designed randomized controlled clinical trials.

Class II. Evidence provided by one or more well-designed clinical studies, such as prospective open, case-controlled studies, etc.

Class III. Evidence provided by expert opinion, nonrandomized historical controls, or case reports of one or more patients.

This is an evidence classification used by M. Hallett and I. Litvan (Evaluation of surgery for Parkinson's disease: A report of the Therapeutics and Technology Assessment Subcommittee of the American Academy of Neurology. The Task Force on Surgery for Parkinson's Disease. *Neurology.* 1999;53:1910–1921).

A newer surgical technique to treat Parkinson's disease uses brain stimulation rather than brain cell destruction. The stimulation can be done at the same small islands of brain tissue that were formerly destroyed. Paradoxically, the stimulation probably blocks the output of cells by overexciting them. The stimulating wires are placed stereotactically. The brain stimulator is attached to a battery and a control unit placed under the skin. Using a magnet held outside the body just over the control unit, the patient or physician can turn the stimulator on and off or adjust it. When patients have bilateral problems, surgeons are often hesitant to operate on both sides of the brain, which is more likely to cause some complications, such as speech difficulty. However, with bilateral stimulators, the surgeon can adjust the stimulators to control these complications.

Brain stimulation does permit some double-blind testing of treatment by comparing patients' status when the stimulator is turned on and when it is turned off. This double-blind approach shows that well-placed bilateral brain stimulation can help patients with advanced Parkinson's disease.[6]

Even with modern stereotactic methods, brain surgery for Parkinson's disease still has risks. Placement of the stereotactic instruments can interrupt arteries, cause bleeding, or introduce infections. A few patients have seizures after the procedures. Cell destruction or brain stimulation can worsen speech, thinking, or movement. The risk of these complications varies from operation to operation and from surgeon to surgeon. Complications are less frequent when the surgical team is experienced. With the best surgeons, less than 3 in 100 patients have permanent worsening from the surgery.

Our current theoretical models do not explain all the results of surgical treatment of Parkinson's disease. For example, why is thalamic cell destruction particularly useful for treatment of tremor, whereas L-dopa therapy is more helpful for treatment of the other aspects of Parkinson's disease? Why does tremor predominate in some patients, whereas tremor is minimal in others? Ongoing microscopic, electrical, and biochemical studies show other defects in the model, and scientists are proposing new, more complex models.

The history of surgical therapy for Parkinson's disease is another example of scientific ebb and flow: A surgical procedure becomes popular, then fades from fashion; a model of brain action seems useful, but its weaknesses prompt searches for a new model; clinicians and basic investigators exchange ideas.

Where does this leave my father, who wants to know if surgery is the right treatment for him? He needs to make an important decision based on imperfect, class-III evidence (Table 8.2). When evidence from class-I controlled trials is unavailable, physicians and patients often use the opinions of experts to guide them. Table 8.3 shows the recommendations of some experts in Parkinson's disease about which patients are most appropriate candidates for surgery.

TABLE 8.3: Recommendations of a Panel of Experts Regarding Stereotactic Globus Pallidus Surgery for Parkinson's Disease

1. The surgery should be done only at centers where the neurologists and neurosurgeons are trained and experienced in the technique.
2. Patients should have disabling idiopathic Parkinson's disease without dementia and should have exhausted options for medical therapy.
3. Patients should be evaluated by standardized rating scales before and after surgery.
4. Symptoms that are most likely to improve are dyskinesias, rigidity, and tremor.
5. The particular center and surgeon's complication rate should be discussed with the patient before surgery.

Adapted from Bronstein JM, DeSalles A, DeLong MR. Stereotactic pallidotomy in the treatment of Parkinson disease: An expert opinion. *Arch Neurol.* 1999;56:1064–1069.

The patient and the physician need to consider whether symptoms are disabling enough to justify the risk of surgery, whether medications have been adjusted for maximum benefit, whether the proposed surgery is designed to benefit the most troublesome symptoms, and whether the surgical team is experienced and has a good safety record.

Dad's most troublesome symptom was his tremor. He did not quite fit the surgical criteria offered in Table 8.3 because he had not exhausted options for medical therapy, but tremor is a symptom that is unlikely to improve with any of the drugs that he had not tried. Most surgical patients are younger than he is, and his age undoubtedly increases surgical risk. However, recommendations in Table 8.3 are from 1999, and experienced clinicians might be more aggressive in recommending surgery now.

My father discussed surgery with his neurologist, who believed that thalamic surgery was likely to benefit his tremor much more than any currently available medication could. The neurologist offered to send him to the neurosurgeon to discuss the risks of surgery, particularly since, at age 87, my father was older than most surgical patients. After mulling the recommendation, Dad decided not to have surgery. He knew that with current techniques a tragedy like Fuller Albright's was extremely unlikely. However, like all of us, he fears stroke or loss of clear thinking. He knew that at his age, even a slight worsening of his speech, swallowing, or memory would be a major setback to his independence. He was unwilling to risk rare but frightening adverse surgical outcomes.

Many of my patients follow a similar pattern. They are usually taking medications. They may be using alternative therapies. They want to know their options, but very few meet criteria for surgical therapy, and even fewer decide to proceed with an operation.

"Brain Transplantation"—Implanting New Brain Cells

Brain transplantation sounds like eerie science fiction. For treatment of Parkinson's disease the idea is to place healthy new cells at local sites in the brain, replacing missing dopamine nerve cells. Only a few cells are placed in the brain with this approach, so *cell implant* is really a more accurate, if less exciting, term than *brain transplant.* These implants, using high-tech stereotactic surgery, raise difficult scientific and controversial ethical issues and have attracted widespread attention in the news media.

Swedish researchers in the early 1980s first operated on animals before placing new cells in human brains. They injected poisons in rat brains to damage dopamine nerve cells. They already knew that if a dopamine relative called 6-hydroxydopamine is injected into one side of the brain, the rat turns toward the injected side when it tries to walk. Before the discovery of the toxic effects of MPTP, these injected rats were one of the few animal models of damage to dopamine nerve cells. The Swedish researchers took cells from the substantia nigra of fetal rats; they then injected these healthy cells into the brains of other rats at the site of toxic damage. The rats that received the fetal cells stopped the abnormal turning behavior.

In the mid-1980s, surgeons followed these rat experiments with the earliest attempts to place healthy cells in the brains of patients who had Parkinson's disease. At first they removed cells from the patient's own adrenal glands. These cells secrete epinephrine and are closely related to the brain dopamine nerve cells. The surgeons injected these cells into the patients' brains. An initial report from Mexico was highly enthusiastic about the results of this surgery: Two patients with Parkinson's disease seemed to improve within days after the surgery.[7] Videotapes taken before and after surgery showed that the patients were much more mobile after the operation.

In the United States, there is little regulation of the spread of new surgical procedures, a marked contrast to the strong control of new drugs under the aegis of the FDA. After the *New England Journal of Medicine* published a report of the Mexican operations, the adrenal tissue implants quickly became popular; however, other centers were unable to obtain the striking results shown in the Mexican videotape, and experimental studies showed that the adrenal cells did not survive in the brain. The adrenal implant technique has been virtually abandoned.

The failure of the adrenal cell implants did not stop research efforts. Attention focused on the cells from substantia nigras of aborted fetuses. Again, the research started on animals. Implants of fetal substantia nigra cells into the brains of monkeys that had MPTP-induced parkinsonism improved the monkeys' movements.[8] After this encouraging experience in animals, Swedish researchers tried the operation in humans. Initial results were promising, and Dr. Langston arranged for two of the Frozen Addicts to fly to Sweden for evaluation.

In August and September 1989, George Carillo, the Frozen Addict, underwent brain implants in Lund, Sweden. First on one side of his brain, then a few weeks later, on the other side, neurosurgeons, using stereotactic instruments, injected cells into his brain. The cells were taken from the substantia nigras of aborted fetuses. A couple months later, Juanita Lopez, another of the Frozen Addicts, had similar surgeries. The addicts initially showed little improvement, but within two years after the surgery, they were more mobile and required less L-dopa medication. They had ^{18}F-dopa PET scans before and after surgery. The scans showed that before surgery, they had decreased ^{18}F-dopa uptake in their putamens. One to two years after surgery, the ^{18}F-dopa uptake had improved.[9] A number of research groups reported similar encouraging results of fetal brain cell implants in patients who had idiopathic Parkinson's disease.

The ethics of fetal cell implants has been fiercely debated. The substantia nigra cells used are obtained from six- to eight-week-old aborted fetuses. For most patients, surgeons place the implants on both sides of the brain, using cells from three or more fetuses for each side. Some people believe strongly that fetal tissue should never be used for experimental or therapeutic purposes. Nonetheless, after considering the arguments, panels of ethicists in Sweden, Great Britain, and the United States approved the implant experiments in Parkinson's disease with specific guidelines. For example, the guidelines indicate that an abortion should never be done solely to obtain fetal tissue. However, if a woman has already decided to have an abortion, she should have the right to donate the fetal tissue for surgical use. She should not be paid for the tissue and should not be allowed to give it to family members or to specify the recipient.

Debates continue about the use of fetal tissue for medical research or treatment. President George Herbert Bush banned U.S. federal funding of fetal cell research, including implants for Parkinson's disease; in contrast, Bill Clinton, early in his presidency, approved the use of federal dollars for fetal cell research.

Once Clinton freed federal money for fetal cell research, the National Institute of Neurological Diseases and Stroke and others funded a research project striving for class-I evidence about fetal cell implants for patients with Parkinson's disease.[10] Forty patients who had severe, long-standing Parkinson's participated. Investigators randomly assigned 20 patients to the implant group and 20 to the control group. Surgeons at the University of Colorado did the surgery, stereotactically inserting fetal brain cells in both putamens of those patients who had the implant operation. The patients flew to New York for pre- and postoperative neurological examinations and PET scans by physicians who did not know if the patients were in the control or treatment group.

Randomized controlled double-blind studies are now a standard part of drug research but are infrequently used in surgical research, despite clear evidence that surgery can have a placebo effect. A placebo surgical effect means that a patient or physician may perceive health improvement, even though an operation fails anatomically to correct the patient's problem. The classic example of the need for controls to evaluate surgery is an operation called the Weinberg procedure that was popular in the 1950s for patients who were having heart pains. The chest pain, called angina, was due to impaired blood flow to the heart. In the Weinberg operation the surgeon did not touch the heart but instead tied off an artery in the chest wall, hypothesizing that this would redirect blood flow to the heart. Many surgeons were performing this operation and raving that after surgery, patients' chest pains improved. Dad and his brother were among the enthusiasts. In 1958 they and two colleagues reported that many patients, for whom my uncle did the Weinberg operation, had excellent relief of chest pain.[11] A couple years later, other physicians did a controlled trial in which some patients underwent the Weinberg operation and others underwent a sham operation of a simple cut in the chest skin.[12] In the controlled trial the Weinberg procedure relieved heart pain no better than the sham surgery did, and the procedure was abandoned.

The fetal cell implant trial included a sham surgical control. The control patients were given general anesthesia, and the surgeons made a cut in their scalps and drilled holes in their skulls, just like those used for the real cell implants. When a patient awoke from the anesthesia, he or she could feel the hole in the skull but could not tell whether fetal cells had been implanted into the brain through the hole. Thus the surgery was double-blinded because neither the patients nor the evaluating physicians in New York knew who had had the implants.

Once again, cell implants stirred a debate. Some criticized this sham surgery as unethical.[13] Federal regulations require that research on human subjects have minimal risk. Minimal risk is explicitly defined as not greater than the ordinary risks of daily life or of routine physical or psychological tests. The research subjects signed documents that they had been informed about the risks of the study, understood that they had a 50/50 chance of receiving sham treatment, and consented to participate. The patients knew that if they had the sham surgery, they would be offered the real implants one year later, if the experiment showed that the operation was safe and beneficial. Fourteen of the 20 sham surgery patients did eventually have the implant surgery, using the skull hole made during the sham surgery. Nonetheless, critics maintained that the sham surgery was riskier than routine daily life and hence failed to meet the federal definition of an ethical research study.

Defenders of the sham surgery design point to the very small risks and discomforts of the procedure and to the greatly increased value of the study for all patients with Parkinson's disease because of the well-controlled design.

Regulations require that institutional review boards (IRBs) approve all federally funded human research. An IRB is a committee that monitors the rights and welfare of human participants in research projects. Each IRB has at least five members, including professionals capable of evaluating the research and community representatives, some of whom must be neither scientists nor affiliates of the institution doing the research. After reviewing all aspects of the study plans, the IRBs of the three hospitals participating in the study and a performance and safety monitoring board appointed by the National Institutes of Health approved the implant experiment, including the sham surgery.

Rating scales, outcome measures, null hypotheses, statistical significance, and the other tools for design of randomized clinical studies are vital for a well-planned assessment of a surgical procedure, just as they are for drug trials. Before a study begins, investigators must specify the primary outcome measure that will determine if the null hypothesis is rejected. The null hypothesis for the study of fetal cell implants was that patients with Parkinson's disease do no better with implant surgery than with sham surgery. Remember that a well-designed experiment has a null hypothesis and a corresponding alternative hypothesis. The alternative hypothesis is what the researchers are trying to prove. In this experiment the alternative hypothesis is that implant surgery is more effective than sham surgery. The alternative hypothesis is supported if the null hypothesis is rejected. For the controlled trial of fetal cell implants, the patients were evaluated before and one year after surgery using rating scales.

When they designed the study, the researchers decided that the primary outcome measure would be a global rating scale through which patients would rate the results of the surgery one year after the operation. The ratings ranged from -3, meaning the parkinsonism was markedly worse, to $+3$, meaning the parkinsonism was markedly better. Each patient's rating expressed the patient's opinion and was not based on any other measurements. The average global rating score for the implanted patients was 0.0; the average for the control patients was -0.4. The difference between the two groups was not statistically significant. Hence, on the basis of the primary outcome measure, the global patient rating scale, the null hypothesis was not rejected. Therefore this study did not provide class-I evidence that the surgery is effective.

The study failed to prove that cell implants were effective but did not prove that they were ineffective. In fact, further analysis provides tantalizing clues that some patients may have benefited and that the surgery had positive physiological effects. For example, the study evaluated patients one year after the surgery. George Carillo, when he had a similar operation years ago in Sweden, had more improvement in the second year after surgery. Many of the implanted patients in this trial had the same pattern of delayed improvement. Unfortunately, the primary outcome measure of the experiment was not designed to detect any changes after the first year.

Another hint of possible surgical value comes from using a different outcome measure; on the basis of the UPDRS, a few patients benefited from surgery, especially for some symptoms. The UPDRS for patients under 60 years old improved for the implant group compared to the sham group, and rigidity and bradykinesia improved, whereas tremor did not. The differences were evident when the patients were tested off medication but not when tested on medication. Because these results are based on secondary analysis rather than on the primary outcome measure, they serve as sources of new hypotheses and impetuses to design new experiments but do not prove the alternative hypothesis of the study.

PET scans, another secondary outcome measure of the study, were particularly interesting because they tested whether the implanted cells were changing brain function. All patients in the study had ^{18}F-dopa PET scans before and one year after surgery. The postoperative PET scans showed that after most implants, ^{18}F-dopa uptake increased, suggesting that the new cells had survived and were metabolically active.

In two instances, pathological examination confirmed that the implanted cells survived and could actively make dopamine. One patient died in a car accident seven months after surgery; another died of a heart attack three years after surgery. Brain autopsies of both these patients showed surviving implanted cells in the putamen.

Like all treatment trials, the cell implant study monitored adverse effects of the treatment. Dyskinesias, the worst complication, occurred in 15 percent of the patients who had implants and often developed in the second year after operation, especially in patients who had improved in the first year after surgery. Dyskinesias are probably due to excessive brain dopamine activity and so are another bit of evidence that the implanted cells were actively making dopamine.

The power of an experiment refers to its ability to answer the question posed by the null and alternative hypotheses. For example, if the study had included 2 patients instead of 40, the results would be very unlikely to be statistically significant. Prior to starting a large study like the implant trial, statisticians can predict how many patients should be enrolled in each group for the best chance of success. For this study to find a statistically significant 1.0 difference in the global rating scale between the two groups of patients, it should have enrolled 64 patients in each group rather than 20. Statisticians would say this study was underpowered to reach its goal. A better study with more patients, longer follow-up, or a better primary outcome measure might have rejected the null hypothesis and provided class-I evidence that implant surgery was beneficial. An underpowered study is one more reason that failure to prove that surgery is effective does not prove that it is ineffective.

Now we can envision a more robust study of cell implant surgery. Perhaps we would follow the patients for two years instead of one and use the UPDRS as the primary outcome measure. We would enroll more patients, asking the statistician for a power calculation. We might decide to study only patients younger than 60. Why did the experienced investigators who designed the original study not take these precautions? After all, the experiences of George Carillo, Juanita Lopez, and others had already shown that postoperative improvement might not be evident until the second year after surgery. Part of the answer is that hypotheses are cheap, but proof is often expensive. Studying 20 patients over one year resulted in a study that cost many millions of dollars. More patients and more years of follow-up would further increase the cost. Furthermore, recruiting patients willing to commit to possible sham surgery can be challenging. Additional demands, like age less than 60 and commitment to an extra year of follow-up exams and scans, makes patient recruitment even more difficult. Physicians joke that the "retrospectoscope" is the best diagnostic tool. Unfortunately, investigators cannot use it when they plan studies. Even after correcting some of these deficiencies, subsequent controlled study of cell implant surgery has failed to prove the benefit of implant surgery.[14]

When the investigators published the results of the controlled implant trial, headlines on the front page of *The New York Times* read PARKINSON'S RESEARCH IS SET BACK BY FAILURE OF FETAL CELL IMPLANTS.[15] The science journalist wrote that the study "failed to show an overall benefit but also revealed a disastrous side effect." A few days later, in an op-ed piece in *The Times,* Dr. Jerome Groopman called the dyskinesias "catastrophic" and urged that implant operations for Parkinson's disease be stopped while efforts concentrated on much more basic research. The science writers' view of the dyskinesias as catastrophic or disastrous is arguably an exaggeration; many of the patients with dyskinesias had had dyskinesias before the surgery, and the operation was a gamble that they took because of the severity of their Parkinson's disease. Some of these patients had subsequent surgery on their globus pallidus, successfully controlling the dyskinesias.

I agree with Groopman that continued basic research on Parkinson's disease is essential. For example, research with stem cells might provide better cells for implantation and more understanding of how to control the growth of the cells once they were implanted in the brain. This is just one example why many patients with Parkinson's disease are avid advocates of stem cell research.

Although a few surgeons still do brain implants and argue that the surgery is justified in young patients who have severe Parkinson's disease, other successful surgical procedures have eclipsed fetal cell surgery.

Undoubtedly, the glamorous possibility of brain transplantation will continue to capture imaginations and attract future investigators. Groopman emphasized that the early attempts at bone marrow transplantation in the 1950s resulted in fatalities, but continued basic research led to bone marrow transplantation techniques that now save many lives. The science fiction of brain transplantation will be closer to reality later in the twenty-first century.

Gene Therapy

Gene therapy, manipulating bad genes or inserting new good genes, is another treatment that is progressing from science fiction to actual medical practice. Scientists have been thinking about how it might apply to Parkinson's disease. Could surgeons stereotactically rearrange the genes in human brain cells? Remember that in a few families a gene called parkin is a cause of autosomal recessive, early-onset Parkinson's disease. If a person had Parkinson's disease due to possessing two bad copies of the parkin gene, would there be any way to replace the bad parkin gene with a normal gene? Would the gene need to be placed in the substantia nigra only, distributed to all nerve cells, or inserted into an embryo very early in development so that the whole body would be protected from abnormal parkin function throughout life?

For an autosomal dominant gene like α-synuclein, those who possess a single bad allele of the gene are likely to develop Parkinson's disease. The bad allele leads to the presence of a defective protein in nerve cells. Gene therapy would need to turn off or prevent function of the defective gene.

So far, manipulation of the parkin or α-synuclein genes in the human body is not feasible, and even if it were possible, it probably would not help patients with idiopathic Parkinson's disease who have normal function of these genes.

A different approach to gene therapy is to add extra genes to protect dopamine nerve cells from death or dysfunction. Imaginative investigators are considering a number of different genes. For example, the gene for a protein called GDNF (glial cell–derived neurotrophic factor) is a potential candidate for this kind of therapy.

Nerve growth factors are proteins that occur naturally in the body and promote cell growth and health. In cell cultures, dopamine nerve cells grow better if the GDNF growth factor is in the culture medium. Animal models can also test GDNF. For example, if GDNF is injected into a rat's brain, the amount of brain dopamine increases. Furthermore, GDNF injected into the brains of monkeys seemed to reverse some of the parkinsonian effects of MPTP poisoning.

On the basis of its benefits in cell cultures and animal models, investigators tested GDNF in patients with Parkinson's disease.[16]

Using stereotactic techniques, neurosurgeons placed plastic tubes through burr holes in the skull into the ventricles of patients with Parkinson's disease. The ventricles are structures deep in the brain that contain spinal fluid. The surgeons injected GDNF through the tubes into the ventricles so that the GDNF would bath the adjacent basal ganglia. This GDNF treatment had seemed to help monkeys poisoned with MPTP, but the human patients with Parkinson's disease had no evident benefit from the injections, and many patients had adverse effects like nausea, vomiting, loss of appetite, and weight loss.

The failure of GDNF to help these patients with Parkinson's disease does not disprove the hypothesis that GDNF can protect or improve dopamine nerve cells. Perhaps the GDNF needs to be delivered closer to the cells. Investigators have tried to do this by infusing the GDNF through plastic tubes placed directly into the putamens of patients with Parkinson's disease.[17] Many of the first few patients treated this way improved, as shown by the following testimonial:

> With his condition deteriorating from Parkinson's disease last year, Steve Kaufman gave up making improvements to his home in Algonquin, Ill. 'I couldn't even hold a nail stable,' he recalled. Earlier this year, after taking an experimental drug in a clinical trial, Mr. Kaufman built new kitchen cabinets and an outdoor deck. He was so steady he could walk across a narrow piece of lumber like an Olympic gymnast on the balance beam.[18]

Just as with fetal cell implant surgery, investigators proceed from individual drug trials to a randomized controlled double-blind experiment. All patients who entered the trial underwent surgery for placement of the tubes into the putamen through burr holes in the skull. They connected the tubes to pumps placed under the patients' skin. For 17 patients the pumps continually sent GDNF into their brains; for the other 17 patients the pumps sent only saltwater. Investigators promised the patients that those receiving saltwater could get GDNF six months later if the treatment was safe and effective. Mr. Kaufman received GDNF and improved miraculously. However, when the data were analyzed from all the patients, those receiving saltwater, on average, did just as well. Eight of the 14 most improved patients had received only saltwater.

The saltwater infusion is another example of a placebo. In Latin, *placebo* means "I shall please," and whether a placebo actually pleases a patient is partly controlled by the patient's expectations. For example, placebo injections are often more potent than placebo pills because most people believe that injected medicines are stronger than swallowed medicines. Placebo surgery can be even more effective than placebo injections.

I have described many placebo-controlled drug and surgical treatment trials. Scientists, reviewing these and similar studies, have learned that placebos can have powerful and long-lasting effects by actually changing brain chemistry. For example, in the controlled trial of fetal cell implants, the effects of implants and of sham surgery were very similar. The results were reanalyzed based on whether the participants, when questioned shortly after the surgery, thought that they had had the implants; nearly equal numbers of those who actually had implants and those who had sham surgery guessed that they had had implants. The surprising and impressive finding was that those who thought that they had had implants did better than those who thought that they had had sham surgery. This placebo effect of surgery was still evident a year after the burr holes were placed. Furthermore, in other trials, PET scans imply that when placebos improve symptoms of Parkinson's disease, patients are actually releasing more dopamine in their brains.

Thirty-four patients participated in the GDNF putamen infusion study. When the six-month experiment ended, patients who had received GDNF could continue to get infusions, and many of those who started on placebo chose to get the GDNF infusions. However, after analyzing the experimental results, Amgen, the manufacturer of the GDNF, stopped supplying it to the patients. Amgen stopped the drug trials partly because GDNF did not have proven value compared to placebo and partly because ongoing animal experiments suggested that GDNF might be toxic to some brain cells. Furthermore, some of the patients who were receiving GDNF started making antibodies against the infused drug. Amgen was concerned that these antibodies could lead to other adverse effects by inactivating natural GDNF elsewhere in the brain or by promoting brain inflammation.

When the trials ended, patients who thought that they had benefited from the infusions were devastated and besieged Amgen with letters. "'It's almost the same thing as a diabetic losing their insulin,' said Mr. Kaufman." Some had used the GDNF for up to three years, had clearly improved in their daily function, and argued that the placebo effect would be unlikely to persist for months or years. Nonetheless, the company refused to provide the drug. Undoubtedly sensitized to criticism of their industry after the Vioxx debacle, they were unwilling to give patients a drug of unproven benefit and unknown dangers. "'How can we ethically justify administering this drug?' said Roger Perlmutter, executive vice president for research and development."

Patients sued Amgen to try to force the release of the drug. On the television show *60 Minutes,* patients described their plight after being deprived of GDNF. Some physicians and organizations like the Parkinson Disease Foundation sided with the patients. They pointed to additional evidence that GDNF might be beneficial. For example, the patients underwent PET scans before and after the infusions; on these scans the dopamine neurons had brighter signals after the GDNF infusions.

I spoke with a woman who had been in the GDNF study and received GDNF rather than placebo infusions. Being a study patient was demanding, particularly for someone already slowed and fatigued by her illness. She had brain surgery under general anesthesia, had multiple MRI scans, traveled twice across the country because PET scans for the study were done in New York rather than in her hometown, and had another operation to remove the pump after the study. She was extremely disappointed when she could no longer get GDNF. She believes the drug was helping her, and she has deteriorated since the drug was stopped, yet we have no way to know how much of her deterioration is the natural course of her Parkinson's disease and how much is due to loss of GDNF benefit. I admire her courage and sacrifice; although she had no long-term benefit, the whole community of patients and investigators has progressed toward a cure of the disease, even with a negative study.

The investigators in the GDNF infusion study naturally reviewed the study results, trying to learn from the failure. Some urged Amgen to continue GDNF trials, looking for more effective doses or better ways to administer the drug, but as of late 2005, the company continued to refuse to provide it. "Mr. Kaufman in Illinois said after several weeks off the drug, he already feels his stamina slipping and his shaking becoming more pronounced. 'I don't think we were given a fair chance,' he said."

Perhaps a fair chance for reversing the cellular changes of Parkinson's disease requires a much more aggressive and imaginative tack. Perhaps the nerve cells need to make the GDNF themselves. Could gene therapy be the way to really get GDNF where it is needed in the brain? Investigators have isolated the gene for GDNF and placed in it a virus. They then inject the virus-GDNF combination into the substantia nigra, caudate, and putamen. The virus infects the dopamine cells so that the extra GDNF gene enables these cells to make more GDNF. The extra GDNF protein is now just where it needs to be to empower the dopamine cells. This approach seems to work in monkeys. Researchers injected monkeys' brains with MPTP. Some of the brains were then injected with a virus carrying a gene for GDNF; other monkeys were injected with a placebo gene, which does not benefit or injure nerve cells, attached to the virus. In the monkeys that got the placebo gene the MPTP-treated brains lost dopamine function. However, monkeys injected with MPTP and then with GDNF genes did not show the MPTP toxicity.[19]

On the basis of these very promising results in the MPTP-treated monkeys, should similar trials proceed in humans? So far, other forms of gene therapy have shown much more promise than proven human benefit. Gene therapy is being investigated for hundreds of different diseases. Myriad research laboratories, journals, scientific societies, and Internet Web sites are devoted to gene therapy. Yet no form of human gene therapy has progressed past the investigative stage to become standard medical care.

Gene therapy is an exciting idea, so naturally, its failures are described vividly in the popular press. As Sheryl Gay Stolberg wrote in *The New York Times Magazine*, "Ever since it became a reality nine years ago, gene therapy has been the bright promise of medicine. Then an experiment went very wrong."[20] Stolberg tells the moving story of Jesse Gelsinger, who died after receiving therapy aimed at correcting a deficiency of a gene called OTC. For Gelsinger the healthy OTC gene was attached to a virus called adenovirus, and the combination was injected into his liver, where this gene normally functions, not into his brain. Tragically, Gelsinger died of liver and lung failure within a few days of the injection. Every investigator who contemplates infecting humans with gene-carrying viruses dreads similar disasters.

Every human gene therapy experiment in the United States must past multiple levels of review. Like all other human experiments, it should be reviewed by an IRB. Because the gene is considered a drug, the regulations and review processes of the FDA apply to gene therapy. Another review committee that is unique to human gene therapy experiments is the Recombinant DNA Advisory Committee of the National Institutes of Health. The committee, known as the RAC to members of the gene therapy community, reviews every proposal for NIH-funded human gene therapy research and sets high standards for ethical and safe research. For example, any proposal for GDNF gene therapy would need to consider not only the surgical dangers common to the stereotactic neurosurgical approaches, but also issues such as the following.

1. Might the virus cause encephalitis?
2. Could the brain react to the injection by forming antibodies or other immune responses that could inflame or damage the brain?
3. Could the virus infect other brain cells besides dopamine nerve cells and cause destructive effects of GDNF in these cells?
4. Should the virus-gene combination include a mechanism to turn the GDNF gene off if the treatment is so successful that it leads to toxic excess of dopamine activity? The gene therapists can engineer clever tricks when they the insert DNA into viruses that allow oral medications to control gene expression.

A very difficult question, which investigators, ethicists, and review committees will undoubtedly debate, is whether GDNF gene therapy trials are more appropriate for patients with early or advanced Parkinson's disease. Traditionally, experimental therapies with unknown dangers are first tried on patients with the bleakest hopes for benefit from conventional treatments. Patients with advanced Parkinson's disease are more likely to gamble on innovative treatments, despairing, like Fuller Albright when he opted for brain surgery, that their lives are so impaired that they have little to lose. The paradox is that a treatment like GDNF gene therapy, aimed at restoring and preserving brain cell function, might succeed in early disease but fail if the brain damage has progressed too far. A failure of gene therapy in patients with severe Parkinson's disease might discourage future research in this area, just as the failure of the fetal cell implant trial has virtually stopped cell implant surgery.

Surgery for Parkinson's disease has had a spectacular history. Investigators and patients have joined on the literal cutting edge of scientific discovery. When surgeons first sliced into the mysterious depths of the brain and early progress came through vague understanding of brain function and serendipitous surgical mishaps, there were no IRB, FDA, or RAC barriers to the surgeon's imagination and patient's courage. One safe gamble is that even with modern attention to ethics and safety, future progress in Parkinson's surgery will feature dramatic failures and successes.

At age 88, a year after he first rejected surgery, my father's tremor was worse so that he sometimes had difficulty eating. Using a fork was hard, and eating soup with a spoon was impossible. He drank through a straw because liquid would slosh all over if he lifted a half-full cup. He was happiest if the meal featured finger foods like hamburgers or ribs. He again asked his neurologist about surgery, and again, the neurologist suggested consultation with the neurosurgeon about stereotactic placement of a small lesion on one side of the thalamus. Relief of tremor in just one hand would make it easier for him to feed himself; however, my father was feeling even more fragile and once more chose to live with the known burdens of his illness, rather than gamble on surgery. These decisions are very personal and difficult. Fortunately, he has been able to carefully consider his options and maintain his intellectual autonomy, despite his increasing physical impairments.

CHAPTER NINE

Living with Parkinson's Disease

The effects of illness on the quality of someone's life is a complex question, dependent not only on the illness and its manifestations, but also on much else, such as the person's personality, caregivers, financial and social resources, past experiences, and other medical problems. Even if I, as a physician, cannot cure a disease, I want to alleviate its symptoms and to comfort and support my patients, so I am particularly interested in research that has investigated factors that influence the quality of the lives of those who have Parkinson's disease. The research uses questionnaires that ask people about many aspects of their lives: mobility, activities of daily living, emotional well-being, the stigma of the disease, social support, cognition, communication, and bodily discomfort.[1] The results suggest that although tremor is the calling card of the shaking palsy, patients find that other aspects of the disease, such as imbalance, risk of falling, depression, constipation, urinary problems, pain, changes in behavior and mental prowess, and disturbed sleep, are much more disruptive of their lives.

Mood, Behavior, and Parkinson's Disease

I asked Dad about his mood. Was he feeling depressed or down or blue? Living with a progressive degenerative neurological disease is a psychological burden. Patients can react to it with a full palette of emotions: anxiety, depression, anger, passion. When Dad answered with a laconic "no," I was not surprised. As long as I have known him, my father has been optimistic, emotionally even keeled, and undemonstrative. He is fortunate because optimism is a personality trait that improves parkinsonians' experience of the quality of their lives. For years Dad has been stoic about medical symptoms. When he wrote *The Doctor* about his experiences with cancer, his editor continually needed to remind him to tell his readers how he was feeling about his illness. I asked him about his mood because I was concerned that he might be feeling depressed but not showing it or talking about it spontaneously.

Patients with Parkinson's disease are often depressed, but assessing their moods requires more than a superficial glance. Most of us guess our friends' moods by watching their faces and actions. We suspect depression when we see bland disinterest rather than smiles and energetic movements. Sometimes family and physicians overlook depression in a patient with Parkinson's disease because a blank stare due to facial masking or apparent apathy due to bradykinesia distort these routine clues to mood. The patient's face is as immobile as a mask, which conceals his emotions rather than hiding his identity. Furthermore, some aspects of serious depression, like disturbed sleep or appetites, can be caused by Parkinson's disease itself rather than by depression. To decide whether a patient with Parkinson's disease is depressed, you need to ask questions about mood rather than rely on outward appearances of expression and activity.

Depression can precede or follow onset of Parkinson's disease. For some, depression develops only after movement is impaired. However, epidemiological studies show that people who have been depressed are more likely to develop Parkinson's disease. Furthermore, subtle changes in personality, such as becoming more introverted or anxious, can precede the classic motor changes of the disease. These patients for whom depression precedes any other manifestation of neurological disease clearly show that the depression is not merely an emotional reaction to having a neurological illness.

Depression and Parkinson's disease are both diseases with abnormal brain chemistry. Just as previous chapters have explored multiple facets of Parkinson's disease, like clinical manifestations, epidemiology, genetics, environmental causes, nerve cell circuitry, brain imaging, and so on, we could have an entire book exploring the same scientific issues in depression. Abnormal levels of neurotransmitters, especially serotonin and norepinephrine, occur in many depressed people, just as dopamine abnormalities occur in those with Parkinson's disease. The pathology of Parkinson's disease extends to some nerve cells that use serotonin and norepinephrine; furthermore, dopamine affects brain control of mood as well as brain control of movement, so there is a chemical basis for the depression in patients with Parkinson's disease. Thus the depression is another aspect of abnormal neurotransmitters, rather than simply a psychological response to dealing with a chronic illness. Fortunately, the mood of patients with Parkinson's disease can improve when they take antidepressant drugs designed to improve the neurotransmitter deficiencies. Physicians need to be sensitive to the easily overlooked emotional aspects of Parkinson's disease, especially because depressed patients lose quality of life and because depression is treatable.

Depression is only one of many psychological manifestations of Parkinson's disease. Other mental processes, such as memory, perception, or behavior, deteriorate in some patients with the disease. Physicians and patients now have extensive experience with these psychological problems; however, despite his skills as a clinical observer, James Parkinson did not detect these changes. He may have overlooked them for a number of reasons. He observed some of his patients only at a distance so would not have known details of their thinking. Or, his small group of patients might have been among the many parkinsonians who never develop psychological problems. Modern patients with Parkinson's disease are living longer, and for many the psychological problems develop late in their illnesses. In addition, some of the changes now seen are caused by or worsened by the medications used to treat the motor aspects of the illness. Dementia, confusion, and hallucinations are particularly common in patients with advanced Parkinson's disease.

Once again, I asked Dad if he was depressed. Again, he answered with a simple "no." I was concerned, however, by subtle changes in his emotional style. He seemed more likely to complain about his tremor. He cried uncharacteristically at a close friend's funeral. He was less resilient about minor daily annoyances. People are sometimes unaware of their own moods. Depression can be expressed by behavior changes or by symptoms of physical illness. But was I being too vigilant? It is commonplace to shed tears at a funeral. A son cannot do a psychiatric assessment of his parents. I asked Dad's neurologist to think about my father's mood on his next office visit.

Can L-Dopa Make People Gamble?

Before returning to the common mental changes of Parkinson's disease, I want to tell the story of a patient with a more unusual condition. He shows how hard it is to know why a patient with Parkinson's disease changes behavior. Perhaps he had a distinctive response to medication for his Parkinson's disease. He shows the challenge of detecting adverse drug effects, recognizing psychological manifestations of disease, and studying the brain chemistry and circuitry of the psyche.

One day, Mr. Norman came to my office with his wife for his usual appointment. I had been seeing him twice a year for the previous four years, treating his Parkinson's disease with L-dopa. On the medication he had a mild bilateral tremor, and although he walked slowly, he remained steady and independent on his feet, so I classified him as Hoehn and Yahr stage II. He was bright, alert, and, at age 75, still worked 20 hours each week. I asked him when he planned to retire. His wife, answering for him, surprised me: "He can't afford to retire because L-dopa turned him into a gambler. He lost all of his IRA playing video poker. I found an article on the Internet about L-dopa and gambling."

I had just learned that Mr. Norman was a pathological gambler. Most Americans do some gambling, and an estimated one or two percent of Americans are pathological gamblers who bet so compulsively that they lose much more money than they can afford or go into excessive debt. Pathological gamblers often disrupt their families, destroy their careers, or pursue crime to pay their debts. Psychiatrists view pathological gambling as a disorder of impulse control, similar to other forms of addiction. Pathological gamblers often have a history of drug or alcohol abuse or of mood disorders such as depression. However, in 25 years as a neurologist, I had neither seen nor heard of blaming excessive gambling on Parkinson's disease or on L-dopa.

After hearing the Normans' story, I wanted to know if anyone else had observed a relationship between Parkinson's disease or its treatment and pathological gambling. I read the article that Mrs. Norman brought me and did a PubMed search on "Parkinson's disease AND gambling" to find three other reports, the earliest from 2000, well over 30 years after L-dopa therapy became standard treatment for Parkinson's disease.

In these four papers, physicians described a few instances of people gambling compulsively while taking L-dopa or dopamine agonist drugs. For example, a 57-year-old woman started gambling pathologically after she began taking selegiline and a dopamine agonist, about 10 years after she developed Parkinson's disease.[2] Before she had taken these drugs, she had been treated with other drugs, including L-dopa, and she had not been gambling. She stopped gambling when she was treated with a dopamine antagonist drug, which unfortunately was likely to worsen her parkinsonian motor impairment.

A group of Spanish clinicians reported more experience with gambling and Parkinson's disease.[3] In a clinic that followed 250 people with the disease, there were 12 pathologic gamblers, 10 of whom started gambling only after being treated with L-dopa. Thus nearly five percent of these Spanish patients were pathologic gamblers, compared to less than two percent prevalence of pathologic gambling, at least among Americans.

The Muhammad Ali Parkinson Research Center in Phoenix, Arizona, reported on a retrospective survey of 1884 patients treated there for

Parkinson's disease.[4] They found nine compulsive gamblers; the highest prevalence (1.5 percent) was among those taking the dopamine agonist pergolide. Other studies have implicated the dopamine agonists pramipexole and ropinerole. These were not formal case-control studies, and prevalence of gambling in some clinics is not very different from the prevalence reported in the general population. Thus the medications are not proven causes of the gambling in every case, but we strongly suspect a causal association because in many instances the gambling seemed to start within in months of beginning the medication.

These reports associating gambling and treatment of Parkinson's disease are not careful epidemiological studies. Furthermore, apparent associations do not prove causation. Hill's four criteria for inferring causation from epidemiological studies are statistical correlation, dose-response relationship, temporal relationship, and biological plausibility. If investigators wish to pursue the gambling–Parkinson's association, they should undertake formal epidemiological studies, either case-controlled or prospective cohort, with more attention to the doses of medication used. Undoubtedly, design of the studies would need to consider various potential biases, and multiple studies would be needed to confirm a statistical association. These studies have not been done, but we can still speculate about whether an association between gambling and treatment of Parkinson's disease is biologically plausible.

Of course, neuroscientists try to understand psychological changes in terms of nerve cell connections and chemistry. Although most dopamine cells in the midbrain send their axons to the putamen, others connect to parts of the brain, such as the frontal lobe, that control mood, memory, and behavior.

Some experimental results about nerve cell function in gamblers make a relationship between gambling and treatment of Parkinson's disease plausible. Even before the reports of parkinsonians gambling compulsively, investigators were studying the role of brain dopamine in gambling. Many of the techniques that are used to study Parkinson's disease, such as brain imaging, genetics, microelectrodes, and animal models, can also yield information about brain activity during gambling.

Scientists study the gambling brain by creating situations in which the subjects, human or animal, have a chance at a reward, which they may or may not receive. For example, monkeys may learn to expect a reward of food in certain circumstances. Experimenters, recording with microelectrodes from dopamine nerve cells in the monkey midbrain, found that the cells fire when the reward is expected, keep firing if the reward is received, but stop firing if the reward is not received. Thus if similar mechanisms work in humans, a human gambler would have active dopamine nerve cell firing while placing a bet or awaiting the outcome of the bet, continue firing these cells after winning bets, but stop firing cells after losing bets.

The microelectrode studies cannot be done in humans. However, brain imaging studies with techniques like functional MRI, PET, or SPECT scanning show that areas of the frontal lobes that receive dopamine nerve cell connections are active during betting or while winning bets but are not active after losing bets.

In another set of experiments, pathological gamblers who did not have Parkinson's disease had less dopamine and more chemical products of dopamine breakdown in their spinal fluid than did nongamblers.[5] Some gamblers had higher levels of dopamine in their blood after a winning streak. Other gamblers, when compared to nongamblers, had variations in blood activity of the enzyme MAO that helps dopamine breakdown.

Genetic studies also support a role for dopamine in gambling behavior. Some pathological gamblers have genetic variations in their dopamine-receptor genes.

The neurobiology of gambling is undoubtedly complex. Other experiments show that many neurotransmitters, including serotonin, epinephrine, and opioids, change in gamblers. Scientific understanding of the gambler's brain is rudimentary. Even though current knowledge suggests a relationship between gambling and brain dopamine, scientists have hardly proven that treatment of Parkinson's disease can cause gambling.

Mr. Norman's experience with gambling and Parkinson's disease introduced me to another intriguing issue about this complex disease. My response to his problem is patient centered rather than purely scientific. Scientifically, I know that a few examples of gambling parkinsonians do not prove an association between gambling and Parkinson's disease. I spoke with him without data from a published, controlled study of the incidence of gambling in healthy people compared to those with various neurological conditions. In recent years, legal gambling has spread widely in the United States, and older Americans are gambling more and more. Perhaps finding people who both gamble and have Parkinson's disease is simple coincidence resulting from this proliferation of gambling.

Clinically, I can respond to Mr. Norman without scientific proof, while intellectually reserving judgment about gambling and Parkinson's disease and awaiting more research on the subject. When I heard Mr. Norman's story, my first concern was his welfare. I wondered whether his medication should be changed just in case doing so would protect him from further losses. Both he and his wife assured me that now that they understood his problem, he had been able to stop gambling by careful self-monitoring and by allowing his wife to control their finances.

His antiparkinsonian medication was controlling his symptoms well, and he did not want to change this medication.

I have already mentioned that James Parkinson found no mental problems in his patients with the shaking palsy. Perhaps he overlooked mental problems because he did not ask the right questions. When taking a medical history, I had never routinely asked my patients about gambling. Now that I have started doing so, I have found other gambling parkinsonians; so far, I have not found them gambling pathologically. I may begin to suspect that the patients with Parkinson's disease gamble more or less than other patients.

If I want to learn the most from my observations, I need to design an experiment in advance, using the methodological care discussed in other chapters: form a null hypothesis, carefully define the patient population, choose an appropriately matched control group, have a prescribed set of questions about gambling and criteria for diagnosing pathological gambling, and use appropriate statistical methods to analyze the results. The requirements of this study exceed my resources and those of most physicians who practice by themselves or in small groups, which is one reason that most clinical research is done in larger institutions or by groups of collaborating investigators.

Mr. Norman's experience shows how hard it is to detect and prove adverse effects of medications. The FDA releases drugs for sale in the United States after phase-III clinical drug trials establish safety and efficacy, usually by testing a few thousand patients for a number of months. After the drug is released, phase-IV monitoring for drug safety begins. All too often, we recognize drug toxicity only after many thousands have taken the drug or after it has been taken for many years.

A striking example made the headlines in 2004. The potential of Vioxx, an inflammatory drug called a COX-2 inhibitor, to increase the risk of heart attacks was not recognized until long after it became one of the most popularly prescribed drugs in America. The heart attacks occurred in two or three of every 1000 people taking Vioxx, compared to one of every 1000 in a control group. Heart attacks are relatively common, so the increased risk was established only after controlled study of thousands of people. Once we are aware of the proven risk, we can easily see, in retrospect, basic science and clinical suspicions of the adverse effect. Now attorneys advertise widely, searching for potential clients who have had a heart attack while taking Vioxx or who had gambling losses while taking drugs for Parkinson's disease, so the courts are participating in the debate on when physicians and drug manufactures knew or should have known the dangers of Vioxx and of drugs for Parkinson's disease.

In November 2004 the FDA approved the new drug called natalizumab (Tysabri) for the treatment of multiple sclerosis (MS). MS can devastate the nervous system, and natalizumab promised to be the best drug ever available to treat it. It was released after clinical trials lasting less than two years in about 2000 patients. This was a so-called fast track release; the drug was rushed to market because of apparent extraordinary benefit for a bad disease. I treat many patients for MS. A few were deteriorating despite the best standard medicines, and I prescribed natalizumab for them within a few weeks of its release. In contrast, the majority of my MS patients had stabilized on the standard medicines. Many of them asked me about natalizumab. After discussing the pros and cons, most of these patients agreed with me that we should delay starting the new medicine until there was more knowledge of its chronic effects.

In February 2005, two MS patients who had taken natalizumab as part of one of the early experimental groups died of a rare brain infection called PML, or progressive multifocal leukoencephalopathy. They were among the 2000 patients who had been on the drug for over two years. PML is rare and is due to failure of the brain's immune system. Natalizumab was designed to turn down the immune system, so it was immediately implicated as the cause of the infection and removed from the market. This rare but fatal side effect was discovered very early in phase IV because it was so unusual and was consistent with the actions of the new drug.

Vioxx and natalizumab are only two of many examples of delayed recognition of adverse events; they have inspired a vigorous debate about how the FDA, the drug companies, and the medical community can improve phase-IV monitoring.

Even though I am personally unable to do my own clinical experiment on gambling and Parkinson's disease, I can still participate in the scientific process. In fact, every physician should report unusual or little known possible adverse effects of drugs to the FDA. Sometimes adverse effects are found only after 10,000 or even 100,000 people have taken a drug. The FDA usually approves a drug for sale after clinical trials in hundreds or at most thousands of patients. Rarer adverse effects come to attention only after thousands more patients take the drugs, so physician reporting of unusual experiences is an important mechanism for continually improving the safety of the drugs that we prescribe.

Throughout this book, I have repeatedly discussed treatments without mentioning a very important process called obtaining informed consent. I will digress to discuss it here because I have been thinking cautiously about what to tell my patients about gambling before I prescribe treatment for their Parkinson's disease.

Every time a physician treats a patient, the physician must tell the patient the details of the treatment, the treatment alternatives, and the treatment risks. When I do this, I encourage the patient to ask questions, which I try to answer. If the patient accepts the treatment after this discussion, the patient's acceptance is called informed consent. For every drug prescription the physician and patient need to discuss the drug, alternatives, and potential adverse effects so that the patient is properly informed before consenting to take the drug.

Having good informed consent discussions with patients is a challenging art. I encourage the patient to bring a family member or friend along for the discussion. Even if the patient has no difficulty with thinking, concentration, or memory, the family member can contribute helpful questions and help the patient remember the discussion. Giving the patient written material about the prescription is also useful.

Table 9.1 shows the more serious and more common potential adverse effects of L-dopa. Most patients who take L-dopa have no serious reactions to it. Others will have to tolerate annoyances such as dry mouth, mild nausea, or light-headedness. The patient needs to know that serious, even deadly reactions can occur, but these are rare, and for the patient with advanced Parkinson's disease, not taking medication can be even more dangerous than taking it, because of complications like falling and breaking bones or poor swallowing leading to choking or lung infections. The friend or family member should be taught to notify the physician promptly if the patient becomes depressed, confused, hallucinatory, or behaves uncharacteristically. Dyskinesias, wearing-off, and on-off reactions do not usually occur until the patient has been taking medication for a few years, but these reactions need to be discussed early in treatment so that the patient can make an informed decision about issues like delaying start of treatment or using dopamine agonists instead of L-dopa. The physician needs to talk about all these issues without inappropriately frightening the patient, causing so much anxiety that the patient imagines ill effects after taking a few pills, or scaring the patient away from taking medication. In fact, cynics might say that there is little truly informed consent because the physician, by slightly shifting the emphasis of the discussion of benefits and adverse effects, can frighten almost any patient into taking or not taking the medication.

With so many issues that need to be part of the informed-consent discussion, should pathological gambling be added to the list of potential adverse effects, even though it is still unproven to be an effect of L-dopa and even though it may be quite rare? Pathological gambling is just one of many behavioral aspects of drug therapy. Some say that men are more prone to pathologically gambling, whereas some women develop pathological shopping. Other patients develop compulsive behaviors or increased sexuality. Rather than specifically mentioning gambling, I warn my patients and their families that behavior can change during Parkinson's disease, with or without therapy, and ask family members to call me if they have any concerns about changes in the patient's behavior, thinking, or personality.

TABLE 9.1: Known Possible Adverse Effects of Taking L-dopa

Rare serious or deadly reactions	More common reactions
Suicide or thoughts of suicide	Drooling or increased production of saliva
Damage to red blood cells, causing anemia	Agitation, confusion, anxiety, hallucinations
Damage to white blood cells, increasing susceptibility to infections	Nausea or vomiting
Damage to blood platelets, increasing susceptibility to bleeding	Headache
Liver damage	Light-headedness, or even fainting, after standing up rapidly
	Malaise
	Fatigue, excessive sleepiness, or napping during the day
	Dry mouth
	Extra movements, dyskinesia
	Muscle spasms
	Wearing-off of drug effect or sudden freezing (on-off)
	Increased sex drive or increased sexual content in dreams
	Leg swelling

When I warned one of my bradykinetic patients and his wife that his medication might change his behavior, he asked me what I meant. "For example," I replied, "some patients who take L-dopa find that it increases their sex drives. Sometimes the medication can cause visions, hallucinations, or confusion. We are wondering if it infrequently leads people to start gambling." He smiled, "If L-dopa lets me start gamboling, I'll be very happy."

Are Parkinson's Disease and Alzheimer's Disease Related?

So far, my mother has had little to say in this narrative of disease. She does have neurological disease, and she likes to tell a good story as much as Dad does. They have been married for over 64 years, and when I was growing up, they often told tales in tandem. The problem is that she cannot remember her stories anymore.

When she was in her seventies, she underwent heart surgery to bypass clogged arteries. When she awoke from surgery, her memory, which once contained every friend's phone number and, more important, every bit of family history, was decimated. Memory loss occurs in a few percent of those who have heart bypasses. There are many other causes of memory loss: brain tumors, strokes, vitamin B12 deficiency, and low activity of the thyroid gland are just a few examples from the list of possibilities, and, of course, she has been checked for these.

After the surgery, she forgot her old recipes, and to everyone's amazement, Dad actually prepared some of his own meals. Their illnesses have strengthened their long-standing symbiosis. He remembers her appointments and gets her to meals on time; she buttons his shirts and cuts his food at dinner.

Now that she is over 85, people often assume that she has Alzheimer's disease. Alzheimer's is the most common cause of memory loss, and nearly one-half of people over 85 have it. Alzheimer's causes very distinctive pathological changes in the brain, distinctly different than the Lewy bodies of Parkinson's. Perhaps now Mom has both Alzheimer's and memory loss due to heart surgery. Short of a brain biopsy, there is no way to know, and with current therapy, there is no need to know.

Patients with advanced Parkinson's disease can also develop dementia that affects their thinking, memory, and behavior. When this happens, there are many possible explanations. In the words of clinical medicine, there is a differential diagnosis for the dementia or confusion. Possible diagnoses for dementia, besides late effects of Parkinson's disease, include Alzheimer's disease, toxic medication effects, Lewy body dementia, and various other toxic, metabolic, or neurological abnormalities.

Parkinson's disease occurs in older people, the same age group that is vulnerable to Alzheimer's disease. These diseases are common enough that some people develop both. If someone who had both Parkinson's disease and Alzheimer's disease died, pathological examination would show not only the Lewy bodies and loss of black pigment in the substantia nigra that are typical of Parkinson's disease, but also other distinctive pathological changes elsewhere in the brain that are characteristic of Alzheimer's. Before death, there is no way to prove whether a patient with Parkinson's disease also has Alzheimer's.

Some patients who die with both Parkinson's disease and dementia have the typical brain pathology of Parkinson's disease in the substantia nigra but do not have the pathological findings of Alzheimer's disease. Instead, their brains show Lewy bodies present in parts of the brain not typically affected by Parkinson's disease, especially in parts of the brain cortex that participate in memory and thinking. These patients are now placed in a separate diagnostic category called Lewy body dementia.

There are pathological and clinical reasons to believe than Lewy body dementia is an illness that is distinct from Parkinson's disease and distinct from Alzheimer's disease. The Lewy bodies of Parkinson's disease and those of Lewy body dementia have identical microscopic appearance and chemical composition, but they differ in their location in the brain. Eventually, we hope to learn more about Lewy body dementia, such as its causes, diagnostic criteria, treatment, and even its prevention. For now, telling whether a demented person has Alzheimer's disease or Lewy body dementia is sometimes impossible while the person lives, and even after death, the pathological diagnosis is sometimes equivocal since some patients with Alzheimer's disease have a few Lewy bodies in their brains and some patients with Lewy body dementia also have some of the pathological changes of Alzheimer's.

Each of the drugs used to treat Parkinson's disease—L-dopa, dopamine agonists, anticholinergic drugs, amantadine, and so on—has the potential to cause adverse psychological effects, such as memory loss, drowsiness, confusion, agitation, and hallucinations. If a patient with Parkinson's disease becomes confused or demented, some antiparkinsonian medications are often cautiously decreased or stopped to see if the mental state will improve. Because Dad's memory now serves him and Mom, he and his doctors have been extremely cautious about increasing his drugs in any way that might impair his thinking.

Hallucinations, perceptions of things that are not present, can trouble patients with Parkinson's disease, particularly as the disease progresses and requires increasing doses of drugs for treatment. The hallucinations are most often visions but can include sounds, tactile feelings, and smells. The visions usually include recognizable objects, particularly people, but are sometimes miniaturized. At times, the visions are illusions, misperceptions of things that are present, rather than pure hallucinations.

Clinical clues about the hallucinations come from observing patients with mild or moderate Parkinson's disease who do not hallucinate. For some of these patients, treatment with L-dopa or with dopamine agonists causes particularly vivid dreams, especially erotic ones. Studies suggest that these patients sleep less soundly than others with Parkinson's disease and that they have more REM sleep. REM, or rapid eye movement, sleep is the stage of sleep when we normally dream. Hallucinations are analogous to dreaming while awake, and one theory is that these hallucinations are associated with REM sleep–like activity in the brain while the patient is awake.

The hallucinations become more common as Parkinson's disease progresses. There is no absolute level of medication or duration of illness that marks patients who hallucinate, but once hallucinations develop, they may decrease if the patient's doses of L-dopa or dopamine agonist drugs are decreased.

Most patients with Parkinson's disease who hallucinate understand that the visions are not real. However, those patients who are convinced of the reality of the hallucinations become increasingly anxious, agitated, or irrational. This is particularly true if the patient has both hallucinations and dementia. Such patients can need treatment with dopamine antagonist drugs to suppress the hallucinations, or at least to control agitated behavior. These patients present a treatment problem called the motion-emotion dilemma. Use of the dopamine antagonists to control the emotional effects of the hallucinations can worsen the motor deficits of Parkinson's disease; use of the antiparkinsonian drugs to improve their motion can worsen the hallucinations and dementia. The motion-emotion dilemma usually does not arise until late in the patient's illness, which is fortunate because agitated and demented patients sometimes need institutional care and treatment with drugs that further impair their mobility.

Psychological aspects of Parkinson's disease can greatly increase patients' distress and impairment. Today, clinicians and patients struggle with social and medication adjustments, balancing on the edge of the motion-emotion divide. Meanwhile, basic neuroscientists, who explore the brain mechanisms of these problems, offer hope of better solutions in the future.

Sleep and Parkinson's Disease

At age 86 my father was living in the large house where I grew up and where he had lived for over 50 years. Dad and Mom drove to the usual gamut of suburban activities, shopping for groceries, running errands, visiting friends and family. Early one afternoon, he was parking his car in his driveway, when a young woman drove up behind him and got out of her car. "I have been following you to be sure you're okay. Do you know that you fell asleep at a red light a mile back? You awoke and drove on before I could stop you, but I was worried that you would fall asleep again and have an accident." My father casually thanked her. As she drove away, he realized that his life had changed. Perhaps he recalled the grotesque joke "I want to die quietly in my sleep like my father, not in utter terror like the passengers in his car." He and Mom had been wondering how long they could stay at home. Now, he realized that he must stop driving. The loss of the freedom to drive prompted my parents to sell their house and move to an assisted-living apartment.

In years past, physicians might have ignored my father's sleep disorder, but now clinicians and investigators are awakening to the neurology of sleep. Many diseases affect sleep, which is not surprising because we sleep nearly one-third of our lives. Sleep patterns often change in neurological diseases because sleep is not just controlled by the brain;

sleep is actually a state of the brain. Just as a switch can be either on or off, the brain can be either awake or asleep.

The on-off switch is really too simple an analogy for the awake-asleep brain. Everyone knows from personal experience that the sleeping brain is not turned off. It actively monitors the body and the surrounding environment and then awakens when it senses a full bladder or a loud noise. It controls muscles so that the sleeper may be calm, tossing, turning, or twitching. It cycles through stages like the soundest deep sleep or the creative exuberance of dreams. A slightly closer, but still very simplistic, analogy for the awake-asleep brain is not a basic switch but a computer, which can be put in "sleep mode" to save power when not in full use.

The study of sleep in Parkinson's disease has followed a typical path of medical scientific inquiry: clinical observation, application of new techniques to clarify the observations, quantification of the clinical findings by epidemiologists, development of animal models, basic science investigation of the underlying anatomy and chemistry, human research on patients with disturbed sleep, and translation of the scientific findings into new methods for diagnosis and treatment.

Some initial observations about relationships between sleep and Parkinson's disease attracted scant attention. Since the 1920s, neurologists have known that those who developed postencephalitic Parkinson's disease often passed through a time of profound sleepiness during the encephalitic brain infection that preceded the parkinsonism, hence the name *encephalitis lethargica*. Another example is that when L-dopa is used to treat Parkinson's disease, some patients dream excessively, often with strongly erotic content, as a side effect of the drug. Despite these findings, most clinicians thought little about connections between sleep and Parkinson's disease.

As recently as the late 1990s, I, like many of my neurological colleagues, was asleep at the wheel about the importance of sleep for patients with Parkinson's disease. I rarely questioned my patients about their sleep habits. Then, in 1999, an article in *Neurology* aroused my attention:

> Abstract: The authors report a new side effect of the dopamine agonists pramipexole and ropinirole: sudden irresistible attacks of sleep. Eight PD patients taking pramipexole and one taking ropinirole fell asleep while driving, causing accidents. Five experienced no warning before falling asleep. The attacks ceased when the drugs were stopped. Neurologists who prescribe these drugs and patients who take them should be aware of this possible side effect.[6]

The patients were all men with stage II Parkinson's disease on the Hoehn and Yahr scale. They were all taking L-dopa in addition to a dopamine agonist drug. Five of the men fell asleep behind the wheel suddenly and recalled no premonition or warning that they were falling asleep. The patients had no dementia, prior sleep problems, or prior driving difficulty. Some of the men stopped taking dopamine agonist drugs and had no further episodes of sudden inappropriate sleep.

Neurologists already knew that dopamine agonists could make people sleepy. The phase-II and phase-III trials, which led to drug approval by the FDA, found that a minority of those taking the drugs had increased drowsiness or napping. However, the 1999 report of unexpected, unheralded, potentially dangerous sleep attacks appeared after the drugs had been released for general prescription. On the basis of this postrelease experience, the drug manufacturers and the FDA modified the drug labeling to warn about the sleep attacks. The manufacturers wrote to all physicians in the United States, alerting us to this newly noted problem. I scrambled to identify all of my patients who were taking dopamine agonist drugs, not an easy task with traditional paper medical records, and wrote letters, passing the warning on to them and inviting them to call me or come in to review their medication.

The article in *Neurology* about drug-induced sleep attacks led to vigorous correspondence in the journal. Dr. Hoehn, junior author of the 1967 Hoehn-Yahr scale and now an old hand among neurologists, wrote that she knew nine patients, six men and three women, who had had similar attacks. In contrast, another neurologist who specialized in Parkinson's disease wrote that he had never heard of similar attacks from his patients. Some wondered whether the sleepiness was really caused by the dopamine agonists. Could it be caused by the Parkinson's disease itself, by L-dopa, or by other drugs? Some writers disparaged the report as anecdotal and called for more formal experimental investigation of the sleep attacks. Correspondents debated whether the best approach was a randomized controlled trial, a prospective or retrospective epidemiological investigation, or sleep laboratory studies. There was consensus, however, that neurologists needed to question their parkinsonian patients more carefully about sleep.

Our perception of the relationship between sleep and Parkinson's disease is clearly very dependent on how we ask about it and on whom we ask. The initial reports of irresistible sleep attacks among patients taking dopamine agonist drugs came from neurologists who specialized in Parkinson's disease, so these reports might provide a view biased toward a more severely ill group of patients. A sense of the magnitude of the problem among all patients with Parkinson's disease can come only from a more widely based survey. German researchers took this approach by mailing a questionnaire to over 6000 members of a club for those with Parkinson's disease.[7] About one-half of those questioned responded, and we cannot be sure if people were more likely to respond if they had sleep problems. Interviewers phoned those who reported sleep attacks and tried to question their caregivers as well.

In their questions the interviewers distinguished between sleep attacks and a more general tendency to nap. They confirmed that patients with Parkinson's disease frequently do nap, even if they do not have sleep attacks. This study offered no controlled questioning of nonparkinsonians of the same age, but other studies show that daytime napping is more common in those with Parkinson's disease.

This epidemiological survey found that about six percent of people with Parkinson's disease had had sleep attacks. The interviewers asked those with sleep attacks if they had warnings such as yawning, droopy eyelids, or sudden sense of sleepiness. They compared the severity of Parkinson's disease and the use of medications for those with and those without sleep attacks. Attacks were more common among men, among patients taking dopamine agonist drugs, among patients with longer duration of Parkinson's disease, and among patients who took more naps. However, there were a few patients who had sleep attacks without warning, even though they were not taking medication and did not have other tendencies toward napping during the day.

My patients rarely spontaneously tell me about their naps, but if I ask them, they readily admit to them. Now that I routinely ask about their sleep habits, I can confirm that they commonly nap more than once a day. Many of them are older, retired, and view the naps as harmless, well-deserved relaxation at a time in their lives when they have no pressing responsibilities or activities. Some, like my father, can fall asleep while driving or at the dinner table while other diners continue conversations around them. Sometimes I hear about the naps from a spouse: "He can fall asleep in midsentence." Obviously, I need to ask specifically about sleep attacks because if these are occurring without warning, the patient should not drive.

Many patients with Parkinson's disease enjoy or at least tolerate their naps. In contrast, physicians, as expected, approach excessive daytime sleepiness with a differential diagnosis (Table 9.2). For some patients the naps are an unavoidable part of the neurological changes of Parkinson's disease. For others, medications like L-dopa and dopamine agonists add to the sleepiness, and the naps decrease after dosage adjustments. In addition, anything that causes insomnia or interferes with sleep at night can increase sleepiness during the day. Insomnia, in turn, has a differential diagnosis, with some of the possible diagnoses more likely in patients with Parkinson's disease. This differential diagnosis can be clarified by watching and measuring sleep in a controlled setting called a sleep laboratory.

Experimental investigation of sleep progressed in the second half of the twentieth century using the polysomnogram, an electrical recording

TABLE 9.2: Differential Diagnosis of Excessive Daytime Sleepiness in Patients with Parkinson's Disease

Primary effect of Parkinson's disease

Medication effect

    L-dopa

    Dopamine agonist

    Anticholinergic

    Many others

Additional sedating medical illness (e.g., narcolepsy)

Sleep deprivation or insomnia

    Tremor or rigidity interfering with sleep

    Medication side effects (e.g., drug-induced dyskinesias, hallucinations) interfering with sleep

    Medical conditions (pain, getting up to urinate, etc.) interfering with sleep

    Sleep apnea

    Restless legs syndrome, periodic limb movements of sleep

    Depression

during sleep of body functions such as brain activity (EEG), heart rate, breathing, and activity in body muscles. Investigators in the early 1950s noted that the eyes move rapidly during certain phases of sleep and added eye movement recordings to the polysomnogram. They divided sleep into stages called REM (rapid eye movement) sleep and non-REM sleep. By waking hundreds of sleepers and asking if they were dreaming, sleep researchers showed that dreaming occurs during REM sleep rather than during non-REM sleep. While the muscles that move the eyes are very active during REM, other muscle activity is turned off. For example, an electrode over the muscles of the chin would show muscle contraction during non-REM sleep but muscle inactivity during REM sleep. The muscles of breathing are active during REM sleep, but arm and leg muscles are inactive.

A polysomnogram can show many aspects of normal sleep, such as how long it takes to fall asleep, how long sleep lasts, or how the brain electrical activity on the EEG changes during sleep. Polysomnograms can also characterize abnormal sleep and have led to better understanding of conditions like sleep apnea, narcolepsy, and restless legs syndrome. These sleep disorders are now recognized not only by physicians but also by the many who suffer from these common conditions.

One day in 2003, I had an appointment with Mr. Powell, a man in his late fifties who had been aware of his tremor for about five years.

I had met him two years after the tremor began and found that he did have Parkinson's disease. Fortunately, his rigidity and bradykinesia were minimal, and he needed only a very low dose of antiparkinsonian medication. When I asked him, as I now routinely do, if he was having any difficulties with sleep, he had no complaints. Then I turned to his wife and asked if he had ever struck out at her while he slept. "How did you know about that?" she asked. "Ten years ago, I moved into a separate bed after he repeatedly punched me while he was dreaming." She was amazed that I had guessed a problem that they had kept secret for a decade. I was wondering how often I had overlooked this problem in other patients by failing to ask the right question.

A few months before my conversation with the Powells, I had spent a morning at a continuing education course on Parkinson's disease and sleep. One of the lectures was on a condition called REM behavioral disorder, a sleep disturbance with distinctive symptoms germane to Mr. Powell. REM behavioral disorder occurs in men four times more often than in woman, typically begins in middle age, and consists of violent behavior during sleep.[8] Violent episodes can occur every few weeks or many times a night. The sleeper may flail, kick, punch, cry out, or fall out of bed. He may cut, bruise, or seriously injure himself or may hurt his sleep partner. Spouses have reported injuries including being punched, slapped, kicked, or even choked. Occasionally, the behavior is more complex, like sleepwalking, shooting a gun, trying to set the bed on fire, or attempting to jump out a window. If the sleeper is awakened and questioned about his activities, he usually explains that during a dream he was protecting himself from attackers, either people or animals. The dreams are usually of self-defense; other dreams like playing a sport, participating in an adventure, or planning offensive aggression are much less common.

Polysomnograms show that REM behavioral disorder occurs, as the name implies, while the sleeper is in REM, the time when we naturally dream. During normal REM sleep, most muscles, including those in the arms and legs, are paralyzed. The defect in REM behavioral disorder is a failure for this normal paralysis to occur, which allows the dreamer to act out his dreams.

Brain stem nerve cells control normal sleep. Specific areas of the brain stem, other than the substantia nigra, direct the different stages of sleep and the varied aspects of REM sleep. In REM behavioral disorder the brain stem nerve cells that should be inhibiting muscular action fail to do their job.

REM behavioral disorder was first discovered in alcoholics going through withdrawal. It was later noted in others, usually men over 50 who had no evident medical or neurological illnesses. However, if these men are watched for a few years, most of those with REM behavioral disorder develop other signs of neurodegenerative diseases, sometimes dementia, sometimes one of the rare degenerative conditions, but most often Parkinson's disease.

After I took the continuing education course, I improved the questions that I asked my patients about their sleep and made an extra effort to question my patients' sleep partners. Suddenly, I was uncovering REM behavioral disorder frequently. The diagnosis was clear once I knew the natural history of the disorder, and I could usually be confident of it without putting the patient through a formal polysomnogram. This is another lesson in the vagaries of observation. Science needs new insights like those of James Parkinson or of the physicians who first discovered REM behavioral disorder, and then clinicians must learn from these pioneers to hone their own observational skills. We do not hear when we do not know how to ask and how to listen.

Mr. Powell followed a very common pattern in that his REM behavioral disorder predated any other visible manifestation of his Parkinson's. He had adapted to it without medical help. We know medication, unrelated to dopamine, that very effectively suppresses REM behavioral disorder. I offered to prescribe it, but Mr. Powell was leery of pills and declined to take it. His wife was long accustomed to their separate beds and did not disagree. For now, this is the end of the story, but when we finally have neuroprotective drugs for Parkinson's disease, physicians may need to look more aggressively for REM behavioral disorder, especially in their middle-aged male patients, trying to identify those at risk for Parkinson's disease who might benefit from neuroprotection.

Investigators using animal models have learned much about the role of different brain stem cells, interlaced brain circuits, and specific neurotransmitters in sleep. The role of dopamine in sleep is obviously relevant to sleep in Parkinson's disease. Serotonin, norepinephrine, acetylcholine, and many other neurotransmitters affect sleep, and dopamine has seemed to play a minor role in sleep biology. Investigators have sought to reconcile this with the clinical sleep changes of Parkinson's disease. Experiments with the knockout mice (Table 9.3) and with narcoleptic dogs (Table 9.4) combine with the results of many other experiments to show that dopamine does promote wakefulness. This is consistent with the clinical observation that patients with Parkinson's disease, in which dopamine deficiency is characteristic, often have excessive daytime sleepiness. The basic science of sleep is incomplete. For example, the experiments with the knockout mice and narcoleptic dogs do not explain why L-dopa or dopamine agonists make some people sleepy.

Experimental observations of people with Parkinson's disease are expanding our understanding of their sleep. For example, PET or

TABLE 9.3: Basic Science of Sleep and Parkinson's Disease: Knockout Mice

Mice with genetic knockouts provide one animal model for studying the role of dopamine in sleep (Wisor JP, Nishino S, Sora I, Uhl GH, Mignot E, Edgar DM. Dopaminergic role in stimulant-induced wakefulness. *J Neurosci.* 2001;21:1787–1794). Knockout mice are mice that are bred to lack activity of a specific gene. Hundred of different kinds of knockout mice, each kind lacking a different gene, are available for research. To study the role of dopamine in sleep, investigators watched the sleep of knockout mice that did not have the gene for the dopamine transport protein. This protein in the wall of dopamine nerve cells recycles dopamine back into the nerve cell after the neurotransmitter has been released into the synaptic cleft. Mice that do not have the gene to make this protein are less able to recycle dopamine, so the dopamine stays active in the synaptic cleft longer than it would in normal mice.

Sleeping mice, like sleeping people, can be studied with polysomnograms. Mice that lack the dopamine transport protein spend more of each day awake than normal mice do. This suggests that the persistence of dopamine in their synaptic clefts promotes wakefulness.

Some drugs that normally keep people awake, like caffeine or amphetamine, a form of speed, also keep normal mice awake. The dopamine transporter knockout mice also stay awake longer when given caffeine but not when given amphetamine. The exact mechanism of caffeine-induced wakefulness is unknown. In contrast, amphetamine seems to work by blocking the dopamine transport protein. The knockout mice have no dopamine transport protein for the amphetamine to block, so the amphetamine does not act as a "speed" for these mice. The absence of amphetamine stimulation in the knockout mice is further evidence that dopamine plays a role in the balance between sleep and wakefulness.

SPECT imaging studies of parkinsonian patients with sleep disorders can show which parts of the brain are active in different sleep and awake states. Neuroanatomical studies after death search for connections between the location of pathological changes, such as Lewy bodies, and the development of sleep disorders. Drug trials check medications to see if they can improve normal sleep and decrease unwanted naps

The results of experiments are conflicting at times, so we still lack a cohesive model of sleep mechanisms in Parkinson's disease. An example of the conflict is the data on orexin, a neurotransmitter than promotes wakefulness (Table 9.5). Individuals with excessive daytime sleepiness due to narcolepsy have low levels of orexin in their spinal fluid, so investigators have naturally wondered whether orexin plays a role in the excessive sleepiness of those with Parkinson's disease. Confusingly, four studies on orexin in people with Parkinson's disease had divergent results, suggesting that only a fraction of those with Parkinson's disease have low orexin levels. If the levels of orexin measured by the different investigators are accurate, we must explain

TABLE 9.4: Basic Science of Sleep and Parkinson's Disease: Narcoleptic Dogs

Narcolepsy is one of the diseases that can cause excessive daytime sleepiness and other changes in sleep. Better understanding of narcolepsy has come from studying families of dogs that inherit the illness. Investigators have used narcoleptic dogs to study the role of dopamine in sleep (Wisor JP, Nishino S, Sora I, Uhl GH, Mignot E, Edgar DM. Dopaminergic role in stimulant-induced wakefulness. *J Neurosci.* 2001;21:1787–1794). The narcoleptic dogs had polysomnograms before and after being given intravenous amphetamine. As expected, when the dogs were given amphetamine, they spent more of their time awake. The experiment was repeated after tubes were placed through burr holes, deep into the dogs' brains, into the caudate. The tubes allowed investigators to measure the amount of dopamine in the fluid surrounding cells in the caudate. The dogs had more dopamine in this fluid when they were given amphetamine. Without the amphetamine, the dopamine would have been taken back into nerve cells and not been in the surrounding fluid. When the amphetamine blocked the dopamine uptake into the nerve cells, more dopamine remained in the synaptic cleft, where it would help keep the dogs awake.

why some patients with Parkinson's disease and sleepiness have normal orexin levels, while other patients with Parkinson's disease have low orexin levels. There are too many variables for us to sort out the answer here. Are the differences due to disease stage, variations in disease physiology (just as some patients with Parkinson's disease have tremor and others do not), differing causes of sleepiness, or effects of medication? This just begins a list of hypothetical explanations for the observations about orexin. No wonder that sleep in Parkinson's disease is now an active area of research.

TABLE 9.5: Orexin—A Neurotransmitter That Promotes Wakefulness

Orexin is a neurotransmitter, first described in 1998, that plays an important role in maintaining wakefulness. A few brain cells in an area called the hypothalamus are the only known source of orexin. The orexin-containing nerve cells send their axons to parts of the brain stem that control the balance between sleep and wakefulness. In animal experiments the orexin nerve cells fire more often when the animal is awake. When orexin is injected into the brain ventricles, animals spend more time awake and less time in REM sleep.

Failure of the orexin system seems to be an important factor in the excessive daytime sleepiness of narcolepsy. Narcoleptic people have abnormally low levels of orexin in their spinal fluid. In contrast, narcoleptic dogs have normal spinal fluid levels of orexin but lack orexinreceptors on their brain stem nerve cells. Either the lack of orexin that occurs in people or lack of orexin receptors that occurs in dogs can interrupt the brain circuitry for wakefulness and result in excessive daytime sleepiness.

As of 2006, research has not yet led to new clinical treatments for sleep problems in patients with Parkinson's disease. However, our increased awareness and understanding of sleep is already beneficial. By asking the right questions, I find some patients who need minor medication changes and others who need some advice about adjusting their sleep habits at night. I send a few patients for polysomnograms to diagnosis more puzzling sleep problems. Some patients just appreciate an explanation of the connections between their sleep experiences and their Parkinson's disease.

For millennia, mankind has been fascinated with sleep and with dreaming, but solving the clinical problems of sleep has occurred chiefly in the last few decades, when it has been a focus of scientific inquiry. Perhaps we will soon have drugs related to orexin to promote wakefulness or neuroprotective drugs to prevent brain degeneration in those with REM behavioral disorder. I expect many exciting solutions in the near future.

Fall and Injury Prevention

I often drive over to the Manor, the assisted-living apartments where my parents live, and pick them up for dinner. They walk slowly, cautiously to the car, usually with their canes or walkers in hand. For years Dad's disease had minimal effect on his walking, but by 2003, he needed his cane for extra support when he first arose or when he turned. He had already fallen a few times, toppling forward and bruising his face and arms. His friends watched him closely when he arose from the breakfast table because right after the meal, he was particularly vulnerable to light-headedness, at times nearly fainting. In late 2004 his neurologist prescribed a specially designed walker for him. Of course, this meant that he was deteriorating, but he took some satisfaction in having the latest high-tech walker, especially because Medicare was paying for it. My mother needs her cane because of severe degenerative arthritis of her knees that makes each step painful and unreliable. She has not had a serious fall, but statistics show that she is more likely than my father to break a hip if she does fall. Hip fractures occur more than twice as often in women than in men. My mother-in-law, who also lives at the Manor, is a case in point. She has had two hip fractures and worked hard in rehabilitations after each; now she must shuffle to the car with her cane or walker.

Our parents fear falling not only because they are unsteady on their feet but also because of what they see at the Manor. Almost weekly, they tell us about fallen and injured friends or neighbors. Their experience is common to the elderly everywhere. More than one-third of people older than 65 years fall each year, and many experience multiple falls.[9] About 1 fall in 10 leads to serious injury.

A broken hip is one of the most common and devastating injuries. Nearly one-third of women who live to age 88 break a hip. A broken hip is costly not only in terms of dollars spent for hip surgery and rehabilitation but also in terms of subsequent lost mobility and failing health. After a hip fracture, at least a quarter of people are unable to walk or are severely disabled, and within a year of the fracture, at least one-sixth of those who break a hip die.[10]

Like many physicians, my father is a teacher. When he tells me about the latest fall among his friends, his bit of gossip is offered as another lesson that my colleagues and I should be doing more to prevent falls and injuries. How can investigators and clinicians work on this problem? If I were researching this problem, I would not start with test-tube experiments or animal models. I would ask epidemiologists and engineers, rather than biologists, to be my coinvestigators.

Arguably, a young investigator, altruistically planning a career for maximum benefit of parents and grandparents, would study fall and injury prevention rather than Parkinson's disease. The investigator might choose not to study genetics, cell biology, neurophysiology, or neurochemistry, but would need the same tools for scientific inquiry that neuroscientists use. The principles that apply to drug experiments, like hypothesis testing, randomized controlled trials, statistical calculations, and power analyses, also apply to evaluating ways to prevent falls and injuries.

Epidemiology provides tools to investigate the problem and its possible causes. One approach is a longitudinal cohort study that observes a selected group of people as time passes. For example, investigators monitored 336 persons who were at least 75 years old and living in the community rather than in institutions.[11] During one year, nearly one-third of the people fell at least once. The investigators then identified risk factors for falling, including use of sedatives, impaired thinking, leg disabilities, poor balance, or foot problems. The more risk factors that a person had, the more likely was a fall. Other prospective cohort studies have shown additional risk factors, including, not surprisingly, arthritis and loss of vision.

Depression, another risk factor, is not so intuitively obvious. Does depression make one more likely to fall because of the medication used to treat it, because the depressed person is less attentive to the surroundings, or because the depression accompanies other impairments? As usual, hypotheses are easier to find than answers.

Once investigators have identified the risk factors for falling, clinicians might help patients make protective changes. Some changes are so obvious that it does not take a neuroscientist to figure them out. It seems that anyone with a little thought could walk through a parent's apartment and see that slippery throw rugs are inappropriate and bright lighting is safer than dim. However, the problem of falling is resistant to simple solutions. One group of geriatric specialists designed a randomized controlled trial of patient counseling.[12] They randomized 165 people older than 65 years into two groups. A recreational therapist visited all the people in the control group at their homes, asked them about their leisure activities, and asked them to keep a diary of their falls. A specialist visited all the people in the treatment group, assessed their risk factors for falling, and then gave them and their physicians written recommendations about possible steps to decrease the risk of falling (Table 9.6). The idea for the specialized counseling is apple-pie simple and wholesome, but in the randomized controlled trial the counseling had no proven value for fall prevention. Notably, the study did not consider whether the people in the treatment group had made any efforts to follow the specialists' advice.

Exercise programs are a more successful tactic for fall prevention. For example, a randomized trial in women older than 80 years compared an exercise group to a nonexercise group. Physical therapists visited each woman in the exercise group at home for four exercise training sessions. The therapists taught the women exercises to do for 30 minutes three times each week. The control group received social visits rather than

TABLE 9.6: Risk Factors for Falling and Suggested Interventions Used by Hogan and Colleagues in Counseling Efforts to Decrease Fall Risk

Risk factor	Intervention
No rails for support getting into or out of the shower or bathtub	Advise on how to obtain grab bars
Abnormal gait	Refer for physical therapy, exercise training, or assistive devices, such as a cane
Visual loss	Refer to an ophthalmologist or optometrist
Unsafe behavior, such as climbing on chairs to change a lightbulb	Advise on risks of this behavior and discuss alternatives
Leg weakness	Suggest exercise program
Use of medications known to increase falls	Suggest medication review with physician for lowest possible doses and fewest possible medications
Drop of blood pressure when standing up	Review medications; advise physical approaches to blood pressure stability, such as sleeping with the head of the bed elevated

See Hogan DB, MacDonald FA, Betts J, Bricker S, Ebly EM, Delarue B, Fung TS, Harbidge C, Hunter M, Maxwell CJ, Metcalf B. A randomized controlled trial of a community-based consultation service to prevent falls. CMAJ. 2001;165:537–543.

exercise-training visits. After a year, the exercise group had about three-eighths fewer falls. In this study the women were actually taught the exercises, a more active approach than the counseling study in which the specialists only suggested exercise.

We would like to decrease the risk of falls and, if falls occur, decrease the chance that they will cause injury. Hip fractures are usually caused by falling directly on a hip, and among older people, perhaps one-quarter of falls on a hip lead to fractures. Women who fracture a hip are on average thinner than their peers who escape fractures. These observations lead to a hypothesis that the heavier women are less likely to have fractures because they have more fat both padding and protecting their hips. Investigators have pursued this hypothesis in the laboratory, dropping weights on slabs of pig tissue. They measured the force transmitted through the tissue and found that thicker tissue transmitted less force. Working from this laboratory observation that soft tissue can decrease the energy that impacts the hipbone in a fall, Lauritzen developed a hip protector, a shield made of foam rubber and plastic sewn into underwear to cover the hip and absorb some of the blow if a fall should occur.

Theoretically, the hip protector can prevent injury. Once the inventor has designed the device and the laboratory investigations show that physically, it might work, the new device needs to be tested in people as rigorously and as carefully as if it were a new drug. Investigators have tried the hip protectors in many older patients. In clinical trials they randomized frail, elderly adults to wear or not wear the protectors. In these trials, there were no sham protectors to use like placebo pills, so the randomized trials could not be double-blind. In initial trials, those given hip protectors had less than one-half as many hip fractures as those in the control group.

The early publications on hip protectors appeared in journals aimed at orthopedists and other bone specialists. Few physicians were aware of the new invention. However, in 2000, the *New England Journal of Medicine* published a larger randomized trial of hip protectors that confirmed their value.[13] After I read this article and an accompanying enthusiastic editorial, I asked my parents if they would try the protectors. My father said he would, but my mother rejected them as too much bother. She was also concerned that the protectors would cause unsightly bulges in her clothes. My father's protectors soon arrived in the mail, and he began to wear them regularly. Of course, day-by-day they seemed an annoyance rather than a therapy because their value is only apparent after a fall on the hip.

A treatment may have proven benefit when used under ideal conditions, yet not be effective in less than ideal settings. A key issue separating treatment of proven value from effective treatment is whether the patient follows the clinician's prescription. Convincing people to wear hip protectors is at least as difficult as convincing them to take their medicine.

Physicians know that their patients frequently do not take medicine as prescribed. Often, a drug treatment fails because a patient is taking the drug incorrectly or not at all. When physicians prescribe a drug, some patients will take it exactly as instructed, but most will not do so. The reasons for not taking medication as prescribed are myriad: high costs that prevent patients from filling the prescription, drug side effects, fears of drug side effects, poor memory or confusion, misunderstandings about what to take or when to take it, disbelief that the drug is beneficial, general reluctance to take pills, or mistakes about medications arising from receiving seemingly countless prescriptions from multiple specialists.

I try to help patients take their medications as prescribed. The patients and I review costs and try to choose the least expensive beneficial drug. We discuss possible side effects and adjust doses to minimize these. We keep the medication schedule as simple as possible. To make the schedule easier to remember, we try to link the medication times to daily activities like meal times or bedtime. I give the patients a written medication schedule, go over the schedule with them, and try to answer their questions. I encourage family members or caregivers to join our discussion so that they can help the patient adhere to the schedule. I encourage them to call me with questions as needed. Nonetheless, I often learn at their next appointment that they have not followed the prescription. There are more reasons for not taking medication correctly than there are patients.

Patients are more likely to take medication regularly if the medication has an easily perceptible benefit. High blood pressure pills are easily skipped or forgotten because the patient cannot feel changes in blood pressure from hour to hour or day to day. In contrast, patients with Parkinson's disease are likely to take their L-dopa or dopamine agonist regularly, especially if their symptoms are better shortly after taking the medication and worse if they forget to take it.

My father was reliably taking his L-dopa. To help him take his medication on schedule, each week, we laid out his pills in a container with separate compartments for the daily morning, noon, and evening doses. No pills are left in the container at the end of the week. However, by the time he turned 90, he realized that he was making errors because of failing vision, imperfect memory, and a more complex regimen, so he asked the medication aides at the assisted-living facility to bring him his pills on schedule.

Fall prevention, like successful drug treatment, requires active patient participation. Despite all the science of randomized controlled treatment trials, the individual patient and individual clinician working together may not achieve the treatment results promised by the experiments. An experimental treatment trial commonly includes ways to remind patients to take the treatment and to measure how often they miss their treatment. For example, the trial of exercise for fall prevention queried the participants monthly to collect diaries of their falls. This simple act of monthly questioning would remind participants of their commitment to exercise three times a week. With my own patients I might advise exercise when I see them in my office only once or twice a year, so they would be less likely to stick with an exercise program.

On the basis of epidemiological studies, controlled treatment trials, and common sense, I advise my parents and my patients about how to prevent falls and injuries. The items in Table 9.6 are a starting point, and I supplement them with a prescription for physical therapy training for gait safety and regular exercise, assessment of the need for assistive tools like a cane or a walker, and advice to buy and use hip protectors. None of these approaches is foolproof, but if exercise can prevent a significant portion of the falls and hip protectors can prevent half of the hip fractures when falls occur, we at least make some progress. Nonetheless, I still get a disturbing number of calls from the emergency room that one of my patients with Parkinson's disease has broken a bone in a fall.

For my father, wearing his hip protectors is not as automatic as taking his L-dopa. He often decides not to bother with the protectors. In 2003 a treatment trial with hip protectors found that there was nearly equal risk of fractures whether or not patients were given the devices. However, most of those who had fractures were not wearing their protectors when they fell and broke their hips. I can warn my father about this, but the protectors are a nuisance, requiring special underwear and extra effort, effort that he does not always make. One study suggested that if 41 frail, elderly adults wore the protectors daily for a year, one of them would be spared a hip fracture. The hip protectors have proven therapeutic value based on well-designed, randomized, controlled studies. The hip protectors are cost-effective therapy: The cost of 41 sets of protectors is much less than the cost of one broken hip. Unfortunately, for my father they cannot be effective therapy because he does not wear them regularly.

I said that fall injury prevention research might start with epidemiologists and engineers; however, they cannot solve the problem themselves. Obviously, psychologists and experts in human motivation and behavior need to be part of the research team, and each patient bears personal responsibility for fracture prevention.

CHAPTER TEN

Conclusions

What Happens to Brain Cells to Cause Parkinson's Disease?

Science is the star of this narrative on Parkinson's disease, heroically working to solve mysteries. We might imagine our hero as a hard-boiled detective, someone like Joe Friday who wants "just the facts, ma'am." Unfortunately, real scientific facts can be much more elusive than the "facts" in works of fiction. Science, the detective, rarely assembles all the suspects at the end of the case to clarify all the clues and seldom points a finger at a single culprit. Science cannot always destroy the villain at the end of the book.

Scientists do try to review the evidence from multiple experiments, improve models, and look for unifying theories that explain the results, setting the stage for new experiments and better treatments. For Parkinson's disease a major goal is neuroprotection: avoiding the cell death and dysfunction that cause the disease. In the twentieth century the model of the synapse gradually improved, eventually leading to L-dopa treatment. Next, better understanding of brain anatomy and neurotransmitters accompanied new operations and new medications to treat Parkinson's disease. Now, we need to examine the cellular and chemical causes of cell death, searching for clues that will assist scientists in preventing the disease.

Parkinson's disease is one of the neurodegenerative diseases, all characterized by premature death of nerve cells. Alzheimer's disease,

TABLE 10.1: Excess Nerve Cell Death Seen in All Four of the Most Common Neurodegenerative Diseases

Disease	Major areas of nerve cell death	Principal clinical features
Alzheimer's disease	Frontal, parietal, and temporal cortex	Dementia
Huntington disease	Caudate	Chorea, psychosis
Lou Gehrig's disease	Motor nerve cells in cortex and spinal cord	Weakness
Parkinson's disease	Substantia nigra	Tremor, bradykinesia, rigidity, postural instability

Lou Gehrig's disease (also known as amyotrophic lateral sclerosis or ALS), and Huntington disease are other common neurodegenerative diseases, and there are many less infamous but equally destructive diseases in this class. For each neurodegenerative disease, specific nerve cells die in specific areas of the brain (Table 10.1). In each of these diseases, there is a gradual loss of the brain functions normally controlled by the dying cells. In Lou Gehrig's disease the dying cells are motor nerve cells from the part of the brain cortex that controls muscle strength and other motor nerve cells in the spinal cord. People who have Lou Gehrig's disease lose strength in the muscles that would normally be controlled by the dying cells, but they do not lose memory, thought, language, sensation, or vision because the cells that participate in these brain activities do not die prematurely.

In Alzheimer's disease, other cerebral cortex cells die, especially in the frontal, parietal, and temporal lobes. People with Alzheimer's disease lose memory and the ability to think clearly. Their personalities and behaviors deteriorate due to the death of these cells, but their motor nerve cells, and hence their strength, are unaffected.

The cell death in Huntington disease is most striking in a deep portion of the brain called the caudate. The clinical results are abnormal movements, called chorea, and mental changes, such as dementia and psychosis.

For Parkinson's disease the chief cell death is deep in the brain in the substantia nigra, and cells also die in a few other brain areas. The mystery of the neurodegenerative diseases is not only why the cells die, but also why different cells die in each disease.

In Parkinson's disease, cells die mainly by a mechanism called apoptosis, which causes relatively subtle microscopic changes in brain tissue. Its pronunciation is debated; I prefer the *snap, crackle,* and *pop* of *ay-pop-toe-sis.* The apoptotic cells shrivel and disappear. Apoptosis derives from a Greek word for "falling leaves," appropriate to this relatively quiet demise.

Apoptosis is sometimes called cellular suicide because the cell death is controlled by complex chemical changes within the cell itself. However, if it is cell suicide, it is assisted suicide because the self-destructive cell processes are often started by signals from outside the cell or chemical disruptions within the cell. Once the process of apoptosis starts, a regular chain of chemical reactions leads to death of the cell, so another term for apoptosis is programmed cell death.

Apoptosis of some cells is a normal, vital part of development and life. During fetal growth, apoptosis removes excess cells. If it were not for apoptosis, we would all be born (if we were born at all) with webs between our fingers and between our toes. Throughout life, extra cells in the blood, immune system, and elsewhere die by apoptosis; if these cells did not die, cancer would be more common, as would so-called autoimmune diseases in which the body has extra immune cells attacking normal tissues.

What causes the excess apoptosis in Parkinson's disease? The cause might not be the same in each case of Parkinson's disease. We know about the unusual cases in which the cell death in Parkinson's disease is clearly due to bad genes, toxic drugs, or infections. Let's look at how these exceptional cases provide clues to the cell death that underlies all the other cases of idiopathic Parkinson's disease.

A protein called ubiquitin seems to be everywhere, at least wherever causes of Parkinson's disease are discussed. It has even made its way into current fiction. In Andrea Barrett's short story, "The Mysteries of Ubiquitin,"[1] Rose, a young investigator, tries at a dinner party to explain her research to a cellist:

> I look at a protein called ubiquitin. It has that name because it is so abundant, and found in all kinds of cells—in people, beetles, yeasts, everything. And it's almost identical in every species. What it does—in your cells, in any cells, proteins are continuously synthesized and then degraded back into their component amino acids. The degradation is just as important as the synthesis in regulating cellular metabolism. Ubiquitin molecules bind to other proteins and mark them for degradation. Without that marking and breaking down, nothing in the cells can work.

Rose was a biochemist, not a clinician, and was not particularly interested in Parkinson's disease, but ubiquitin may be a vital clue to the mechanism of cell death in Parkinson's disease. Investigators have made antibodies against ubiquitin and used these antibodies to stain brain tissue, showing where the protein is most abundant. As Rose said, it is found in all brain cells, but in patients with Parkinson's disease, ubiquitin concentrates in large clumps in the Lewy bodies.

Ubiquitin is important to the genetics of Parkinson's disease. The α-synuclein mutation was first associated with Parkinson's disease in 1996; over the next decade, investigators found at least a dozen other genes that could cause Parkinson's disease. Only a minority of patients with Parkinson's disease has mutations in these genes. However, researchers can study the proteins produced by these genes, trying to understand the function of the proteins in the normal brain and searching for clues to the cause of run-of-the-mill, idiopathic Parkinson's disease. The first three genes found to cause Parkinson's disease were α-synuclein, parkin, and UCH-L1. Each of these is closely linked to ubiquitin and protein breakdown. Of course, this observation has prompted many experiments on the role of ubiquitin in Parkinson's disease.

A mutation in the gene for α-synuclein was the first proven genetic cause of Parkinson's disease. The gene is autosomal dominant: An individual who inherits one bad copy of the gene will develop Parkinson's disease as an adult. After geneticists linked the α-synuclein mutation to Parkinson's disease, investigators made antibodies against α-synuclein, labeled the antibodies, and used them to stain brain tissue. The antibody staining showed that Lewy bodies are rich in α-synuclein, just as they are rich in ubiquitin. Lewy bodies are filled with α-synuclein not only in people with dominantly inherited Parkinson's disease, but also in those with sporadic Parkinson's disease who have normal α-synuclein genes. Lewy bodies also contain other proteins, including UCH-L1.

The techniques that molecular geneticists use to study the role of these mutations are ingenious. Investigators can breed animals, including primates or rodents or fruit flies, that have copies of the mutant gene or lack both the normal and the mutant genes. They can look at genetic changes in cells in test tubes or in living animals.

Investigators, trying to understand how genetic defects in α-synuclein, parkin, or UCH-L1 can cause Parkinson's disease, have focused attention on how nerve cells in the substantia nigra control their own protein content. Our genome is our collection of genes; our proteome is our collection of proteins. The genome and proteome are closely linked since specific genes synthesize each protein, and DNA and RNA regulate protein synthesis. Once a protein is synthesized, details such as how it is activated, modified, or folded; how long it lasts in the cell; and how it is destroyed or inactivated are important to the life of the cell. Intense recent interest in genomics is now being matched by attention to proteomics.

Inside cells, the proteasome, a small structure or organelle, is part of the system for degradation of proteins. Enzymes repeatedly attach the small ubiquitin protein to the other proteins scheduled for destruction. Once many ubiquitin molecules have been attached, other enzymes working with the proteasome cut the protein into small fragments.

Mutant α-synuclein appears to interfere with normal proteasome function, leading to premature cell death. Abnormal parkin or abnormal

UCH-L1 also can prevent the proteasome system from ridding the cell of proteins that are no longer needed. Finding α-synuclein, ubiquitin, and UCH-L1 in Lewy bodies of patients with idiopathic Parkinson's disease has prompted hypotheses that these proteins facilitate premature apoptosis in idiopathic Parkinson's disease, even when these proteins are coming from normal rather than mutant genes.

In a family from Iowa that has autosomal dominantly inherited Parkinson's disease, the gene defect causes excess production of normal α-synuclein, another bit of evidence that the normal α-synuclein protein, which everyone has, may be important in Parkinson's disease.

After Rose tried to explain ubiquitin to her dinner companion, she mused to herself that "she'd left out everything important but still the cellist looked mystified." The role of ubiquitin and protein breakdown in Parkinson's disease is still mysterious, a subject of intense investigation. One theory is that failure of protein breakdown causes the apoptosis that underlies Parkinson's disease. However, much remains to be explained. Why, for example, do those who develop Parkinson's disease because they inherit two bad copies of the parkin gene not have Lewy bodies as part of their pathology? A competing theory is that, at least in idiopathic Parkinson's disease, the protein breakdown products in the Lewy body are debris left behind by dying cells but are not the primary cause of the apoptosis.

The MPTP story has highlighted the role of toxins, particularly those that damage mitochondria. This toxicity is not caused directly by the MPTP, but by MPP+, a breakdown product that poisons mitochondria. Any theory of toxins causing Parkinson's disease needs to explain why dopamine nerve cells are specifically injured. MPP+ is one of the molecules that can bind to the dopamine transport protein, so dopamine nerve cells take it up much more than other nerve cells do. MPP+ poisons mitochondria by blocking normal action of complex I of the series of enzymes that generate energy for the cell.

Recently, investigators have developed a new animal model of Parkinson's disease. They injected rats with rotenone, a common pesticide that poisons energy-producing enzymes of the mitochondria. The rats treated with rotenone developed an illness somewhat like Parkinson's disease. They were less active, moved with a flexed posture, and became rigid. Their brains had abnormal dopamine nerve cells, which contained inclusions, like Lewy bodies, filled with α-synuclein. This model is tantalizing because it dovetails with previous observations: epidemiological studies that show that pesticide exposure is a risk factor for developing Parkinson's disease and cellular studies that show that mitochondrial enzyme complex I is less active than normal in some patients with Parkinson's disease.

Some people believe that antioxidants guarantee good health. Seemingly, every skin cream, potion, elixir, or vitamin is advertised as an antioxidant. Antioxidants are touted as preventing cancer, heart disease, aging, and Alzheimer's disease. There are innumerable antioxidant drugs. Most health food stores offer ample supplies of vitamins C and E, selenium, coenzyme Q_{10}, *Gingko biloba,* and β-carotene, to name a few.

There are some truths behind the hype. Oxidation is the chemical reaction that adds oxygen to molecules and occurs naturally and frequently throughout the body. Excessive oxidation can damage cells and seems to occur in many neurodegenerative diseases, including Parkinson's disease. However, if we could totally prevent oxidation with drugs or health foods, the chemical reactions in the body would grind to a deadly halt.

Because vitamin E fights oxidation, it was chosen as one of the potentially neuroprotective drugs for Parkinson's disease used in the DATATOP trial. Vitamin E was not proved effective in that study. There has even been a suggestion in other analyses that large doses of vitamin E might be dangerous, but the failure of vitamin E has not deterred neuroscientists from further studies of oxidation in Parkinson's disease. Perhaps, someday, the right dose of the right antioxidant drug will be an important treatment for Parkinson's disease. Of these, coenzyme Q_{10} is the leading candidate for a neuroprotective antiparkinsonian drug, but if it is effective, it may work by improving mitochondrial complex I, rather than by antioxidant action.

Some of the genes, other than parkin, identified as causes of early-onset Parkinson's disease affect the mitochondria or protect the cell from excessive oxidation, rather than modifying the ubiquitin-proteasome system. These are more evidence that mitochondrial failure and oxidation figure in the causation of at least some cases of Parkinson's disease.

Excitotoxicity is another theory that has been offered as a cause of Parkinson's disease. Excitotoxicity refers to a possible bad effect of some neurotransmitters. Dopamine and many other neurotransmitters cross the synapse and stimulate or excite nerve cells as part of the normal, nontoxic, everyday work of the brain. The theory of excitotoxicity is that these same neurotransmitters, if released in excess or if stimulating cells that are already partially injured, can become toxins rather than routine messengers between healthy nerve cells. One hypothesis is that dyskinesia and other late side effects of long-term L-dopa therapy are prompted by excitotoxicity of excess dopamine created by the drug therapy.

One more theory is that cells die in the substantia nigra in Parkinson's disease because of excitotoxicity of the neurotransmitter glutamate. The bodies of the glutamate nerve cells are in other parts of the brain and send their axons to the substantia nigra. In a rat model of Parkinson's disease, drugs that block some glutamate receptors are neuroprotective, slowing deterioration of the diseased rats.[2] If this truly happens in humans, is the excitotoxicity the primary cause of the Parkinson's disease or a secondary promoter of cell death, once something else like mutant α-synuclein or MPTP has already damaged the nerve cells in the substantia nigra?

Rose's boyfriend was an older scientist, who specialized in whole organisms—beetles, in his case—rather than in cells and molecules. Unlike the cellist, he had studied science for years, yet he did not quite understand Rose's research. When she tried to explain it, "he smiled and held out his hands palm up, in a gesture of incomprehension. 'Different generation,' he said, 'And a whole different field.'"

As a clinician with over a quarter century of experience, I share his bemusement. Clinicians and basic scientists have different viewpoints. I look at the new experiments, struggle to understand the basic science, and realize that each area is just part of the puzzle. I listen to the excitotoxicity theories with hope tinged by pessimism. Although excitotoxicity has been a fashionable topic in neuroscience research, so far, it has not led to useful new treatments. Repeatedly, blockers of excitotoxins have emerged from animal experiments as possible treatments for other diseases, like Lou Gehrig's disease or stroke; have been tested in elaborate human clinical trials; and have failed to show clinical benefit. These treatment trial failures reflect the complexity of human disease. Successful treatment of diseases like Parkinson's will probably require strategies aimed not just at excitotoxins, or oxidation, or ubiquitin, but also more broadly at multiple interlocking causes of the disease.

Apoptosis, abnormal protein breakdown, environmental toxins, mitochondrial failure, neurotransmitter excitotoxicity, and excessive oxidation are all popular areas for Parkinson's disease research. This list is hardly exhaustive, and within each of these topics, there is no end to details, refinements, hypotheses, and future experiments. Like Rose, some would say that the explanation in this chapter leaves out everything important. We can, however, try to link these ideas as building blocks for a model of the causes of Parkinson's disease, a model that recognizes that for each person with the disease, both environment and genetics play some role. Undoubtedly, year by year, this model will become more detailed, more specific, and more useful. Science, the detective, is learning that Parkinson's disease is not a single villain but a conspiracy, a complex conjunction of a genetically unique, vulnerable human body and the environmental stresses—infections, chemicals, oxidants, or even emotional events evoking extra neurotransmitters—that mark a lifetime.

Living Better with Parkinson's Disease

My ill father, despite his long years of medical training and practice, is more interested in practical issues of living with the disease than in experimental details. When he wrote *The Doctor* about his experiences with cancer, he emphasized his rights to be treated by his physicians as a person, not just as a patient. The European Parkinson's Disease Association offers a charter of these rights for those with Parkinson's:[3]

1. to be referred to a doctor with a special interest in Parkinson's disease
2. to receive an accurate diagnosis
3. to have access to support services
4. to receive continuous care
5. to take part in managing the illness.

To Be Referred to a Doctor with a Special Interest in Parkinson's Disease

Anyone who has read this book is familiar with the many complexities of Parkinson's disease. Diagnosis, prognosis, cause, treatment with drugs or surgery, and management of complications all require expertise, which includes knowledge from specialty training and experience from caring for patients. In general, neurologists are the specialists who have the most expertise in this area, but some internists, gerontologists, rehabilitation specialists, and others also make the commitment to know and treat Parkinson's disease well. Patients should never hesitate to ask about their physicians' training and experience, nor should they hesitate to consult specialists in their illnesses.

To Receive an Accurate Diagnosis

The right to accurate diagnosis means both that the diagnosis should be correct and be clearly explained to the patient. For some patients with Parkinson's disease the physician knows the diagnosis at a glance; for others, accurate diagnosis requires repeated examinations over time, medication trials, or brain imaging. This is another reason that patients should seek out physicians with a special interest in Parkinson's disease and other movement disorders. When I am puzzled by findings that are not classical for Parkinson's disease, I will ask one of my colleagues for a second opinion. Even the best neurologists can make diagnostic errors, and no patient needs to feel embarrassed to ask about the certainty of the diagnosis, the need for more testing, or the desirability of another opinion. When my patients ask me for a second opinion, I am delighted to guide them to the subspecialist most likely to help with their problem, whereas if they are afraid to offend me and instead choose a consultant on their own, they often receive a less expert answer.

To Have Access to Support Services

No one with Parkinson's disease needs to face the illness alone. My patients often bring their spouses or close friends with them to appointments, and these caregivers are their first line of support. A patient with mild illness might need no physical assistance but only a partner to ask questions of the physician, remember medications, and provide solace. As the illness progresses, a caregiver helps tie shoes or provides a steadying arm on a walk. If the disease worsens, causing markedly impaired mobility, frequent falls, or dementia, the partner often needs help from professional caregivers.

Over the years my parents have gradually gotten more help in their assisted-living facility. At first they lived in the Manor as if it were an ordinary apartment house. My mother helped Dad with buttoning his shirts. When his hands were too shaky to write or use the computer, my son helped him send out the checks for his monthly bills. Later, when my father found that he was most likely to fall shortly after breakfast, he arranged for an aide to accompany him from the dining room to his apartment after the meal. Most days, he could use his walker; on bad days he was pushed by wheelchair. Eventually, he arranged for a caregiver to walk beside him on his daily walks. He found that he was forgetting to take his medications and asked that the medication aides bring them to him on schedule. Of course, over time, some patients become even more dependent.

Each patient with Parkinson's disease has evolving needs for physicians as the illness progresses. Early in the illness, a physician's visit once or twice a year may be the only care needed. Even when patients are seeing Parkinson's disease specialists, most will also need to maintain contact with another primary physician or other care provider. My father needs his internist to help with varied medical problems typical of those his age. The internist helps him with issues like his diabetes, and if he were to get pneumonia or another infection, his internist, rather than his neurologist, would treat it.

I usually send my patients to a physical therapist if they are having trouble with walking or balance. The therapists can teach exercises to make walking safer and advise about assistive devices like canes and walkers. I expect that a few therapy sessions will meet these initial goals, but the patient will need to continue exercising regularly after the therapy ends. Early in his illness, my father exercised by hiking alone or with friends; later, he patiently pushed his walker around the grounds of the assisted-living complex. His walker has a seat so that he can rest as needed. Now we encourage him never to go out alone because he often needs a steadying hand. Others with Parkinson's disease swear by Tai Chi for balance or yoga for flexibility. In our community the YMCA provides a special exercise group for parkinsonians, and the Parkinson's Resources of Oregon offers exercise and movement classes that I recommend to my patients.

Depending on specific needs, parkinsonians may also need other rehabilitation specialists. Occupational therapists can facilitate daily activities, teaching exercises to improve coordination, ways to eat despite tremor, or the best tricks for dressing and bathing. Speech therapists are very important if swallowing becomes difficult.

Dad's physician arranged for an occupational therapist to go my parents' apartment in the Manor and survey it for safety. Dad says bluntly, "At first I thought it was bunk," but he was impressed by improvements the therapist recommended, like adding night-lights, moving phone and extension cords that might trip him, and removing throw rugs that could slip underfoot.

I tell my patients about community support groups where they can meet regularly with others facing similar problems. Some, particularly those with mild disease, avoid these groups; perhaps they are shy about their illnesses or fear that seeing others with more advanced disease will be discouraging. Many patients benefit from sharing their challenges and often return to my office with new questions about the medicines or therapies they hear about from group members. Spouses or the caregivers also find support in these groups, and some prefer groups for caregivers without patients present so that they can vent their frustrations and challenges.

For patients with Parkinson's, depression and other disorders of mood, behavior, or thinking can be the greatest barriers to enjoying life. When this happens, I can provide initial treatment. We now have a wide selection of psychiatric medications and can manipulate myriad neurotransmitters to improve memory, mood, delusions, hallucinations, and similar problems. Choosing the best treatment for an individual patient can be complex. My patients and I often consult psychiatrists for their expertise in adjusting psychotherapeutic drugs and in other forms of psychotherapy. The patients' primary care physicians also play an important role since drugs for Parkinson's disease must be adjusted based on each individual's other medications and illnesses.

To Receive Continuous Care

In the course of a chronic illness lasting many years, someone with Parkinson's disease is likely to work with many caregivers, support people, therapists, and physicians. Continuity can be lost through moves, retirements, and changes in medical insurance. I think patients are most comfortable and best treated when they can maintain contact with a single physician, whether neurologist or primary care physician, throughout their illnesses.

To Take Part in Managing the Illness

I hope that I have made it clear that every patient with Parkinson's disease has a distinct illness and has more expertise in his or her personal needs than any physician has. Patients need to choose their physicians with care and then talk freely with them. I encourage patients to take notes, to read about their illnesses, and to ask me questions. I am delighted when they bring their caregivers to appointments so that we can have another source of information about the patients' conditions, another questioner, and another memory about what we decide together.

Every physician knows that patients do not always take their medications as prescribed. They fail to fill a prescription because of its cost or for fear of adverse effects. They forget to take their medication or, worse still, take something else instead. I know how easy this is because I have done it myself, even after a simple tooth extraction. Patients with Parkinson's disease probably actually do better than many others in taking medications on time because a missed dose or an extra dose can have such a marked effect on tremor and other movements.

When their medication schedule is at all complex, I give my patients a written list of when to take which pills. I try to teach them about intended drug effects and possible side effects and urge them to keep me informed about their response so that together, we can adjust doses and timing of drugs. However, even when my prescriptions are precisely planned and patients adhere to them perfectly, Parkinson's disease will often defy our teamwork. The symptoms of Parkinson's disease usually wax and wane unpredictably, so we rarely control them totally. With few exceptions I urge my patients not to adjust medication on their own because trying to increase medication whenever symptoms worsen often leads to overmedication and more adverse effects.

Patients with Parkinson's can improve their health by good nutrition and regular exercise. Exercise helps with balance, flexibility, and fatigue; it is good for the brain, not just for the heart and other muscles. If patients' walking becomes unsteady, they should be aggressive about fall prevention. This includes asking for physical therapy training; using assistive devices, such as canes and walkers; and considering the use of hip protectors. Table 9.6 lists some other ways to decrease the risk of falling.

When parkinsonians are depressed, they have extra need to facilitate their own care. Physicians can help improve depression only when patients seek help with mood and pursue prescribed therapies. This alliance between patient and physician is especially important when depression is impairing the patient's quality of life.

Patients need to tell their physicians about all their symptoms. At an office visit I can see how a patient moves or shakes, but I learn about mood, thinking, sleep, pain, constipation, and all the other nonmotor symptoms only if the patient or caregiver tells me. I try to ask about all these nonmotor symptoms at every visit with a patient, but if a physician does not ask these questions, the patient should insistently talk about his or her problems.

The expanding research on so many aspects of Parkinson's disease is a source of hope. As new drugs become available, patients should participate, whenever possible, in experimental drug trials. Probably less than one patient in a hundred with Parkinson's disease currently does this, and investigators will need many more patients to adequately test promising new treatments. Of course, before becoming a research volunteer, patients need to confer with their physicians to be sure that the experiment does not have undue risks and will not interfere with their usual treatments.

Patients can also battle Parkinson's disease politically. For example, the Parkinson's Action Network (PAN) (www.pan.org) is a patient-centered organization that lobbies Congress and other parts of the government not only about research funding, but also about scientific policies, like how the FDA should regulate new drugs and where the NIH should concentrate it resources. When I went to Washington with the PAN, I was inspired by walking the halls of Congress with hundreds of patients with Parkinson's disease and their caregivers.

The Story of Parkinson's Disease Is Not Finished

Parkinson's disease is fractally fascinating. We can take any aspect of it, study it in detail, then break that detail into many smaller details. A PubMed search finds over 11,000 articles on parkinsonism published in peer-reviewed medical journals in the first six years of the twenty-first century. Each basic scientist with a specific research area, such as genetics or pathology or cell biology, can explore a fraction of the disease and will never run out of experiments to look more deeply.

Patients want prevention and cure without delay; they need answers before they lose more nerve cells. To them, scientists seem bradykinetic and dyskinetic, progressing too slowly and digressing randomly from the search for a cure. In 2006, at the first World Parkinson Congress, Michael J. Fox chided researchers that despite their prolific experiments, "I can't tie my tie any better."

Each patient has unique problems and will never run out of challenges as the disease progresses. This gap between the needs of patients and the slow, measured pace of science is inevitable; however, when patients and their caregivers understand the illness, when they comprehend the experiments of the scientists and the thinking of their physicians, they are at least better equipped to take part in managing the illness and to live a little more easily with Parkinson's disease.

Appendix: Reading about Parkinson's Disease

> Read not to contradict and confute; not to believe and take for granted; nor to find talk and discourse; but to weigh and consider.
>
> Francis Bacon, *Essays*, 1597

There are hundreds of books, thousands of articles, and myriad Web sites about Parkinson's disease. In the endnotes I cite many of the sources that I have used in writing this book. I list here just a sample of the books on Parkinson's disease that are well written and easily read without medical training.

Fox MJ. *Lucky Man*. New York: Hyperion; 2002.

Havemann J. *A Life Shaken: My Encounter with Parkinson's Disease*. Baltimore, MD: The Johns Hopkins University Press; 2002.

Langston JW, Palfreman J. *The Case of the Frozen Addicts*. New York: Vintage Books; 1996.

Morgan E. *Defending against the Enemy: Coping with Parkinson's Disease*. Fort Bragg, CA: QED Press; 1997.

Sacks O. *Awakenings*. New York: Harper Collins; 1990.

A number of books deal more concretely with living with and caring for Parkinson's disease. Examples follow.

Lieberman A. *100 Questions and Answers about Parkinson's Disease*. Sudbury, MA: Jones and Bartlett; 2003.

Lieberman A, Williams F, Imke S, Moscinski E, Falwell PB, Gordon H, LeVert S. *Parkinson's Disease: The Complete Guide for Patients and Caregivers.* New York: Simon & Schuster; 1993.

Weiner WJ, Shulman LM, Lang AE. *Parkinson's Disease: A Complete Guide for Patients and Families.* Baltimore, MD: The Johns Hopkins University Press; 2001.

The American Academy of Neurology has published a set of practice parameters that evaluate the best medical evidence on a number of issues about diagnosis, prognosis, and treatment of Parkinson's disease.

Miyasaki JM, Shannon K, Voon V, Ravina B, Kleiner-Fisman G, Anderson K, Shulman LM, Gronseth G, Weiner WJ; Quality Standards Subcommittee of the American Academy of Neurology. Practice parameter: evaluation and treatment of depression, psychosis, and dementia in Parkinson disease (an evidence-based review): report of the Quality Standards Subcommittee of the American Academy of Neurology. *Neurology.* 2006;66:996–1002.

Pahwa R, Factor SA, Lyons KE, Ondo WG, Gronseth G, Bronte-Stewart H, Hallett M, Miyasaki J, Stevens J, Weiner WJ; Quality Standards Subcommittee of the American Academy of Neurology. Practice parameter: treatment of Parkinson disease with motor fluctuations and dyskinesia (an evidence-based review): report of the Quality Standards Subcommittee of the American Academy of Neurology. *Neurology.* 2006;66:983–995.

Suchowersky O, Gronseth G, Perlmutter J, Reich S, Zesiewicz T, Weiner WJ; Quality Standards Subcommittee of the American Academy of Neurology; Practice parameter: neuroprotective strategies and alternative therapies for Parkinson disease (an evidence-based review): report of the Quality Standards Subcommittee of the American Academy of Neurology. *Neurology.* 2006;66:976–982.

Suchowersky O, Reich S, Perlmutter J, Zesiewicz T, Gronseth G, Weiner WJ; Quality Standards Subcommittee of the American Academy of Neurology; Practice parameter: diagnosis and prognosis of new onset Parkinson disease (an evidence-based review): report of the Quality Standards Subcommittee of the American Academy of Neurology. *Neurology.* 2006;66:968–975.

The Internet has given patients and their families powerful tools for learning about their illnesses. The challenges are choosing what to read, assessing the reliability of what is written, and knowing when to stop reading to go on to more important things. Patients frequently arrive in my office very knowledgeable about their illnesses, carrying a list of questions about the latest research and newest treatments reported on the Internet.

An Internet search can produce a bewildering cornucopia of possibilities. Using the Google search engine, a search for the word "Parkinson" gives over 900,000 hits. Of course, this search yields not only Web sites about Parkinson's disease, but also Web sites that mention anyone named Parkinson. By searching for "Parkinson's disease," I winnowed the possibilities to 186,000. Choosing the reliable Web resources is difficult not only because of the excessive possibilities, but also because the Web sites vary greatly in quality.

For good sites on Parkinson's disease, start with organizations such as the National Parkinson's Foundation (www.parkinson.org), the Parkinson's Disease Foundation (www.pdf.org), the Michael J. Fox Foundation (www.MichaelJFox.org), and the American Parkinson Disease Association (www.apdaparkinson.com).

PubMed (www.ncbi.nlm.nih.gov/entrez/query.fcgi) is an excellent Internet site to start searching the professional medical literature. PubMed provides access to Medline, the National Library of Medicine's database of nearly 4,500 journals devoted to biomedicine and health. Over 11 million articles have been indexed on this database since 1966. A PubMed search selects over 28,000 of these using the search term "Parkinson's disease." Google Scholar (scholar.google.com) is another access point for searching medical literature.

Debate and criticism among scientists is an important part of scientific progress. Many forms of peer review facilitate scientific critique. Under the auspices of the National Institutes of Health or other agencies, peer committees assess scientists' requests for research funding. A journal is classified as a peer-reviewed journal if it uses expert scientists to review scientific articles prior to publication. Committees of scientists examine peer-reviewed journals to decide if they merit inclusion on Medline.

One way to assess quality of writing about science is to rely on journals that use peer review. When a scientist sends a new research report to a peer-reviewed journal, the editor will ask a few scientists working in the same field to read and comment on the manuscript. On the basis of the reviewers' comments, the manuscript might be accepted or rejected for publication or sent back to the authors with comments and an invitation to revise and resubmit the manuscript. Even after publication, the process of criticism continues; frequently, journal readers respond to research articles with letters to the editor that identify weaknesses in the paper or that raise issues for future research. Of course, the subsequent research projects and papers that build on and cite articles are part of this interactive scientific criticism. One measure of the impact of a scientific article is how often it is cited in subsequent articles.

Almost every scientific article has references linking it to previous articles. All authors hope that other investigators will cite their articles, linking them to the fabric of evolving scientific thought. The word *hyperlink* entered the English language through its usage on the Internet. When you click a reference on a Web page, you automatically connect to another Web page through hyperlinks. Careful readers of the scientific literature have been hyperlinking for years, albeit with a slower process of following leads from one book or journal to the next.

This interconnected web of articles mirrors the evolution of scientific thought. Philosophers of science debate whether scientific progress comes from the knowledge accumulating gradually from myriad experiments or from sudden bursts of insight, like Darwin's theory of evolution and Einstein's theory of relativity. But even Darwin and Einstein derived their ideas from a thorough knowledge of the scientific work of their predecessors, a deep enough understanding to let them see and overcome the shortcomings of preceding theories.

Sir William Osler, one of the most famous physicians and humanists of the early twentieth century, cautioned, "To study the phenomena of disease without books is to sail an uncharted sea, while to study books without patients is not to go to sea at all."[1] A medical student learns more about the diagnosis of Parkinson's disease from examining patients than can ever be learned about the diagnosis in books. Ramón y Cajal, the father of neuroscience, warned young investigators about personalities who might go astray in a research career and put bibliophiles high on the list. Although reading is important, the actual experimental and clinical aspects of science are even more so. Science has always been a continual process of experimentation, communication, and cooperation among investigators with varied interests and talents. People with Parkinson's disease should also be part of this investigative team.

Glossary

acetylcholine An important neurotransmitter in both the brain and the peripheral nervous system.

agonist When referring to neurotransmitters, a chemical that mimics the action of a neurotransmitter at its receptor.

ALS See *amyotrophic lateral sclerosis.*

amantadine (trade name Symmetrel) A drug used to treat Parkinson's disease; at least part of its action is blocking some receptors for the neurotransmitter glutamate.

amyotrophic lateral sclerosis (ALS or Lou Gehrig's disease) A neurodegenerative disease that causes progressive muscle weakness because of death of nerve cells in the brain and spinal cord that control muscles.

angiogram An X ray or other imaging study that visualizes blood vessels.

antagonist When referring to neurotransmitters, a chemical that blocks the action of a neurotransmitter at its receptor.

antioxidant A chemical that prevents addition of oxygen or the removal of hydrogen or electrons from other molecules.

apoptosis A way in which cells die through a complex series of chemical reactions within the cell rather than because of attack by inflammatory cells.

Artane Trade name for trihexyphenidyl.

arteriogram An angiogram that concentrates on visualizing arteries, often just used synonymously with angiogram.

Atropa belladonna   One of the plants in the nightshade family from which belladonna can be extracted.

atropine   A chemical, derived from the herbal belladonna, that blocks the actions of acetylcholine at some of its receptors.

autoradiography   A method of imaging tissue by exposing it to radioactive chemicals, letting the chemicals bind to portions of the tissue, then recording where in the tissue the radioactivity accumulates. Autoradiography is done on slices of tissue; PET or SPECT scans provide autoradiographs of living organisms.

basal ganglia   Areas of gray matter deep in the brain, separate from the gray matter of the cerebral cortex. Examples include the caudate, putamen, globus pallidus, thalamus, subthalamic nucleus, and substantia nigra.

belladonna   An herbal drug that contains compounds that block many acetylcholine receptors.

benztropine (trade name Cogentin)   A chemical, related to the herbal belladonna, that blocks that the actions of acetylcholine at some of its receptors and is used to treat some symptoms of Parkinson's disease.

bias   In statistical studies, an error that can lead to incorrect results. There are many potentials for bias. For example, errors in diagnosis can lead to misclassification bias, whereas memory errors by study participants can introduce recall bias.

biological plausibility   The basic scientific explanation of how something in living organisms happens. When epidemiologic studies show statistical associations, biological plausibility is needed to consider why the association occurs.

blood-brain barrier   The structures that separate the brain and spinal cord from the blood flow in the body. These structures prevent many substances in the blood from entering the brain.

bradykinesia   Slow movement.

bromocriptine (trade name Parlodel)   A dopamine agonist drug, derived from ergot and useful for treatment of Parkinson's disease.

carbidopa   A chemical that inhibits the enzyme dopa decarboxylase. Carbidopa is usually given with L-dopa, thereby preventing the breakdown of L-dopa in the blood and thus allowing more to enter the brain.

case-control study   A research study that tests a hypothesis by comparing in retrospect a group of patients who have a particular illness with a control group of people who are similar in many respects but do not have the illness.

CAT scan   See *CT scan.*

catechol   Also know as catecholamine, a type of neurotransmitter; examples include dopamine, epinephrine, and norepinephrine.

catechol O-methyltransferase   See *COMT.*

caudate   One of the basal ganglia. Most dopamine nerve cells in the substantia nigra send their axons to the caudate or putamen. The caudate is the chief site of cell loss in patients with Huntington disease.

chlorpromazine (trade name Thorazine)   An antagonist at dopamine receptors used to treat schizophrenia and other forms of psychosis and prone to causing parkinsonism as a side effect.

chorea A movement disorder characterized by abnormal writhing of the body. The word derives from the Greek word for "dance." One of the best-known causes of chorea is Huntington disease. The dyskinesias that occur as a toxic effect of L-dopa or other drugs can be a form of chorea.

coenzyme Q$_{10}$ A vitamin (also called ubiquinone) that facilitates energy production in the mitochondria and has antioxidant properties.

Cogentin Trade name for benztropine.

complex I Part of an enzyme system in mitochondria that is important for cellular energy production.

COMT An enzyme that helps break down dopamine.

Comtan Trade name for entacapone.

confounders Factors that can provide alternative explanations for a statistical association other than direct causation.

consistency of association Similarity of findings among multiple statistical studies.

CoQ$_{10}$ See *coenzyme Q$_{10}$*.

cortex The surface layers of the brain. The cortex is a form of gray matter. The color comes from its high content of nerve cell bodies.

Creutzfeldt-Jakob disease A severe neurogenerative disease caused by abnormal proteins called prions. The most common form causes rapidly progressive dementia. Some cases are inherited; other are dues to infection with prions.

CT scan Computerized tomographic scan, a method of using X rays and computer processing to display slices of the brain or of other parts of the body.

DATATOP The acronym for a large randomized controlled double-blind study that investigated the value of vitamin E and selegiline for treatment of Parkinson's disease.

dominant inheritance The pattern of inheritance in which having one copy of a gene is sufficient to cause that gene to be expressed as a trait. When the person has a dominant gene, half of his or her offspring will inherit the gene and express the trait controlled by that gene.

dopa Dihydroxyphenalanine, an amino acid that can be converted in the body to dopamine. There are L and D forms of dopa; L-dopa, also called levodopa, is the form that is now used to treat Parkinson's disease.

dopa decarboxylase An enzyme that helps convert dopa to dopamine.

dopa decarboxylase inhibitor See *carbidopa*.

dopamine An important neurotransmitter, particularly important in nerve cells whose bodies are in the substantia nigra of the midbrain and whose axons synapse in the caudate and putamen. Loss of these nerve cells is one of the chief pathological effects of Parkinson's disease.

dopamine nerve cell Nerve cells that use dopamine as their chief neurotransmitter.

dopamine receptor antagonist A chemical that blocks the dopamine receptor, thereby preventing dopamine from stimulating it. Chlorpromazine and haloperidol are examples of strong dopamine receptor antagonists.

dopamine receptors   Molecules that protrude from the outer membrane of a cell and that bind to dopamine when it is present. When the dopamine binds to the receptor, a message is passed to the inside of the cell, allowing the dopamine to affect the cell.

dorsal raphé nucleus   An area of gray matter in the midbrain, separate from the substantia nigra. Although the chief neurotransmitter of its cells is serotonin rather than dopamine, the dorsal raphé also loses cells in patients with Parkinson's disease.

dose-response relation   A change in a response based on the amount of a stimulus. A dose-response relation occurs for most drugs, where taking more of the drug increases the effects on the body. In statistical studies the amount of a variable, like how much a person smokes, might have a dose-response effect on the outcome, like the risk of getting cancer.

dyskinesia   Abnormal, excessive body movements, which can be writhing, like chorea, or stiff, in which case it is called dystonia.

Eldepryl   Trade name for selegiline.

encephalitis   Any brain disease caused by inflammation.

encephalitis lethargica (von Economo's encephalitis)   A specific brain disease characterized clinically by severe sleepiness and pathologically by inflammation in the midbrain.

entacapone (trade name Comtan)   A drug that blocks the action of the enzyme COMT, which would otherwise break down dopamine.

epinephrine   An important neurotransmitter, also called adrenaline, chemically related to dopamine.

GABA   A common brain neurotransmitter.

gamma amino butyric acid   See *GABA*.

Ginkgo biloba   A tree or the herbal drug derived from it, often simply called ginkgo, sometimes used to treat Alzheimer's disease and other forms of memory loss.

globus pallidus   Part of the basal ganglia, adjacent to the putamen and divided into internal and external portions. Although it is not a primary site of pathology in patients with Parkinson's disease, the internal globus pallidus is a site for surgical treatment of Parkinson's disease because of its role in brain circuits between the putamen and cerebral cortex.

glutamate   A common brain neurotransmitter.

gray matter   Areas of the brain where nerve cell bodies are concentrated, such as the cerebral cortex and the basal ganglia. The rest of the brain is called white matter, which is rich in the axons connecting different areas of gray matter.

Haldol   Trade name for haloperidol.

haloperidol   An antagonist at dopamine receptors used to treat schizophrenia and other forms of psychosis and prone to cause parkinsonism as a side effect.

Huntington disease   A dominantly inherited neurodegenerative disease that causes chorea, psychosis, and dementia due to loss of brain cells, especially from the caudate.

hydroxydopamine   A chemical that is chemically similar to dopamine but is toxic to dopamine nerve cells when injected near them in the brain. It can be injected into rodents and other animals to create an animal model of Parkinson's disease.

hyoscyamine   A drug, related to atropine, that blocks the actions of the neurotransmitter acetylcholine.

L-dopa   See *dopa.*

levodopa   See *dopa.*

Lewy bodies   Abnormal inclusions in brain cells (see Figure 2.1C). They are visible by microscope in the nerve cells of the substantia nigra of patients with Parkinson's disease but can also be seen in various parts of the brain in other conditions, such as in Lewy body dementia.

Lewy body dementia   A neurodegenerative disease characterized by dementia and parkinsonism. The pathology includes Lewy bodies in a number of areas of the brain beyond the areas, like the substantia nigra, that are typically affected by Parkinson's disease.

Lou Gehrig's disease   See *amyotrophic lateral sclerosis.*

mad cow disease   A variant of Jacob-Creutzfeldt disease caused by eating meat from cows carrying infectious abnormal prions.

MAO   Monoamine oxidase, an enzyme that facilitates breakdown of dopamine and of many other neurotransmitters, such as serotonin and epinephrine.

Mirapex   Trade name for pramipexole.

mitochondria   A small organelle or structure with cells. A cell contains many mitochondria, which are the centers for production of energy for the cell.

monoamine oxidase   See *MAO.*

motor cortex   The part of the brain cortex that sends axons to the areas of the brain stem and spinal cord that directly connect to muscles.

MPP+   A chemical formed in the body when the enzyme MAO breaks down MPTP. MPTP does not cause parkinsonism if the formation of MPP+ is prevented.

MPTP   A chemical (1-methyl 4-phenyl 1,2,3,6-tetrahydropyridine) that can cause irreversible parkinsonism if swallowed or injected.

MRI   Magnetic resonance imaging, a method of taking detailed pictures of slices of the brain or other parts of the body using a large magnet and a computer.

multiple systems atrophy   A neurodegenerative disease that can cause some findings of parkinsonism but is different from Parkinson's disease in many of its clinical findings, such as lack of response to L-dopa, and in its pathology.

natural history   When referring to a disease, the course the disease would take if untreated.

neurodegenerative disease   A progressive disease of the nervous system characterized by loss of cells from specific areas of the brain. Each neurodegenerative disease has unique symptoms depending on which cells are lost. The best-known examples are Parkinson's disease, Alzheimer's disease, Huntington disease, and Lou Gehrig's disease.

neurotransmitter   A chemical released by one nerve cell that spreads across a synapse to carry a message to another nerve cell or to a muscle cell.

norepinephrine   An important neurotransmitter, also know as noradrenaline, chemically related to dopamine.

on-off   A pattern of symptoms that can occur when taking medication for Parkinson's disease. When the medication is working well, the patient is "on" and has less symptoms of parkinsonism; when the medication is not working well, the patient is "off" so that symptoms like tremor, rigidity, and bradykinesia are at their worst.

paralysis agitans   The name for the "shaking palsy" used by James Parkinson, from the Latin for "tremulous weakness."

Parlodel   Trade name for bromocriptine.

PARK1   The gene for one form of dominantly inherited Parkinson's disease. The gene is for the protein α-synuclein and was first described in a family from Contursi, Italy.

PARK2   The gene for one form of recessively inherited Parkinson's disease. The gene is for the protein parkin.

PARK4   One form of dominantly inherited Parkinson's disease related to extra copies of the gene for α-synuclein.

PARK5   The gene for one form of dominantly inherited Parkinson's disease. The gene is for the protein UCH-L1.

parkin   An enzyme that participates in breakdown of proteins inside cells. The gene that codes for parkin is called parkin or PARK2; mutations in this gene can cause recessively inherited Parkinson's disease.

parkinsonism   Clinical findings including some combination of tremor, slow movement (bradykinesia), stiff muscles (rigidity), and unstable posture. Parkinsonism can be due to Parkinson's disease or to a number of other medical conditions.

parsidol   A chemical, related to the herbal belladonna, that blocks the actions of acetylcholine at some of its receptors and is used to treat some symptoms of Parkinson's disease.

pergolide (trade name Permax)   A dopamine agonist drug, derived from ergot and useful for treatment of Parkinson's disease.

peripheral nervous system   The nerves that run throughout the body apart from the brain and spinal cord.

Permax   Trade name for pergolide.

PET (positron emission tomography)   A method of imaging metabolic activity in the brain or other organs by injecting radioactive chemicals, using detectors of radioactivity to find where the radioactivity localizes in the body and computer processing to show slices of the body where the radioactive chemical is being metabolized.

polio   A disease caused by a virus (poliovirus) that inflames the brain and spinal cord and can leave severe residual muscle weakness after the acute inflammation resolves.

postencephalitic Parkinson's disease A disease that includes findings of parkinsonism and occurs after an episode of encephalitis, especially after encephalitis lethargica.

postural instability One of the cardinal features of Parkinson's disease, manifested by difficult sitting or standing steadily. Postural instability can also occur in many other neurologic conditions that affect strength, balance, or sensation.

pramipexole (trade name Mirapex) A dopamine agonist drug useful for treatment of Parkinson's disease.

programmed cell death See *apoptosis.*

progressive supranuclear palsy A neurodegenerative disease that can cause some findings of parkinsonism but is different from Parkinson's disease in many of its clinical findings, such as trouble moving the eyes, and in its pathology.

prospective cohort study A scientific study that forms a hypothesis then tests it by observing a group of related people over time.

proteasome An organelle or structure inside cells that is important for breaking down proteins that are no longer needed by the cell.

Prozac Trade name for fluoxetine.

PubMed The Web site of the National Library of Medicine, which provides an excellent search engine for peer-reviewed medical journals (available at: http://www.ncbi.nlm.nih.gov/entrez/query.fcgi).

putamen One of the basal ganglia. Most dopamine nerve cells in the substantia nigra send their axons to the caudate or putamen. In patients with Parkinson's disease the putamen is the chief area of loss of dopamine nerve cell connections.

RAC The Recombinant DNA Advisory Committee of the National Institutes of Health that must review and approve any human gene therapy experiments done in the United States.

rasagiline A drug used to treat Parkinson's disease that acts by blocking the enzyme MAO-B, which would otherwise break down dopamine.

Requip Trade name for ropinerole.

recessive inheritance The pattern of inheritance in which having two copies of a gene is necessary to cause that gene to be expressed as a trait.

Recombinant DNA Advisory Committee See *RAC.*

REM behavioral disorder A condition in which REM sleep is abnormal and lacks the normal paralysis. Therefore a person with REM behavioral disorder will often be physically active, even violent, during some dreams.

REM sleep The part of sleep normally characterized by rapid eye movements, paralysis of other muscles, and dreaming.

reserpine A drug, derived from rauwolfia plants, that can be used to treat high blood pressure or as a sedative but that can have the adverse effect of causing reversible parkinsonism by depleting brain dopamine.

reverse causation When A is being investigated as a possible cause of B by epidemiological studies, and an association between A and B is found, B might cause A, rather than A causing B.

rigidity   Increased stiffness in muscles during passive movement.

ropinirole (trade name Requip)   A dopamine agonist drug useful for treatment of Parkinson's disease.

schizophrenia   A severe psychosis, characterized by abnormal personality, poor understanding of reality, and difficulty getting along in society.

selegiline (trade name Eldepryl)   A drug used to treat Parkinson's disease that acts by blocking the enzyme MAO-B, which would otherwise break down dopamine.

serotonin   An important neurotransmitter.

Sinemet   Trade name for a drug containing both L-dopa and carbidopa.

SPECT (single photon emission computerized tomograph)   A method of imaging metabolic activity in the brain or other organs by injecting radioactive chemicals, using detectors of radioactivity to find where the radioactivity localizes in the body and computer processing to show slices of the body where the radioactive chemical is being metabolized.

Stalevo   Trade name for a drug containing L-dopa, carbidopa, and entacapone.

substantia nigra   An area of brain gray matter in the midbrain, named for its black appearance when healthy. The substantia nigra is the chief brain location of the bodies of dopamine nerve cells. In Parkinson's disease these cells die in the substantia nigra, and it loses its usual blackness.

subthalamic nucleus   One of the basal ganglia. Although it is not a primary site of pathology in patients with Parkinson's disease, it is a site for surgical treatment of Parkinson's disease because of its role in brain circuits between the putamen and cerebral cortex.

Symmetrel   Trade name for amantadine.

synapse   The point of connection between two nerve cells or between a nerve cell and a muscle cell. The synapse is a very narrow gap between the cells, and neurotransmitters carry information across the gap.

Tasmar   Trade name for tolcapone.

temporal relation   A link in the timing of events.

thalamus   One of the basal ganglia. Although it is not a primary site of pathology in patients with Parkinson's disease, it is a site for surgical treatment of Parkinson's disease because of its role in brain circuits between the putamen and cerebral cortex.

Thorazine   Trade name for chlorpromazine.

tolcapone (trade name Tasmar)   A drug that blocks the action of the enzyme COMT, which would otherwise break down dopamine.

trihexyphenidyl (trade name Artane)   A chemical, related to the herbal belladonna, that blocks the actions of acetylcholine at some of its receptors and is used to treat some symptoms of Parkinson's disease.

ubiquitin   A protein found in cells all over the body (and present in high concentration in Lewy bodies), which plays an important role in the breakdown of other proteins.

UCH-L1 A natural body enzyme. When the enzyme is inherited in mutant form, it is likely to cause dominantly inherited Parkinson's disease.

Unified Parkinson's Disease Rating Scale (UPDRS) A method to quantify the severity of Parkinson's disease by recording a patient's motor activity, mental capacity, and ability to do daily activities.

vagus nerve (also called the 10th cranial nerve) A nerve that originates toward the end of the brain stem and sends axons to the heart, stomach, intestines, and other internal organs. Acetylcholine is the chief neurotransmitter for these axons.

ventricle Areas deep in the brain where spinal fluid is stored. The caudate and thalamus abut the ventricles, and the other basal ganglia are nearby.

von Economo's encephalitis See *encephalitis lethargica.*

wearing-off Gradual decreased effectiveness of medications for Parkinson's disease in the hours after the drugs are taken.

α-synuclein A natural body protein. When the protein is inherited in mutant form, it is likely to cause dominantly inherited Parkinson's disease. Most patients with Parkinson's disease have extra α-synuclein in their Lewy bodies.

Notes

Chapter 1. The Diagnostic Conversation —Diagnosis and Prognosis of Parkinson's Disease

1. Parkinson J. *An Essay on the Shaking Palsy*. London: Sherwood, Neely, and Jones; 1817:1, 5.

2. Parkinson, 5.

3. Charcot JM. On paralysis agitans. In: *Leçons sur les maladies du système nerveux*. Paris: Delehaye; 1872/1973:105–128.

4. Hughes AJ, Daniel SE, Kilford L, Lees AJ. Accuracy of clinical diagnosis of idiopathic Parkinson's disease: A clinico-pathological study of 100 cases. *J Neurol Neurosurg Psychiatry*. 1992;55:181–184.

5. Hughes AJ, Ben-Shlomo Y, Daniel SE, Lees AJ. What features improve the accuracy of clinical diagnosis in Parkinson's disease: A clinico-pathologic study. *Neurology*. 1992;42:1142–1146.

6. Fox MJ. *Lucky Man*. New York: Hyperion; 2002:1.

7. Hoehn MM, Yahr MD. Parkinsonism: Onset, progression, and mortality. *Neurology*. 1967;17:427–442.

8. Cotzias GC, VanWoert MH, Schiffer LM. Aromatic amino acids and modification of parkinsonism. *New Engl J Med*. 1967;276:374–379.

9. Gancher S. Scales for the assessment of movement disorders. In: Herndon R, ed. *Handbook of Neurologic Rating Scales*. 1st ed. New York: Demos Vermande; 1997:81–106.

10. Shults CW, Oakes D, Kieburtz K, Beal MF, Haas R, Plumb S, et al. Effects of coenzyme Q_{10} in early Parkinson disease: Evidence of slowing of functional decline. *Arch Neurol*. 2002;59:1541–1550.

Chapter 2. Pathology of Parkinson's Disease

1. Parkinson J. *An Essay on the Shaking Palsy*. London: Sherwood, Neely, and Jones; 1817:i.

2. Golgi C. The neuron doctrine—Theory and facts. In: *The Nobel Lectures, Physiology or Medicine, 1901–1921*. Amsterdam: Elsevier; 1967:189–217. Available at: http://www.nobel.se/medicine/laureates. Accessed April 1, 2006.

3. Ramón y Cajal S. The structure and connexions of neurons. In: *The Nobel Lectures, Physiology or Medicine, 1901–1921*. Amsterdam: Elsevier; 1967:220–253. Available at: http://www.nobel.se/medicine/laureates. Accessed April 1, 2006.

4. Ramón y Cajal S. *Recollections of My Life*. Philadelphia, PA: American Philosophical Society; 1937: 324.

5. Ibid: 549.

6. Ibid: 363.

7. Tello Valdivieso F. Some aspects of Cajal's personality. In: Grisolía S, Guerri C, Samson F, Norton S, Reinoso-Suárez F, eds. *Ramón y Cajal's Contribution to the Neurosciences*. Amsterdam: Elsevier; 1983:23–27.

8. Carlsson A. Perspectives on the discovery of central monoaminergic neurotransmission. *Annu Rev Neurosci*. 1987;10:19–40.

9. Carlsson A. Lecture at Oregon Health and Sciences University. October 9, 2002.

10. Hornykiewicz O. Chemical neuroanatomy of the basal ganglia—Normal and in Parkinson's disease. *J Chem Neuroanat*. 2001;22:3–12.

11. Birkheimer H, et al. Brain dopamine and the syndrome of Parkinson and Huntington: Clinical, morphological and neurochemical correlations. *J Neurol Sci*. 1973;20:415–455.

Chapter 3. Is There an Epidemic of Parkinson's Disease?

1. Ben-Shlomo Y. How far are we in understanding the cause of Parkinson's disease? *J Neurol Neurosurg Psychiatry*. 1996;61:4–16.

2. Snow J. *On the Mode of Communication of Cholera*. London: John Churchill; 1856:38. Available at: http://www.ph.ucla.edu/epi/snow.html (an excellent Web site that reviews Snow's contribution to epidemiology). Accessed July 8, 2006.

3. Kumar A, Calne SM, Schulzer M, et al. Clustering of Parkinson disease: Shared cause of coincidence? *Arch Neurol*. 2004;61:1057–1060.

4. Stone R. Parkinson's disease: Coincidence or connection? *Science*. 2002;296:451–452.

5. Gajdusek C. Unconventional viruses and the origin and disappearance of kuru: Nobel Lecture, December 13, 1976. In: Lindsten J, ed. *The Nobel Lectures in Physiology or Medicine, 1971–1980*. Singapore: World Scientific; 1992:305–354. Available at: http://www.nobel.se/medicine/laureates/1976/gajdusek-lecture.pdf. Accessed March 31, 2006.

6. Hill AB. The environment and disease: Association or causation? *Proc. R. Soc. Med.* 1965;58:295–300.

7. Benedetti MD, Bower JH, Maraganore DM, McDonnell SK, Peterson BJ, Ahlskog JE, Schaid DJ, Rocca WA. Smoking, alcohol, and coffee consumption preceding Parkinson's disease: A case-control study. *Neurology.* 2000;55:1350–1358.

8. Hernán MA, Zhang SM, Rueda-deCastro AM, Colditz GA, Speizer FE, Ascherio A. Cigarette smoking and the incidence of Parkinson's disease in two prospective studies. *Ann Neurol.* 2001;50:780–786.

9. Gorell JM, Johnson CC, Rybicki BA, Peterson EL, Richardson RJ. The risk of Parkinson's disease with exposure to pesticides, farming, well water, and rural living. *Neurology.* 1998;50:1346–1350.

10. Williams DB, Annegers JF, Kokmen E, O'Brien PC, Kurkland LT. Brain injury and neurologic sequelae: A cohort study of dementia, parkinsonism, and amyotrophic lateral sclerosis. *Neurology.* 1991;41:1554–1557.

11. Bower JH, Maraganore DM, Peterson BJ, McDonnell SK, Ahlskog JE, Rocca WA. Head trauma preceding PD: A case-control study. *Neurology.* 2003;60:1611–1615.

Chapter 4. Causes of Parkinson's Disease

1. Dickman MS. Von Economo encephalitis. *Arch Neurol.* 2001;58:1696–1698.

2. Poskanzer DC, Schwab RS. Cohort analysis of Parkinson's syndrome: Evidence for a single etiology related to subclinical infection about 1920. *J Chronic Dis.* 1963;16:961–973.

3. Rail D, Scholtz C, Swash M. Post-encephalitic Parkinsonism: Current experience. *J Neurol Neurosurg Psychiatry.* 1981;44:670–676.

4. Festinger L. *When Prophecy Fails: A Social and Psychological Study.* New York: Harper Collins; 1964.

5. Schwab RS, Poskanzer DC, England AC Jr, Young RR. Amantadine in the treatment of Parkinson's disease. *JAMA.* 1969;208:1168–1170.

6. Sacks O. *Awakenings.* New York: Harper Collins; 1990.

7. Langston WJ, Ballard P, Tetrud JW, and Irwin I. Chronic parkinsonism in humans due to a product of mederidine-analog synthesis. *Science.* 1983;219:979–980.

8. Langston JW, Palfreman J. *The Case of the Frozen Addicts.* New York: Vintage Books; 1996.

9. Davis GC, Williams AC, Markey SP, Ebert H, Caine ED, Reichert CM, Kopin IJ. Chronic parkinsonism secondary to intravenous injection of meperidine analogues. *Psychiatry Res.* 1979;1:249–254.

10. Huntington G. On chorea. *Med Surg Rep.* 1872;26:317–321.

11. Wexler A. *Mapping Fate: A Memoir of Family, Risk, and Genetic Research.* Berkeley: University of California Press; 1999.

12. Bennett DA, Beckett LA, Murray AM, Shannon KM, Goetz CG, Pilgrim DM, Evans DA. Prevalence of parkinsonian signs and associated mortality in a community population of older people. *New Engl J Med.* 1996;334:71–76.

13. Langston JW, Palferman J. *The Case of the Frozen Addicts.* New York: Vintage Book; 1996:126

14. Ward CD, et al. Parkinson's disease in 65 pairs of twins and in a set of quadruplets. *Neurology.* 1983;33:815–824.

15. Marttila RJ, Kaprio J, Koskenvuo M, Rinne UK. Parkinson's disease in a nationwide twin cohort. *Neurology.* 1988;38:1217–1219.

16. Golbe LI, Di Iorio G, Bonavita V, Miller DC, Duvoisin RC. A large kindred with autosomal dominant Parkinson's disease. *Ann Neurol.* 1990;27:276–282.

17. Golbe LI, Di Iorio G, Sanges G, Lazzarini AM, La Sala S, Bonavita V, et al. Clinical genetic analysis of Parkinson's disease in the Contursi kindred. *Ann Neurol.* 1996;40:767–775.

18. Polymeropoulos MH, Higgins JJ, Golbe LI, Johnson WG, Ide SE, Di Iorio G, et al. Mapping of a gene for Parkinson's disease to chromosome 4q21-q23. *Science.* 1996;274:1197–1199.

19. Polymeropoulos MH, Lavedan C, Leroy E, Ide SE, Dehejia A, Dutra A, et al. Mutation in the alpha-synuclein gene identified in families with Parkinson's disease. *Science.* 1997;276:2045–2047.

20. Farrer M, Gwinn-Hardy K, Muenter M, DeVrieze FW, Crook R, Perez-Tur J, et al. A chromosome 4p haplotype segregating with Parkinson's disease and postural tremor. *Hum Molec Genet.* 1999;8:81–85.

21. Leroy E, Boyer R, Auburger G, Leube B, Ulm G, Mezey E, et al. The ubiquitin pathway in Parkinson's disease. *Nature.* 1998;395:451–452.

22. Bembi B, Zambito Marsala S, Sidransky E, Ciana G, Carrozzi M, Zorzon M, et al. Gaucher's disease with Parkinson's disease: Clinical and pathological aspects. *Neurology.* 2003;61:99–101.

23. Aharon-Peretz J, Rosenbaum H, Gershoni-Baruch R. Mutations in the glucocerebrosidase gene and Parkinson's disease in Ashkenazi Jews. *New Engl J Med.* 2004;351:1972–1977.

24. Ozelius LJ, Senthil G, Saunders-Pullman R, Ohmann E, Deligtisch A, Tagliata M, Hunt AL, Klein C, and Henick B. LRRK2 G2019S as a cause of Parkinson's disease in Ashkenazi Jews. *New Engl J Med.* 2006;354:424–425.

25. Lesage S, Dürr A, Tazir M, Lohmann E, Leutenegger A-L, Janin S, Pollak P, Brice A. LRRK2 G2019S as a cause of Parkinson's disease in North African Arabs. *New Engl J Med.* 2006;354:422–423.

26. Slatkin M. A population-genetic test of founder effects and implications for Ashkenazi Jewish diseases. *Am J Hum Genet.* 2004;75:282–293.

Chapter 5. Medications for Parkinson's Disease

1. PubMed. National Library of Medicine Web site. Available at: http://www.ncbi.nlm.nih.gov/entrez. Accessed April 1, 2006.

2. Vaidya AB, Rajagopalan TG, Manoki NA, et al. Treatment of Parkinson's disease with the cowhedge plant—*Mucuna pruriens* Bak. *Neurol India.* 1978;26:171–176.

3. Damodaran M, Ramaswamy R. Isolation of L-dopa from the seeds of *Mucuna pruriens. Biochemistry.* 1937;31:2149–2151.

4. Chan K. Jimson weed poisoning: A case report. *Permanente J.* 2002;6(4):28–30. Available at: http://xnet.kp.org/permanentejournal/fall02/Fall02.pdf. Accessed July 8, 2006. Italicized text added.

5. Eisenberg DM, Davis RB, Ettner SL, Appel ZSZ, Wilkey S, Rompay MV, Ressler RC. Trends in alternative medicine use in the United States, 1990–1997: Results of a follow-up national survey. *JAMA.* 1998;280:1569–1575.

6. Rajendran PR, Thompson RE, Reich SG. The use of alternative therapies by patients with Parkinson's disease. *Neurology.* 2001;57:790–794.

7. Saper RB, Kales SN, Paquin J, Burns MJ, Eisenberg DM, Davis RB, et al. Heavy metal content of Ayurvedic herbal medicine products. *JAMA.* 2004;292:2868–2873.

8. Specter M. Miracle in a bottle. *The New Yorker.* February 2, 2004:64–75. Quoting Don Atkinson, vice president of sales for Basic Research.

9. Fontanarosa PB, Lundberg GD. Alternative medicine meets science. *JAMA.* 1998;280:1618–1619.

10. Cotzias GC, Van Woert MH, Schiffer LM. Aromatic amino acids and modification of parkinsonism. *New Engl J Med.* 1967;276:374–379.

11. Birkmayer W, Hornykiewicz O. Der L-Dioxyphenylalanin (= L-dopa)—Effeckt beim der Parkinson-Akinese. *Wien Klin Wochenschr.* 1961;73:787–788.

12. Cotzias GC, et al. Modification of parkinsonism—Chronic treatment with L-dopa. *New Engl J Med.* 1969;280:337–345.

13. Sacks O. *Awakenings.* New York: Harper Collins; 1990:208.

14. Green MF. *Schizophrenia Revealed.* New York: W. W. Norton; 2001. This is an excellent review, written for nonprofessionals.

15. Deniker P. From chlorpromazine to tardive dyskinesia (brief history of neuroleptics). *Psychiatr J Univ Ottawa.* 1989;14:253–259.

16. Tuller D. Julius Axelrod dies at 92; Won Nobel Prize in Medicine. *The New York Times.* December 31, 2004. Obituary, citing *The Toronto Star.*

17. From test tube to patient. *FDA Consumer Magazine.* 2006. Available at: http://www.fda.gov/fdac/special/testtubetopatient/trials.html. Accessed April 1, 2006.

18. Birkmayer W, Knoll J, Riederer P, Youdim MB, Hars V, Marton J. Increased life expectancy from the addition of L-deprenyl to Madopar treatment in Parkinson's disease: A longterm study. *J Neural Transm.* 1985;64:113–127.

19. Parkinson Study Group. Effects of tocopherol and deprenyl of the progression of disability in early Parkinson's disease. *New Engl J Med.* 1993;328:176–183.

20. Ben-Shlomo Y, Churchyard A, Head J, Hurwitz B, Overstall P, Ockelford J, et al. Investigation by Parkinson's Disease Research Group of the United Kingdom into excess mortality seen with combined levodopa and selegiline treatment in patients with early, mild Parkinson's disease: Further results of randomised trial and confidential inquiry. *BMJ.* 1998;316:1191–1196.

21. Shults CW. Study suggests coenzyme Q10 slows functional decline in Parkinson's disease. NIH news release. 2002. Available at: http://www.nih.gov/news/pr/oct2002/ninds-14.htm. Accessed April 1, 2006.

22. Shults CW, Oakes D, Kieburtz K, Beal MF, Haas R, Plumb S, et al. Effects of coenzyme Q_{10} in early Parkinson disease: Evidence of slowing of functional decline. *Arch Neurol.* 2002;59:1541–1550.

23. Pure Prescriptions Web site. Available at: http://www.purepre-scriptions.com. Accessed April 1, 2006.

24. Zhang J, Qu FR, Nakatsuka A, Nomura T, Nagai M, Nomoto M. Pharmacokinetics of L-dopa in plasma and extracellular fluid of striatum in common marmosets. *Brain Res.* 2003;993:54–58.

25. Rascol O, Brooks DJ, Korczyn AD, De Deyn PP, Clarke CE, Lang AE. A five-year study of the incidence of dyskinesia in patients with early Parkinson's disease who were treated with ropinirole or levodopa. *New Engl J Med.* 2000;342:1484–1491.

Chapter 6. Images of the Brain—A Picture of the Brain Is Worth a Thousand Words

1. Piccini P, Burn DJ, Ceravolo R, Maraganore D, Brooks DJ. The role of inheritance in sporadic Parkinson's disease: Evidence from a longitudinal study of dopaminergic function in twins. *Ann Neurol.* 1999;45:577–582.

2. Berendse HW, Booij J, Francot CM, Bergmans PL, Hijman R, Stoof JC, et al. Subclinical dopaminergic dysfunction in asymptomatic Parkinson's disease patients' relatives with a decreased sense of smell. *Ann Neurol.* 2001;50:34–41.

3. Whone AL, Watts RL, Stoessl AJ, Davis M, Reske S, Nahmias C, et al. Slower progression of Parkinson's disease with ropinirole versus levodopa: The REAL-PET study. *Ann Neurol.* 2003;54:93–101.

Chapter 7. A Better Model of Parkinson's Disease

1. Sacks O. *Awakenings.* New York: Harper Collins; 1990:375–386.

2. Double K, Rowe DB, Hayes M, Chan DK, Blackie J, Corbett A, et al. Identifying the pattern of olfactory deficits in Parkinson disease using the brief smell identification test. *Arch Neurol.* 2003;60:545–549.

Chapter 8. Brain Surgery for Parkinson's Disease

1. Speelman JD, Bosch DA. Resurgence of functional neurosurgery for Parkinson's disease: A historical perspective. *Mov Disorders.* 1998;12:582–588.

2. Meyers R. Historical background and personal experiences in the surgical relief of hyperkinesia and hypertonus. In: Fields WS, ed. *Pathogenesis and Treatment of Parkinsonism.* Springfield, IL: Charles C. Thomas; 1958:229–270.

3. Axelrod L. Bones, stones and hormones: The contributions of Fuller Albright. *New Engl J Med.* 1970;283:964–970.

4. Fuller Albright (1900–1970). *New Engl J Med.* 1970;282:280–281.

5. Hallett M, Litvan I. Evaluation of surgery for Parkinson's disease: A report of the Therapeutics and Technology Assessment Subcommittee of the American Academy of Neurology. The Task Force on Surgery for Parkinson's Disease. *Neurology.* 1999;53:1910–1921.

6. Deep-Brain Stimulation for Parkinson's Disease Study Group. Deep-brain stimulation of the subthalamic nucleus or the pars interna of the globus pallidus in Parkinson's disease. *New Engl J Med.* 2001;345:956–963.

7. Madrazo I, Drucker-Colin R, Diaz V, Martinez-Mata J, Torres C, Becerril JJ. Open microsurgical autograft of adrenal medulla to the right caudate nucleus in two patients with intractable Parkinson's disease. *New Engl J Med.* 1987;316:831–834.

8. Taylor JR, Elsworth JD, Roth RH, Sladek JR Jr, Collier TJ, Redmond DE Jr. Grafting of fetal substantia nigra to striatum reverses behavioral deficits induced by MPTP in primates: A comparison with other types of grafts as controls. *Exp Brain Res.* 1991;85:335–348.

9. Widner H, Tetrud J, Rehncrona S, Snow B, Brundin P, Gustavii B, et al. Bilateral fetal mesencephalic grafting in two patients with parkinsonism induced by 1-methyl-4-phenyl-1,2,3,6-tetrahydropyridine (MPTP). *New Engl J Med.* 1992;327:1556–1563.

10. Freed CR, Greene PE, Breeze RE, Tsai WY, DuMouchel W, Kao R, et al. Transplantation of embryonic dopamine neurons for severe Parkinson's disease. *New Engl J Med.* 2001;344:710–719.

11. Brill IC, Rosenbaum WM, Rosenbaum EE, Flanery JR. Internal mammary ligation. *Northwest Med.* 1958;57:483–486.

12. Beecher HK. Surgery as placebo: A quantitative study of bias. *JAMA*. 1961;176:1102–1107.

13. Bakay RAE. Is transplantation to treat Parkinson's disease dead? *Neurosurgery*. 2001;49:576–580.

14. Olanow CW, Goetz CG, Kordower JH, Stoessl AJ, Sossi V, Brin MF, et al. A double-blind controlled trial of bilateral fetal nigral transplantation in Parkinson's disease. *Ann Neurol*. 2003;54:403–414.

15. Kolata G. Parkinson's research is set back by failure of fetal cell implants. *The New York Times*. March 8, 2001:1.

16. Nutt JG, Burchiel KJ, Comella CL, Jankovic J, Lang AE, Laws ER Jr, et al. Randomized, double-blind trial of glial cell line-derived neurotrophic factor (GDNF) in PD. *Neurology*. 2003;60:69–73.

17. Lang AE, Gill S, Patel NK, Lozano A, Nutt JG, Penn R, et al. Randomized controlled trial of intraputamenal glial cell line-derived neurotrophic factor infusion in Parkinson disease. *Ann Neurol*. 2006;59:459–466.

18. Pollack A. Many see hope in Parkinson's drug pulled from testing. *The New York Times*. November 26, 2004.

19. Palfi S, Leventhal L, Chu Y, Ma SY, Emborg M, Bakay R, Déglon N, Hantraye P, Aebischer P, Kordower JH. Lentivirally delivered glial cell live-derived neurotrophic factor increases the number of striatal dopaminergic neurons in primate models of nigrostriatal degeneration. *J Neurosci*. 2002;22:4942–4954.

20. Stolberg SG. The biotech death of Jessie Gelsinger. *The New York Times Magazine*. November 28, 1999.

Chapter 9. Living with Parkinson's Disease

1. Peto V, Jenkinson C, Fitzpatrick R, Greenhall R. The development and validation of a short measure of functioning and well being for individuals with Parkinson's disease. *Qual Life Res*. 1995;4:241–248.

2. Seedat S, Kesler S, Niehaus DJ, Stein DJ. Pathological gambling behaviour: Emergence secondary to treatment of Parkinson's disease with dopaminergic agents. *Depress Anxiety*. 2000;11:185–186.

3. Molina JA, Sainz-Artiga MJ, Fraile A, Jimenez-Jimenez FJ, Villanueva C, Orti-Pareja M, Bermejo F. Pathologic gambling in Parkinson's disease: A behavioral manifestation of pharmacologic treatment? *Mov Disorders*. 2000;15:869–872.

4. Driver-Dunkley E, Samanta J, Stacy M. Pathological gambling associated with dopamine agonist therapy in Parkinson's disease. *Neurology*. 2003;61:422–423.

5. Bergh C, Eklund T, Sodersten P, Nordin C. Altered dopamine function in pathological gambling. *Psychol Med*. 1997;27:473–475.

6. Frucht S, Rogers JD, Greene PE, Gordon MF, Fahn S. Falling asleep at the wheel: Motor vehicle accidents in patients taking pramipexole and ropinirole. *Neurology*. 1999;52:1908–1910.

7. Paus S, Brecht HM, Koster J, Seeger G, Klockgether T, Wullner U. Sleep attacks, daytime sleepiness, and dopamine agonists in Parkinson's disease. *Mov Disorders*. 2003;18:659–667.

8. Olson EJ, Boeve BF, Silber MH. Rapid eye movement sleep behavior disorder: Demographic, clinical, and laboratory findings in 93 cases. *Brain*. 2000;123:331–339.

9. Tinetti ME. Preventing falls in elderly persons. *New Engl J Med*. 2003;348:42–49.

10. Lauritzen JB. Hip fractures: Incidence, risk factors, energy absorption, and prevention. *Bone*. 1996;18:65S–75S.

11. Tinetti ME, Speechley M, Ginter SF. Risk factors for falls among elderly persons living in the community. *New Engl J Med*. 1988;319:1701–1707.

12. Hogan DB, MacDonald FA, Betts J, Bricker S, Ebly EM, Delarue B, et al. A randomized controlled trial of a community-based consultation service to prevent falls. *Can Med Assoc J*. 2001;165:537–543.

13. Kannus P, Parkkari J, Niemi S, Pasanen M, Palvanen M, Jarvinen M, et al. Prevention of hip fracture in elderly people with use of a hip protector. *New Engl J Med*. 2000;343:1506–1513.

Chapter 10. Conclusions

1. Barrett A. *Servants of the Map*. New York: W. W. Norton; 2002:171–194.

2. Blandini F, Nappi G, Greenamyre JT. Subthalamic infusion of an NMDA antagonist prevents basal ganglia metabolic changes and nigral degeneration in a rodent model of Parkinson's disease. *Ann Neurol*. 2001;49:525–529.

3. EPDA Charter for People with Parkinson's Disease. 1997. Available at: http://www.epda.eu.com/worldPDDay/worldPDDay_epdaCharter. shtm. Accessed April 1, 2006.

Appendix

1. Bean RB, Bean WB. *Sir William Osler: Aphorisms from His Bedside Teaching and Writings*. Springfield, IL: Charles C. Thomas; 1968.

Index

Acetyl L-carnitine, 92
Acetylcholine: atropine's influence on, 105; Loewi's discovery of, 89–90, 105; and memory, 123; and sleep, 193
Adverse effects, of L-dopa, 98–99, 101, 183, 184
Aging, and coenzyme Q_{10}, 118
Albright, Fuller, 157, 172
Albright's syndrome, 157
Alcoholism, and REM behavioral disorder, 192–93
Ali, Laila, 71, 72
Ali, Muhammad, 51, 71, 72. *See also* Muhammad Ali Parkinson Research Center
Alternative/complementary therapies, 91–92, 161; hope provided by, 93; possible conflicts with, 92
Alzheimer, Alois, 25
Alzheimer's disease: cell death in, 204; new treatments for, 2; and Parkinson's disease, 184–87. *See also* Lewy body dementia
Amantadine, 151
American Parkinson's Disease Association, 53

Aneurysms, 137
Angiograms, 137, 157
Animal research: and drug safety, 110; on GDNF, 170; on L-dopa, 125, 131; on MPPP, 66; on MPTP, 110; and new cell implantation, 162. *See also* Knockout mice; Monkeys
Anticholinergic drugs, 130, 186
Apoptosis, and cell death, 205
Archives of Neurology, 119
Arm weakness, from strokes, 23
Ashkenazic Jews: diseases common to, 78, 79; and Founder effect, 80
Atmagupta, 91
Atropine, 88, 90, 105
Autoradiography, 106; and dopamine recognition, 138–39, 147. *See also* Positron emission tomography; Single photon emission tomography
Autosomal dominant inheritance, 80
Awakenings (Sacks), 59, 60; and L-dopa therapy, 94–102
Axelrod, Julius, 32, 33
Ayurvedic medical system (India), 87, 90

Bacteriologic studies, 42
Ballard, Phillip, 61
Banisterine (hallucinogen), 90–91
Basal ganglia, of brain, 146; GDNF
    bathing of, 169; neurotransmitters
    of, 150–51; surgical experimenta-
    tion on, 158
Behavior: and Parkinson's disease,
    175–77; and REM sleep, 192–93
Belladonna, 83, 87–90, 88
Bell's palsy, 2
Benztropine (Cogentin), 90
"Black substance" of brain. *See* Substan-
    tia nigra
Blood-brain barrier, 95, 107
Brady, Roscoe, 77
Bradykinesia, 5–6, 61, 68, 126
Brain surgery: on basal ganglia, 158;
    consequences of, 160; on globus
    pallidus, 158, 161; for Parkinson's
    disease, 155–73; risks of, 160, 161;
    sites for, 159; stereotactic, 156–57;
    on subthalamic nucleus, 158; on
    thalamus, 158, 161; and UPDRS,
    166
Brain(s): autoradiography imaging
    of, 106; awake-sleep cycles of, 188;
    basal ganglia of, 146; cells, losses
    of, 151–53; cerebral cortex of, 147,
    148; communication cells of, 27;
    and Creutzfeldt-Jakob disease, 45;
    and dopamine, 35, 45, 95, 146–47,
    149–50; dorsal raphé nucleus of,
    152; early theories of, 22; electrical
    stimulation of, 160; frontal lobes
    of, 180; immune system of, 182;
    localized functions of, 22; magnetic
    stimulation of, 123; as mass of jelly,
    23; motor cortex of, 147, 148, 149;
    new cell transplantation in, 162;
    and Parkinson's disease, 21–27,
    56; post-mortem examination of,
    22–23; psychiatry and chemistry of,
    108; purposeful destruction of, 155;
    radiologic imaging of, 135; stroke's
    scarring of, 23. *See also* Lewy bodies;
    Substantia nigra
Bromocriptine, 107
Bush, George Herbert, 163

Ramón y Cajal, Santiago: as father of
    neurosciences, 30–31; microscope
    usage of, 28, 29, 30; neuron theory
    of, 28, 31; synapse model of, 31
Cannibalism, of Fore tribe, 44, 45
Carbidopa/levodopa (Sinemet), 100,
    159
Carillo, George, and Frozen Addicts,
    60–67
Carlsson, Arvid, 34, 35, 104
The Case of the Frozen Addicts (Langs-
    ton), 60
Case study, Leonard L., 101
Catechol O-methyltransferase
    (COMT), 33; blocking of, 126
Catechols, 4, 34. *See also* Catechol
    O-methyltransferase; Dopamine;
    Epinephrine; Monoamine oxidase;
    Norepinephrine
Causation: association v., 47–48; re-
    verse, 50
Causes, of Parkinson's disease, 55–82
Cell implantation, in brains, 162–68;
    and dyskinesias, 166; and PET, 166
Centers for Disease Control, 41
Cerebral cortex, and substantia nigra,
    147, 148
Charcot, Jean, 24, 87, 102; belladonna
    research of, 90; and better examina-
    tions, 6–7
Chemical anatomy: of putamen, 35,
    37; of substantia nigra, 35, 37
Chemical pathology, of Parkinson's
    disease, 31–37
Chlorpromazine (Thorazine), 9, 104,
    105
Cholera: epidemic, 40–41; *Vibrio cholera*
    as cause of, 42
Chorea, hereditary, 67–68
Clinical trials, of drugs: and coenzyme
    Q_{10}, 119–21; DATATOP, 111–17;
    phase-I-clinical trial of, 110; phase-II
    / III-clinical trials of, 111
Clinton, Bill, 163
Clusters: epidemiologist's study of, 41;
    of Parkinson's disease, 43–44
Coenzyme Q_{10}, 81–82, 92; and aging,
    118; Parkinson's progression slowed
    by, 117, 121

College of Physicians and Surgeons (NY), 15

Color blindness, 23–24

Complementary and Alternative Medicine, National Center, 91

Computed tomography (CT) scans, 135, 136; anatomical slices displayed by, 137; limitations of, 138; and Parkinson's disease, 137; and stereotactic surgery, 158; and strokes, 137

COMT. *See* Catechol O-methyltransferase

Comtan. *See* Entacapone

Conversation, neurologists/patients, 12–13, 20

Cooper, Irving, 156

Cormack, Allan, 136

Cotzias, George, 17; and L-dopa, 94–97; Parkinson's treatment revolutionized by, 31

COX-2 inhibitors, 181

Creutzfeldt-Jakob disease, 44–46; brain influenced by, 45; infectious nature of, 44

CT scans. *See* Computed tomography (CT) scans

Dale, Henry, 32

DATATOP clinical trials, 111–17; and L-dopa, 113; and neuroprotection issue, 115–16; null hypothesis of, 112, 113; shortcomings of, 159; and Vitamin E, 208

De Niro, Robert, 59, 150

DEA. *See* Drug Enforcement Agency

Defending Against the Enemy: Coping with Parkinson's Disease (Morgan), 129

Depression: abnormal brain chemistry of, 176; facial masking v., 176; and falls/injuries, 197

Diagnosis: Charcot's influence on, 6; checking for accuracy of, 7–9; clinician's comparisons of, 8; Hippocrates insight about, 14; imaging and, 136–41; as knowing distinctions, 14; methods used in, 5; as neurologist/patient conversation, 12–13, 20; presymptomatic, 141–43; and prognosis, 14; self-evident, 12;

as specialty of neurologists, 2–3; specificity/sensitivity balance in, 10; 21st century methods of, 6; variations in, 39

Diagnosticians, non-perfect skills of, 11

Digitalis purpura (foxglove plant), 86

Disease, infectious, and Koch's postulates, 48

Disease Control, Centers for, 41

DNA identification, 11

The Doctor (book), 14

The Doctor (movie), 14

Doll, Richard, 46

Dominant inheritance theory (Mendel), 68

Dopa decarboxylase, 100

Dopamine: abnormal scans for, 142–43; autoradiography recognition of, 138–39; and brain, 34, 35; bromocriptine's influence on, 107; chemical structure of, 96; and dyskinesias, 166; key points about, 31; L-dopa's conversion to, 94; and parkinsonism, 35; receptors of, 106–7; and sleep, 193

Dopamine agonists, 104; importance of, 108; and sleep, 189

Dopamine synapses: and multiple brain connections, 146–47, 149–50; scans of, 139, 140, 141

Dorsal raphé nucleus, 152

Dreaming, and L-dopa, 188

Drug Enforcement Agency (DEA), 62

Drug interactions, 92

Drugs: FDA approval of, 114; off-label use of, 114; phase-I-clinical trial of, 110; phase-II / III-clinical trials of, 111

Drug therapy. *See* Rational drug therapy

Dyskinesias (movements), 68, 74, 99; causes of, 100; and cell implantation, 166; and dopamine, 166; and globus pallidus surgery, 167; L-dopa's influence on, 101; types of, 126

Early-onset parkinsonism, 75

Economo, Constantin von, 56

18F-dopa PET scan, 139, 141–42, 166

18F-haloperidol, 153
Electron microscopy, 34
Encephalitis lethargica (Sleeping sickness), 56, 58, 60, 101, 188
Entacapone (Comtan), 126
Enzyme(s): defined, 33, 117; L-dopa's interaction with, 96; replacement therapy, 79
Epidemics: of AIDS, 40; of cholera, 40–41
Epidemiologic maps, 45
Epidemiologists: causation v. association issue of, 47–48; collaboration of, 42; illness clusters studied by, 41; methodologies of, 43
Epidemiology: causation v. association issue of, 47–48; and neurological research, 44; of Parkinson's disease, 4, 39–40, 48–50, 71; as scientific discipline, 40; of smokers v. non-smokers, 46; Snow, as father of, 40–42
Epinephrine, 32
Ergot (fungus), 87, 91, 107
Ergotism, 107
An Essay of the Shaking Palsy (Parkinson), 4
Euler, Ulf von, 32
Examination, as specialty of neurologists, 2–3

Facial weakness, 2, 70; L-dopa's influence on, 99; and masked face, 61
Falls/injuries: and depression, 197; hip protection for, 201; prevention of, 196–201; risk factors for, 198
False positives: delayed treatment v., 11; false negatives v., 10; and scan for dopamine, 143; for throat cancer, 13
Family studies, 69–74; Contursi (Italy) families, 72–74, 76; Iowa family, 74; twin studies, 72; Venezuelan family, 69
FDA. *See* Food and Drug Administration
Fetal cell implants, 163–64; *New York Times* article on, 167; null hypothesis for, 165
Food and Drug Administration (FDA): drug approval process of, 181, 182;

phase-III trials required by, 121–22; selegine approval by, 114–15
Fore tribe (of New Guinea), 44, 45
Founder effect, and Ashkenazic Jews, 80
Fox, Michael J.: and cluster factor, 43; initial misdiagnosis of, 15; progressive symptoms of, 11–12; tremors as first symptom of, 19
Freud, Sigmund, 102
Frozen Addicts, 60–67; early research on, 109–10; and "new heroin," 61, 63; and substantia nigra cell implantation, 163; treatment of, 64

Gajdusek, Carlton, 44–45
Galen (Greek physician), 4
Gambling: and dopamine antagonists, 178; and frontal lobes of brain, 180; and L-dopa, 177–84; and MAO, 180
Gamma amino butyric acid (GABA), 69, 151, 152
Gaucher, Pierre, 77, 79
Gaucher's disease, 77; and Ashkenazic Jews, 78, 79; and Parkinson's disease, 78–80
GDNF. *See* Glial cell-derived neurotrophic factor
Gene therapy, 168–73; failures of, 172; and GDNF, 170–71; NIH funding of, 172
Genes/genetics: disease as, 77–82; and environmental interaction, 76; and familial diseases, 71; and Huntington disease, 69; localization studies, 74; LRRK2, 81; PARK1, 73; PARK2, 75; PARK5, 74; parkin, 75; and Parkinson's disease, 67–77; -synuclein, 73, 75, 206; UCH-L1, 74, 206–7
Gingko biloba, 92
Glial cell-derived neurotrophic factor (GDNF), 168; double-blind study, 169; putamen infusion study, 170
Globus pallidus: and brain surgery, 158, 161; and dyskinesias, 167
Glucocerebrosidase, 77
Glutamate, 151
Goldberg, Sheryl Gay, 172
Golgi, Camillo, 25, 26, 32
Groopman, Jerome, 167

Hallucinations, 186, 187
Haloperidol (Haldol), 9
Handwriting, tremor's influence on, 6–7
Head trauma, and Parkinson's disease, 51–52
Health Professional Follow-Up Study, 50
Hench, Philip, 85
Herbal medicines, 84–94
Heroin: and morphine addiction, 62; "new," 61; synthesizing, 63. *See also* MPPP
Herpes virus, 2
Hill, Austin, 46, 47
Hip fractures, 196
Hippocrates, diagnostic insight of, 14
Hoehm, Margaret, 15–17
Hoehm and Yahr Scale, 15–17; prognostication problems with, 17; stage II classification, 178, 188; UPDRS v., 19
Hope, importance of, 93–94
Hounsfield, Godfrey, 136
Human beings: GDNF testing in, 168–69; IRB research monitoring on, 165; L-dopamine research on, 97–98; substantia nigra cell transplantation in, 162–63
Human Genome Project, 70
Huntington, George, 67
Huntington disease: and brain atrophy, 69; cell death in, 204; dominant gene association of, 72; Parkinson's disease v., 69; partial success in treating, 68. *See also* Chorea, hereditary
Hurt, William, 14

Illness: clusters, 41; unique development patterns of, 15
Imaging, of brain: and diagnosis, 136–41; and disease progression, 143–44; and presymptomatic diagnosis, 141–43
Implantation, of cells: animal research on, 162; in brains, 162–68; in Frozen Addicts, 163; NIH approval of, 165
Infectious diseases, and Koch's postulates, 48

Information system, of nervous system, 33
Informed consent, 182–83
Inheritance: autosomal dominant, 80; of Parkinson's disease, 70, 72
Institutional review boards (IRBs), 165
IRBs. *See* Institutional review boards

Journal of the American Medical Association, 64–65

Katz, Bernard, 32
Key-lock analogy, of neurotransmitters, 105–6
Knockout mice, 194
Koch, Robert, 42–43
Koch's Postulates, 42–43; and Creutzfeldt-Jakob disease, 44; and infectious disease, 48
Kuru, 44–45

Langston, J. William, 60, 61, 63, 70, 163
Late-onset parkinsonism, 75
Lauterbur, Paul, 136
L-dopa: adverse effects of, 98–99, 101, 183, 184; and animal research, 125, 131; in beans, 87; blood levels of, 125, 130; challenges of taking, 122–27, 129–33; chemical structure of, 95, 96; conversion difficulties of, 96; Cotziaz's paper on, 17; and DATATOP clinical trials, 113; dosage modifications of, 127; and dreaming, 188; enzyme interaction with, 96; and fast cell loss, 144; and gambling, 177–84; and hallucinations, 186; and high-protein foods, 92; L-dopa/selegine v., 116; life span increases from, 101; on-off pattern of, 124; oral v. injection of, 99; and symptom reduction, 31, 32, 72, 74; therapy, 94–102; tremors influenced by, 97–98, 102, 123; wearing-off pattern of, 123, 124, 126, 127, 130; and white blood cells, 99–100. *See also* 18F-dopa PET scan
Levodopa. *See* L-dopa
Lewy, Freiderich, 25

Lewy bodies, 25, 64, 151; of brain, 21, 25; in dorsal raphé nucleus, 152–53; improved stains for, 25

Lewy body dementia, 185

Limb rigidity: L-dopa's influence on, 101; as symptom of Parkinson's, 7

Lister, Joseph, 42

Loewi, Otto, 32; acetylcholine discovered by, 89–90, 105; pharmaceutical research of, 88–90; vagus nerve experimentation of, 89

Lou Gehrig's disease, 203–4; cell death in, 204

LRRK2 gene, 81

Lung cancer, epidemiological studies of, 46–47

Magnetic resonance imaging (MRI), 136; and false negatives/false positives, 143; invention of, 138; and radioactive labeling of water, 150; and stereotactic surgery, 158

Mansfield, Peter, 136

MAO. See Monoamine oxidase

Mapping Fate (Wexler), 69

Maps, epidemiologic, 45

Masked face, 61

Mayo Clinic, 49

Medical history, as stylized conversation, 5

Medicine/medication: art/science of, 12; carbidopa/levodopa, 102; herbal tradition of, 84–94; for Parkinson's disease, 83–133; tincture of Belladonna, 83

Memory: and acetylcholine, 123; and heart bypass surgery, 185

Men, and Parkinson's disease, 39

Mendel, Gregor, dominant inheritance theory of, 68

Meyers, Russell, 156

Microelectrode studies, on monkeys, 147, 179

Microscopy: and Ramón y Cajal, 28, 29; electron, 34; importance of, 24; staining advances in, 25

Misdiagnosis, possibility of, 15

Monkeys: fetal substantia nigra cells in, 162; GDNF injection in brains of, 168; and microelectrode studies,

147, 179; and MPTP-induced parkinsonism, 147

Monoamine oxidase (MAO), 33, 66; Banisterine inhibition of, 91; B-blockers, 67; and gambling, 180

Mood, and Parkinson's disease, 175–77

Morgan, Eric, 129

Morphine, 61; and opium poppies, 90; synthesizing, 63

Motion-emotion dilemma, 187

Motor cortex, of brain, 147, 148, 149

MPP+, 66

MPPP ("new heroin"), 61, 63; animal research on, 66; and parkinsonism, 66

MPTP, 63, 66, 70

MRI. See Magnetic resonance imaging

MS. See Multiple sclerosis

Mucolipidosis IV disease, 78

Muhammad Ali Parkinson Research Center, 178–79

Multiple sclerosis (MS), 181–82; new treatments for, 2

Narcolepsy, 191

Narcoleptic drugs, 195

Natalizumab (Tysabri), 181

National Center for Complementary and Alternative Medicine, 91

National Institutes of Health (NIH), 33, 77, 91; on cell implantation, 165; on coenzyme Q_{10}, 117; gene therapy funding by, 172

National Library of Medicine, 85

National Parkinson Foundation, 53

Nerve cell connections, 27–28, 30–31; in gamblers, 179

Nerve cells: death of, 203–4; of peripheral nervous system, 32–33; of sympathetic nervous system, 32–33

Nervous system: anatomy of, 34; information system of, 33; peripheral, 32; sympathetic, 32–33; virus damage of, 57

Network theory, neuron theory v., 31

Neurologists: atypical consultations by, 3; case study conferences of, 23; characteristics of, 2; and conversation with patients, 12–13, 20; examination/diagnosis by, 2–3

Neurology, growth of modern, 24
Neurology journal, 188
Neuron theory: of Ramón y Cajal, 28, 31; network theory v., 31
Neuropathologists, 23
Neuroprotection: and coenzyme Q_{10}, 117–22; and selegine, 115–16
Neuroradiologists, 135
Neurosciences: Ramón y Cajal as father of, 30–31; complexity of, 21
Neurosurgeons, 155–56
Neurotransmitters, 89–90, 150–51; acetylcholine as first, 89–90; actions of, 90; of basal ganglia, 150–51; and depression, 176; γ amino butyric acid, 69; and gambling, 180; key-lock analogy of, 105–6; and nervous system, 32–33; and opiate research, 62; and schizophrenia, 103; and sleep, 193; sound wave activation of, 108; specificity of, 105. *See also* Dopamine; Epinephrine; Gamma amino butyric acid; Glutamate; Norepinephrine; Orexin
New England Journal of Medicine, 64, 99, 162
New York Times, 167
New York Times Magazine (Goldberg), 172
New Guinea, kuru in, 44–45
Niemann-Pick disease, 78
NIH. National Institutes of Health
Nobel Prize winners, 32, 33; Carlsson, Arvid, 34; Cormack, Allan, 136; Dale, Henry, 32; Euler, Ulf von, 32; Golgi, Camillo, 25, 26; Hench, Philip, 85; Hounsfield, Godfrey, 136; Katz, Bernard, 32; Lauterbur, Paul, 136; Loewi, Otto, 32; Mansfield, Peter, 136; Pruisner, Stanley, 44; Ramón y Cajal, Santiago, 26; Roentgen, William, 136
Norepinephrine, 32, 176; radioactively labeled, 34; reuptake of, 34; and sleep, 193
Null hypothesis: of cell implantation, 165; of DATATOP clinical trials, 112, 113
Nurses' Health Survey, 50

On the Shaking Palsy (Parkinson), 24
On-off pattern, of L-dopa, 124
Opiate receptors, 62
Opium poppies, 61, 90
Oregon Health and Sciences University, 155
Orexin, 194, 195

Paralysis agitans, 4, 6
PARK1 gene, 73
PARK2 gene, 75
PARK5 gene, 74
Parkin gene, 75
Parkinson, James, 3–6, 24; incomplete studies of, 22; shaking palsy described by, 3–6, 21, 108
Parkinson Disease Foundation, 170
Parkinsonism: and brain trauma, 51; differential diagnosis of, 9; and dopamine, 35; early-onset/late-onset, 75; idiopathic Parkinson's v., 9; monkeys and MPTP-induced, 147; MPPP induction of, 66; MPTP induction of, 67; and natural cell loss, 139; and rauwolfia/reserpine, 35; and sense of smell, 142
Parkinson's Action Network, 53
Parkinson's disease: age onset of, 141; and Alzheimer's disease, 184–87; and brain, 21–27; causes of, 55–82; Charcot's naming of, 7; chemical pathology of, 31–37; daily variations of, 98; early signs of, 27; endemic nature of, 39; epidemiology of, 4, 39–40, 48–50; eventual cure for, 20; German survey of, 189–90; herbal treatments of, 86–94; Hoehm and Yahr stages of, 16; improved model of, 145–53; Indian physician's descriptions of, 4; insidiousness of, 14; L-dopa's influence on, 31, 32, 72, 74; Lewy bodies as hallmark of, 25; limb rigidity as symptom of, 7; living better with, 209–10; living with, 175–201; and neurologists, 2; new treatments for, 2; paralysis agitans as original name of, 4, 6; parkinsonism v. idiopathic, 9; pathological characteristics of, 27, 29; possible

causes of, 43; postencephalitic v.
idiopathic, 58; postural instability as symptom of, 7; preventing
progression of, 109–17; prognosis
for, 13–15; psychological manifestations of, 177; recognizing signs of,
1; and sleep, 74, 75, 152, 187–96;
and smoking, 46–47, 48–50; stroke's
influence on, 22; surgical history
of, 155–56; surgical sites for, 159;
testing patient's for, 5; timing of, 22;
unexplained aspects of, 141–42
Parkinson's Disease Foundation, 53
Parkinson's Institute (Sunnyvale, CA),
61
Parsidol, 90, 122
Pasteur, Louis, 42
Pathology, of Parkinson's disease, 27,
29, 31–37
Patients: informed consent from, 182–
83; motion-emotion dilemma of,
187; risk taking of, 157, 160; surgical
choices of, 160
Peripheral nervous system, 32, 35
Pesticides, and Parkinson's disease,
51–52, 76–77
PET. *See* Positron emission tomography
Pharmacogenetics, 131–32
Pharmacokinetics, 124, 125
Physicians: *primum non nocere* training
of, 11; showing caring by, 12
Physicians and Surgeons, College of, 15
Placebo effect, 169–70
Plants: fox leaf plant, 85–86; history of
therapeutic, 86–91; medicinal value
of, 85, 90
PMI. *See* Progressive multifocal leuko-
encephalopathy
Pneumoencephalograms, 157
Polio encephalomyelitis, 57
Positron emission tomography (PET),
139; and cell implantation, 166; and
18F-dopa, 139, 141–42; and 11C-
WAY radioactive molecule, 153; and
false negatives/false positives, 143;
and motor cortex activity, 149; and
radioactive labeling of water, 150
Poskanzer, David, 55, 56; hypothesis of,
58–60; medication discovery of, 59

Postulates, of Koch, 42–43
Postural instability, as symptom of
Parkinson's, 7
Pramipexole, 179
Primum non nocere ("first do no harm"),
11
Prions, 44
Prognosis: for Parkinson's disease,
13–15; UPDRS and, 19; variabilities
in, 16
Progressive multifocal leukoencepha-
lopathy (PML), 182
Pruisner, Stanley, 44
Psychiatric diseases, brain chemistry
of, 108
Psychiatric Research, 65
PubMed, 85, 178
Putamen, chemical anatomy of, 35, 37
Putamen infusion study, 170

Radioactive molecule 11C-WAY, 153
Radiology reports, 135
Rational drug therapy, 109–17; drug test-
ing component of, 109; steps of, 124
Rauwolfia, 35
Receptor agonists/antagonists, 64
Recombinant DNA Advisory Commit-
tee, 172
REM sleep, 186, 191
Reserpine (drug), 35, 104, 105
Restless leg syndrome, 191
Risks: of brain surgery, 160, 161; of
falls/injuries, 198
Roentgen, William, 136
Ropinirole, 179

Sabin oral polio vaccine, 57
Sacks, Oliver, 59, 94, 101, 150
Salk polio vaccine, 57
Schizophrenia: chlorpromazine for,
104; and drug therapy, 102–3; and
neurotransmitters, 103; symptoms
of, 103–4
Schwab, Robert: hypothesis of, 58–60;
medication discovery of, 59
Science, 65, 66
Selegiline, 110; and DATATOP clinical trials, 111–17; L-dopa v. L-dopa
plus, 116

Selenium, 92
Serotonin, 153, 176, 193
Shaking palsy, 3–6, 21, 108
Sherrington, Charles, 28, 30
Sickle cell anemia, 78
Single photon emission tomography
    (SPECT), 139; and false negatives/
    false positives, 143; progression dis-
    played via, 143
60 Minutes, 170
Sleep: differential diagnosis of, 191;
    diseases affecting, 187–88; and
    dopamine, 193; and dopamine
    agonists, 189; experimental investi-
    gation of, 190–91; and narcoleptic
    drugs, 195; and neurotransmitters,
    193; and Parkinson's disease, 74,
    75, 152, 187–96; REM, 186, 191;
    and SPECT imaging studies, 194;
    tremor's disruption of, 158
Sleeping sickness. *See* Encephalitis le-
    thargica
Slow movement. *See* Bradykinesia
Smell, sense of, and Parkinson's, 142,
    152
Smoking: epidemiological studies
    of, 46–47, 48–50; and Parkinson's
    disease, 46–47, 48–50; and throat
    cancer, 46
SPECT tomography. *See* Single photon
    emission tomography
Stages, of Parkinson's disease, 16
Staining: advances in, 25, 30; and brain
    study, 28; fluorescent, 34, 37
Stanford Medical School, 61
Stem cells, of brains, 193
Stereotactic brain surgery, 156–57,
    160; and human GDNF testing,
    168–69; and MRI/CT, 158
Strokes: arm weakness from, 23;
    brain scars from, 23; brainpower
    loss from, 22; and CT scans, 137;
    expected improvements from, 15;
    new treatments for, 2; Parkinson's
    influenced by, 22; timing of, 22; and
    tremors, 22
Substantia nigra: in Alzheimer's dis-
    ease, 185; of brain, 21; brain inflam-
    mation and, 56; cell transplantation

of, 162; and cerebral cortex, 147,
    148; chemical anatomy of, 35, 36;
    and CT scan/MRI, 138; dopamine
    cells in, 139; Frozen Addicts and,
    163; Lewy bodies of, 21, 25, 64, 151;
    location of, 24; new heroin's influ-
    ence on, 63; Parkinson's partial
    destruction of, 24, 27, 35, 72–73;
    surgical avoidance of, 158
Subthalamic nucleus, 146; and brain
    surgery, 158
Sympathetic nervous system, nerve
    cells of, 32–33
Symptoms, of Parkinson's disease: bra-
    dykinesia, 5–6, 61, 68; early aware-
    ness of, 27; facial weakness, 2, 70.
    See also Bradykinesia; Shaking palsy;
    Tremors
Synapse: Ramón y Cajal's model of, 31;
    evolving model of, 28, 30

Tasmar. *See* Tolcapone
A Taste of His Own Medicine, 14
Tay-Sachs disease, 78
Thalamus, 146; and brain surgery, 158,
    161
Thorazine. *See* Chlorpromazine
Throat cancer, and smoking, 46
Tolcapone (Tasmar), 126
Toxins, and Parkinson's disease, 60–67
Tremors, 1; as cause of embarrass-
    ment, 15; constancy of, 69; Galen's
    mention of, 4; and handwriting,
    6–7; L-dopa's influence on, 97–98,
    102, 123; and magnetic stimulation
    of brain, 123; and sleep disruption,
    158; and strokes, 22
Tretiakoff, C., 24
Trihexyphenidyl (Artane), 90
Twins: and 18F-dopa PET scan, 141–
    42; and Parkinson's disease, 72
Tysabri. *See* Natalizumab

Ubiquitin, 205
UCH-L1 gene, 74, 206–7
Unified Parkinson's Disease Rating
    Scale (UPDRS), 17–20; description
    of, 119; divisions/categories of, 18;
    early illness tracking via, 19; Hoehm

and Yahr Scale v., 19; and prognosis, 19; sample items, 120; scoring, 18; and surgery, 166
University of Iowa, 156
UPDRS. *See* Unified Parkinson's Disease Rating Scale

Vaccines, 57
Vibrio cholera, 42
Vioxx (rofecoxib), 83, 181
Viruses: nervous system damaged by, 57; West Nile, 60
Vitamin E, 93; and DATATOP clinical trials, 111–17, 208; oxidation reactions blocked by, 114
Von Economo, Constantin von

Wakefulness, and Orexin, 195
Wearing-off pattern, of L-dopa, 123, 124, 126, 127, 130
West Nile virus, 60
Wexler, Alice, 69
When Prophecy Fails (Festinger), 59
White blood cells, and L-dopa, 99–100
Williams, Robin, 59
Withering, William, 86

X rays, 157

Yahr, Melvin, 15–17

Zinc, 92

About the Author

RICHARD B. ROSENBAUM, M.D. is a Clinical Professor of Neurology at Oregon Health Sciences University, and a practicing Neurologist at The Oregon Clinic. He is an elected member of the American Neurological Association, and a Diplomate of the American Board of Internal Medicine as well as the American Board of Electrodiagnostic Medicine. He earned his medical degree at Harvard University Medical School.